PRAISE FOR

WHAT WERE THEY THINKING?

"This book, What Were They Thinking?, *is the need of the hour. It should be read by all families so they can instruct the next generation to restore individual liberty and self-government and reclaim the greatness and goodness that has made America the land of the free and the home of the brave."*

Rev. Lou Sheldon
Traditional Values Coalition

"It is rare nowadays for one to really educate themselves on the principles of the history of our nation and its founders. It is rarer still to commit to writing a book that accurately teaches what has been learned. Carol Sewell is rare! She has produced a tremendous book that gives us such an accurate picture of where we came from that we can actually discover where we should be going. With this information we can take corrective measures that just might prevent disaster. I pray that this book becomes a deterrent to the potential to forget to water our roots and in the process lose our desired harvest. Thank you, Carol. History will record that your work made a difference."

Pastor Mike Hayes
Founding & Senior Pastor – *Covenant Church*

"This book is an earnest endeavor to recover the meaning of the great principles summarized by the expression 'the laws of nature and of nature's God' and to support the great principles of civil and religious freedom that are the American blessing to the world. That this freedom is the gift of God is part of what Lincoln called 'our ancient faith.'"

Dr. Larry Arnn, President – *Hillsdale College*

What Others Are Saying

~ **Rabbi Daniel Lapin**, American Alliance for Jews and Christians - " This outstanding resource reminds us that some of us recognize Judeo-Christian values as vital for our nation's survival while others see them as primitive obstructions to progress."

~ "**What Were They Thinking?** will benefit anyone who reads these pages, and if taken seriously, this book has the potential to turn our nation back from destruction. - **Chuck D. Pierce**, *President, Global Spheres, Inc.; President, Glory of Zion International Ministries, Inc.*

~ **John P. Kelly**, LEAD Servant Leadership Ministry, "This is a must read for all leaders, ministers, and parents."

~ "… a significant book on the principled founding of the United States of America. It is a book that can make a great difference in the future of this nation." **Dr. Ronald E. Cottle**, Christian Life Educators Network

~ "It's the people who must capitalize upon what the Founding Fathers did 200 years ago. That's why Carol Sewell wrote her book. And that's why Americans should read it." *Penna Dexter is a conservative activist and frequent panelist on the "Point of View" syndicated radio program. Her weekly commentaries air on the Bott and Moody Radio Networks.*

~ Carol Sewell has captured in "What Were They Thinking?" the history of our great nation and the values that undergirds the strength of who we are. 'What Were They Thinking?' gives the first steps necessary in winning our nation back to its founding principles." *Pastor Stephen E. Broden; Sr. Pastor Fair Park Bible Fellowship; Dallas, Texas*

CAROL SEWELL

WHAT WERE THEY THINKING?

• ON TRUTH, LIBERTY & LEGACY

Foreword by
David Barton

Contact Information: carolsewell@g2g.org
Phone: 214-995-0240

*What Were They Thinking? On Truth, Liberty and Legacy - **formerly**
published as*: We, the People: Know the Past, Understand the Present, Secure
the Future*

Published by G2g [Generation to generation]
1208 Serenade Circle, Plano, TX 75075
www.G2g.org

Printed in USA.

Unless otherwise indicated, all Scripture references used in this book are from
the New King James Version of the Bible.

Cover Design by Gaston Digital Marketing
Interior Design by Brian Ballard
Edited by Naida Johnson

ISBN # 978-0-9907689-0-6

CONTENTS

DEDICATION

To my three grandsons:
Reagan, Graham and Landry,
and their future children
and their children's children.

FOREWORD

America is unlike any other nation in the world. Born in 1776 with the Declaration of Independence, she has had only one form of government since the U. S. Constitution was ratified in 1789. Neither our closest allies nor our fiercest enemies have experienced the stability with which America has been blessed.

Some describe this accomplishment as "American Exceptionalism" – a term coined in 1831 by Alexis De Tocqueville, a famous French visitor to America who declared:"The position of the Americans is quite exceptional, and it may be believed that no democratic people will ever be placed in a similar one."

This description is not an indication of American superiority. To the contrary, as President John Adams observed, it should always be a source of national humility: "It must be felt that there is no national security but in the nation's humble acknowledged dependence upon God and His overruling providence."

American Exceptionalism is the result of distinctive Biblical ideas such as God-given inalienable rights, limited government, full republicanism, separation of powers with checks and balances, and especially, an educated and virtuous citizenry. Because of the stability America has experienced, eight-five percent of the resources committed to the worldwide propagation of Christianity over the past two centuries has come from America.

Yet, the blessings we currently enjoy are not merely a result of what famous Founding Fathers did two centuries ago. We enjoy today's blessings because every generation since the Founders has cherished, preserved, and transmitted their unique values and institutions from one generation to the next – they have been good stewards of our civil government.

Christians in previous generations fully understood the scope of Jesus' command in Matthew 22:21 – a command frequently turned on its head today. Too many mistakenly think that the conjunction in that verse is "or" – that is, "render unto Caesar the things that are Caesar's, or unto God the things that are God's," but that is not what the verse says. To the contrary, it deliberately uses the conjunction "and" – that is, *"Render unto Caesar the things that are Caesar's, and unto God the things that are God's."* Christians are commanded to do their duty in both the spiritual and the civil arenas – to fulfill a dual responsibility in both areas.

Understanding that Christians would account to God for their role in both the civil and spiritual arenas; in 1803, the Rev. Matthias Burnet charged believers in his generation:
"To God and posterity you are accountable for [your rights and your rulers]. Let not your children have reason to curse you for giving up those rights and prostrating those institutions which your fathers delivered to you."

Founding Father William Prescott similarly warned:

"Our forefathers…spent their blood and treasure that they might enjoy their liberties, both civil and religious, and transmit them to their posterity… Now, if we should give them up, can our children rise up and call us blessed?"

It is time for Christians to reengage and once again become salt and light in the civil arena, and *What Were They Thinking?: On Truth, Liberty & Legacy* equips Christians to be effective citizens, thus preserving both our civil and religious liberties.

- David Barton, WallBuilders

"A Christian cannot fail of being useful to the republic, for his religion teacheth him that no man 'liveth to himself.'"

- Benjamin Rush, signer of the declaration, ratifier of the U.S. Constitution, founder of America's first Bible Society.

"We electors have an important constitutional power placed in our hands: we have a check upon two branches of the legislature. . . . It becomes necessary to every subject [citizen], then, to be in some degree a statesman and to examine and judge for himself …the… political principles and measures. Let us examine them with a sober … Christian spirit."

> - John Adams, signer of the Declaration, signer of the Bill of Rights, U.S. president.

"Every member of the State ought diligently to read and to study the constitution of his country. . . . By knowing their rights, they will sooner perceive when they are violated and be the better prepared to defend and assert them."

> - John Jay, original Chief Justice U.S. Supreme Court, president of the American Bible Society.

"Suppose a nation in some distant region should take the Bible for their only law book and every member should regulate his conduct by the precepts there exhibited. . . . What a Eutopia – what a Paradise would this region be!"

> - John Adams, signer of the Declaration, signer of the Bill of Rights, U.S. President.

"I have always considered Christianity as the strong ground of republicanism. . . . It is only necessary for republicanism to ally itself to the Christian religion to overturn all the corrupted political and religious institutions in the world."

> - Benjamin Rush, signer of the Declaration, ratifier of the U.S. Constitution, founder of America's first Bible Society.

What Were They Thinking?

ACKNOWLEDGMENTS

No one ever accomplishes anything on her own without the help of many others to encourage by words and deeds. I could not have written this book without God's direction, inspiration and those He put in my life to come alongside to help. Without the support of my husband, daughter, parents and brother, I could not have finished this book. Special thanks to my son-in-law for the hours of work on the interior design.

I would like to thank Pastor Tom Barkey, Pastors Gerald and Ginny Brooks, David Barton and Rev. Lou and Beverly Sheldon for listening to my initial idea for this book and giving valuable insight, resource material and advice in pursuing this dream.

Special thanks to Dianne Davega for supporting this work both financially and with her knowledge and business expertise. Dianne, the book is finally finished! Also, I want to thank Beth Edgell for sowing seed into this project and providing encouragement that kept me going.

I would also like to thank:

- Joan Hunter for your prayers, encouragement and advice.
- Pastors Debbie and Daniel Erickson for believing this information was important and needed to be taught.
- A big thank you to Jo Cason, Emma Trimble, my mother, my daughter and son-in-law, and my husband. You have prayed and supported me throughout this process with your love, encouragement and advice.
- Sheila Ninowsky and her Life Team for going through the manuscript and giving their feedback, suggestions, and encouragement.
- Kathryn Jankowitz for prayer support, practical advice and editing.
- My special 'What Were They Thinking?' prayer partners.
- Pastors Dennis Steeger, Joel Scrivner and Ricky Texada for taking time to look at the work and give valuable feedback.

INTRODUCTION

"What Were They Thinking?: On Truth, Liberty & Legacy" was
written out of a heartfelt cry to the Lord to understand how and why
this once great nation was now failing. The Lord spoke to my heart
very clearly saying that we, the Body of Christ, have failed to pass on
our faith to our children and grandchildren. God commanded the
Israelites to teach their children and grandchildren the Word of God
and all His greatness. Because they did not obey, each succeeding
generation increasingly fell into idolatry. This resulted in all the curses
of Deuteronomy 28 coming to pass. In the same way, the Lord said
that not only had we, American Christians, not passed on our faith; but
we had failed to pass on America's true Christian heritage embodied
within both the Declaration of Independence and the Constitution.

God is always right, and I knew His words were true when I heard His
voice. I then asked, "How can we restore knowledge of America's
Christian heritage and of basic civic responsibilities?" and "How will
our system be saved?"

His response to me was a very astounding, "The church has to teach
it."

Having been involved in both denominational and non-denominational
churches, I questioned how this could be accomplished. This topic
would not exactly be welcomed as Sunday School material even
though it teaches Biblical truths and can (if we allow it) challenge our
walk with the Lord. The Lord was unrelenting in stressing the
church's need to learn, understand and teach this material to everyone
who would listen.

God believes that if we, the people of God, understand the Founding
Father's Biblical worldview, we could better understand the Biblical
nature of the United States' founding documents – The Declaration of
Independence and Constitution. This book was birthed out of my
conversation with the Lord. Since writing a book or even curriculum
did not come naturally to me, this challenging project put me well out
of my comfort zone. However, a passion for America and our political
system began to develop when I attended "Washington for Jesus" in
1980.

From that time forward, God has taken me on a journey of educating myself about the true history of this nation, our political system and my responsibility as a Christian and citizen of the USA. Therefore, the basic research for much of this project had already been completed when the vision for the book was dropped into my heart. I had to dig deeper both in prayer and research to find the right mix of information that could concisely be presented for the most powerful impact. There is no lack of information on the founding of this nation from a Judeo-Christian perspective and there are more and more books cropping up regarding a Biblical worldview.

The reality is that most of us are not willing to take the time to find the necessary resources, study the information and use what we learn. American Christians, as a whole, are lazy and spoiled. We live in a microwave society where everything happens quickly and taking time to study any subject is not the norm. Based on that precept, I have set out to compile all the information needed to encourage believers to become educated, active and empowered in order to impact our culture within a relatively short and hopefully interesting read.

My prayer is that you will allow the Holy Spirit to speak through this book and bring you to a place of conviction and commitment to change the culture beginning within your own family and environment. The material is meant to transform the nation by equipping the saints to transform the nation. As this information is passed down from generation to generation, it will insure the foundational Judeo-Christian values used to build this great nation are never forgotten and/or abandoned. Each generation is responsible to leave the next generation with more faith in Christ, blessings, opportunity, liberty, and prosperity. Most importantly, we, the people of God, need to be unified in order to win the very real war for the heart and soul of this nation.

Disclaimer

Let me take a moment to state emphatically that **God is not a Democrat, a Republican nor an Independent!** His desire is that we treat political issues with His perspective in mind and see them as He does and vote accordingly. Also, let me state my priority. I am a Christian first, conservative second and then a Republican. I long for more statesmen and less politicians in both parties. Discerning God's viewpoint should be our priority. His priorities will benefit all the people. We must remember that government is not our provider and if we ever look to government instead of God to meet our needs then we are destined to become another Roman Empire.

Foundational Truth – Chapter 1

"Freedom is never more than one generation away from extinction. We didn't pass it to our children in the bloodstream. It must be fought for, protected, and handed on for them to do the same, or one day we will spend our sunset years telling our children and our children's children what it was once like in the United States where men were free."

- President Ronald Reagan

Chapter 1

Why Christian Citizenship

Overview and Introduction

The purpose of this book is to equip Christians with the information they need to articulate their beliefs and to understand the American system of government and its foundation in Biblical principles. Then they can put their beliefs into action by becoming involved in the cultural and civic arena, and ultimately pass their beliefs and knowledge on to their children and grandchildren.

In the Old Testament, Moses instructed the Israelites to teach their children the scriptures and pass their faith in God and His greatness to each generation. This was a command that they did not always obey. Consequently, they were at war with their enemies, oppressed, continually drawn away to worship idols, and finally carried off to Babylon. Likewise, we have not been faithful in passing on our Christian heritage to our progeny. Consequently, there has been a lack of knowledge of the true foundation on which this nation was birthed.

Before we can fully comprehend the Constitution and the men who wrote it, we first have to understand their worldview. The founding fathers were well educated in the Bible, and most of them were religious. They learned to read from the Bible and they studied its truths. Men equally well versed in the Bible wrote most of the other books that they read. Therefore, the

> *"The only foundation for a useful education in a republic is to be laid in religion. Without this there can be no virtue, and without virtue there can be no liberty, and liberty is the object and life of all republican governments. Without religion, I believe that learning does real mischief to the morals and principles of mankind."*
>
> **Dr. Benjamin Rush**, Signer of Declaration, founder of the Bible Society, Philosophical Society, Academy of Arts and Sciences, Abolitionist Society, Father of Modern Medicine, Father of Public Schools.

founding fathers approached everything they did from a Biblical worldview. These men believed that the Bible was the basis for good and just laws, the instrument for truth and liberty. True freedom, they believed, was a gift from God. Our constitution was written from a Biblical worldview perspective by men of God. However, it is not enough to know only what the founders believed. We must examine what we truly believe about God and the Bible. The first three chapters were designed to help us establish, believe and better understand our Christian heritage. Then, and only then, can we truly adopt our belief system into a congruent and consistent lifestyle that will glorify God. Chapters 4-7 deal with the historical Christian heritage of this nation. Chapters 8-11 deal with the Constitution, our political system, how we have lost our way, why we should be concerned and why we must get involved. When we gain these foundational understandings, we can begin to effectively steward our civic responsibilities in ways that truly make a difference in both our culture and our government. The last lesson is devoted to practical application and ways to get involved.

Why Vote?

Taking freedom and liberty for granted, Americans have grown fat and lazy. Forgotten are the sacrifices that make it possible to live in the most free and prosperous country in the world. Many people around the world do not have a voice in their government and, instead, live in fear without freedom to worship as they choose, to own property, to speak freely or to control their economy. The early American colonists cherished these basic rights that we take for granted. We are blessed to live in the United States of America. It is time for us to step up and take responsibility to protect what has been given to us.

Did we not all rejoice in the early 2000's, when we watched the Afghan and Iraqi people set free and then participate in free elections? After deliverance from oppressive regimes, they turned out in massive numbers to vote in free elections for their new leaders and representatives. Even with the threat of death by sniper fire or suicide bombers, they willingly risked their lives to stand in line and exercise their right to vote. For the women, this intimidation was particularly fierce since the role of women in these cultures, especially

Afghanistan, has been so oppressive. Covered by their native attire from head to toe, the women in Afghanistan conquered their fear and voiced their opinion by voting for the first time. Yet, in America, we let little things like bad weather keep us from voting. Heaven forbid that we might have to stand in a long line in the rain. This form of apathy is especially evident at the local and state levels.

As registered voters, we are able to bring about change in our nation. As the preamble to the Constitution reads, we are a nation of "We, the people." Voting is both a privilege and a responsibility and should not be taken lightly or for granted. There are many places around the world where the privilege to vote is absent; in other areas the elections are rigged in advance so the people actually have no voice in their government at all. It is only through prayer and vigilance that the United States is still a nation of "We, the people". Our votes can and do make a difference.

Many people choose not to vote because they do not think their vote will make a difference. However, if just one person on every street or in every voting precinct had thought that way through the years, the course of history would have been very different. Many elections were won or lost by only one vote. In fact, several of our states, including California, Idaho, Oregon, Texas and Washington, became states by just ONE vote. In 1948, Lyndon B. Johnson, our 36th president, became a U.S. senator by ONE vote. The Declaration of Independence hinged on just ONE vote. These are just a few examples of how one vote made a huge difference. Each and every vote represents the voice of a citizen of the United States of America. One voice speaking out can change the course of history.

With this in mind, voting should be considered a very important privilege. Not voting should never be considered a viable option. Up until we reach voting age, our lives revolve around our relationships with God, family, friends, teachers and peers. The question "What would Jesus do in this situation?" has often applied only to these few areas as we lived out our faith. However, once we become an adult, we have to accept added adult responsibilities which must be taken seriously. "What would Jesus do?" also applies to first educating ourselves on the important issues of our society, learning the truth of the history of our Founding Fathers, understanding our political process and how it applies to us on a daily basis as well as the consequences of our actions. Once educated, we can follow "What would Jesus do?" and truly become salt and light in our civil society.

With each season of life, our responsibilities vary in degree of importance and difficulty. Many people are so involved with fun, work, family and life in general that the idea of civic duty is forgotten or ignored. As Christians, what is our role in a secular society and government? Is God really involved in government?

God and Government

Does the Bible deal with human/earthly government? Yes. God instituted human government in the beginning with Adam. In Genesis, God created the world and established Adam as the head of the world government at that time. God gave Adam dominion over all the animals, plants and every living thing.

> *Be fruitful and increase in number; fill the earth and subdue it.*
> *Rule over the fish of the sea and the birds of the air*
> *and over every living creature that moves on the ground.*
> (Genesis 1:28)

> *...and whatsoever Adam called every living creature,*
> *that was the name thereof.*
> (Genesis 2:19)

By this action, God ratified Adam's authority. This principle of authority is evident in the New Testament when God told Joseph to name baby Jesus. In Hebrew culture, the father always named the first-born. God put Joseph in the position of Jesus' earthly father, and gave him that authority in Jesus' life. God established a divine order of authority for men as well as a divine order for the family (Isaiah 33:22). The father has the ultimate authority in the family unit and answers to God for his leadership decisions. God expects the father/husband to execute this authority with benevolence, wisdom, and a Christ-like attitude.

When God established Adam as the head of His creation, He set in motion the principal foundation for God's people to be involved in human government. Jesus tells us in Matthew 22:21, *Give to Caesar what is Caesar's and to God what is God's.* In this verse, Jesus acknowledged and confirmed the authority of civil government and its demands on its citizens.

Sadly, few in our culture acknowledge this truth and many Christians do not think it important or necessary to become an informed voting citizen. Some do not believe their one vote will affect the outcome even though historical facts prove otherwise. They also think politics and politicians are self-serving and corrupt. Some think that it makes no difference whom is in office. In many of our presidential elections only 50% of the population turned out to vote. Mid-term (non-presidential) elections draw an even smaller percentage. Local elections have a voter turnout of less than 10% of the population. A small group of voters determines who gets elected in your city and county. This should not be happening in our free nation.

In both the recent free elections held in Afghanistan and Iraq, voter turnout was 80 – 90%. Under threat of death for going to the polls, they realized how important every vote was and considered the privilege to vote more valuable than the threat against their life.

In Genesis, we read how Adam's decisions have affected all of us. Even though Eve was equally as guilty as Adam was, God held Adam to a higher standard because he was the head of the family. Adam's refusal to accept responsibility for his disobedience resulted in the perpetual sinful state of all of humankind. The actions of one man impacted and forever changed the entire universe. Animals die, stars burn out and plants decay because of Adam and Eve's actions. Look at what resulted:

> *...cursed is the ground for thy sake;*
> *in sorrow shalt thou eat of it all the days of thy life.*
> (Genesis 3:17)

Adam's actions affected all of us. The most common belief is that Adam sinned by eating the forbidden fruit. Actually, his sin was his refusal to take responsibility for his actions. God gave him a chance to confess, repent, receive forgiveness and, thus, be restored to favor with God. Instead, Adam blamed Eve, indirectly blaming God.

If we confess our sins, He is faithful and just to forgive us our sins
and to cleanse us from all unrighteousness.
(I John 1:9)

God wants us to avoid sin, because it has negative consequences in the earth. If we do sin, He simply wants us to admit our sin and repent. Sin separates us from Him. Repentance allows Him to forgive us and reconciles us to Him once again.

Pharaoh is an example of a leader who made decisions that seriously affected his people and land. When he refused to allow the Israelites to leave, all Egypt suffered through ten plagues. King David brought about a similar calamity on his people when he ordered the people "be numbered" against God's will. Israel was and still is affected by many decisions made by its leaders or kings throughout history.

David said to God,
"Was it not I who ordered the fighting men to be counted?
I am the one who has sinned and done wrong. These are but sheep.
What have they done? O Lord my God, let your hand fall upon me
and my family, but do not let this plague remain on your people."
(Chronicles 21:17)

The Israelite kings brought blessings to their people when they obeyed God. Conversely, they brought judgment when they rebelled against Him. Wise leaders will reap positive results and unwise leaders will reap negative results. Solomon recognized this principle when he wrote in Proverbs 29:2, *When the <u>righteous</u> are in authority, the people rejoice: but when the <u>wicked</u> man <u>rules</u>, the people groan.* Because of Abraham's obedience and faith, God blessed him. Through his actions, God's blessings also flowed to the children of Israel, to his seed, Jesus Christ, and onward to all who believe. There are many examples of this principle throughout the Old Testament.

Throughout history, you can see the two sides of this coin played out. People's disobedience and rebellion against God always brought death. In this country, we see a type of death through the moral and spiritual decay of our society. Death is not always physical. Daily, we see the death of marriages, the death of the family, the death of innocence and the death of absolute truth. When our leaders are corrupt in their lifestyles or behavior, death spreads slowly, but surely, throughout this nation. Death of our values and beliefs will ultimately kill the one thing that sets this nation apart from all others – "We, the people."

If we do not vote for leaders who will stand up for righteousness, our nation will continue to decline and our way of life will wither and die. Christians must be informed and vote their beliefs/values to maintain the life we so cherish.

Some say politics is dirty and, yes, it certainly can be. However, in the end, men/women in public life who lack integrity and moral absolutes are the ones who contribute to the notion that politics is dirty. When Christians who live lives that exhibit honesty, integrity, loyalty, and morality get involved, society prospers.

The Apostle Paul's philosophy in I Timothy 2:1-2 instructs us to pray

R.J. Rushdoony says in *Law and Liberty*, p. 59 that to the founders *"The word government meant, first of all, the self-government (see definition in glossary) of the Christian man, the basic government in all history. Second, and very closely and almost inseparably linked with this, government meant the family. Every family is a government; it is man's first church and first school, and also his first state. The government of the family by God's appointed head, the man, is basic to society. Third, the church is a government, with laws and discipline. Fourth, the school is an important government in the life of a child. Fifth, business or vocations are an important area of government. Our work clearly governs us and we govern our work. Sixth, private associations, friendships, organizations, and the like act as a government over us, in that we submit to these social standards and we govern others by our social expectations. Seventh, the state is a form of government, and, originally, it was always called civil government in distinction from all these other forms of government."*

But, tragically, today when we say *government* we mean the state, the federal government, or some other form of civil government. And, more tragically, civil government today claims to be *the* government over man, not one government of many, but one over-all government. Civil government claims jurisdiction over our private associations, our work or business, our schools, and churches, our families, and over ourselves. The word government no longer means self-government primarily and essentially; it means the state"..

first for our leaders so our government may be used by God to provide peace and safety. Then we are to obey the laws of the land when they are consistent with the will of God. As the Bible clearly indicates in Genesis (Joseph), Daniel, Esther and Nehemiah; the people of God have favor and wisdom to rule righteously. These obedient believers were promoted to high levels of influence in pagan governments. We can have the same favor and influence if we choose to follow His directions.

God called Moses to lead his people to freedom and into the Promised Land. At that time, God gave His people His law, The Ten Commandments. These commandments formed the basis for all laws of western civilization. Keep in mind that God did not institute government to meet our needs or provide for us. We are to trust God to do that. Government is to provide leadership and promote peace and safety for its citizens.

The Ten Commandments [i]

God gave us the Ten Commandments as a standard by which to live. At that time in history, man was doing what was right in his own eyes. Today, most of our laws as well as those of other nations are based on these commandments whether the government leaders admit it or not. Before going any further, take a brief look at the ten simple rules God put into place for us and for the good of society in Exodus 20:1-17.

1. *You shall have no other gods before me* (Exodus 20:3). We are to worship the one true God. Why? Because He is a Holy God and a jealous God, He wants our affection and attention first before anything else. Nations who worship God will experience the blessing of stability, peace and security. He meets the needs of those who worship Him and helps them reach their true potential. When we honor Him, we honor and respect ourselves. Sadly, today, "self" is the god honored by many. Actually, many false gods are worshiped within our nation. We have the gods of intellect, psychology, materialism, self-help, environmentalism and even the god of tolerance/multiculturalism.

2. *You shall not make for yourself a carved image – any likeness of anything that is in heaven above, or that is in the earth beneath, or that is in the water under the earth: you shall not bow down to them nor serve them* (Exodus 20:4-6). Because of the massive influx of immigrants from around the world, an abundance of world religions that worship idols has permeated our American culture. Political correctness harnesses the truth from going forth by labeling anyone who protests as narrow minded and bigoted. It has become un-American to criticize anyone's religion, unless it is Christianity. For example, pastors have been subject to investigations (for possible hate speech) for speaking the truth about Islam.

    > Does it seem to you, as it does to me, that there is one religion in particular that is mocked, belittled, and criticized in America today? ...Christianity.

3. *You shall not take the name of the Lord your God in vain* (Exodus 20:7). We are to honor God's Name. There are many ways to dishonor or take God's name in vain besides using it with a curse word. Surprisingly, it is quite common for Christians to use God's name in vain. Some use God's name to manipulate other people with words like "God told me…" Others utilize Christian lingo when trying to impress others or to entice new business. You dishonor the name of God when you claim to be Christian but live like the world. When we honor the name of God, we experience the blessing of His presence, as our transformed spirits become a blessing to others. We show forth His righteousness in the earth. Is your life honoring God's name?

4. *Remember the Sabbath day, to keep it holy* (Exodus 20:8-11). God wants us to set aside one day a week to worship Him and rest from our work. This refreshment prepares us for a new week physically and spiritually. This nation used to honor God on Sundays by closing all businesses (blue laws), however, in the early 1960's, the Supreme Court ruled that these blue laws should be under the control of the individual states. That single

ruling began the demise of honoring God on the Sabbath. Today, it is a day of sports, shopping and movies to many across the country.

5. *Honor your Father and your Mother* (Exodus 20:12). The only commandment with a promise, God will bless us with long life if we honor our parents. Today, honoring your father and mother is an offense to many in the United States. "Modern" thinkers believe the "individual" is supreme and independent. Over the past 50 years, parental authority has systematically been undermined. The world has failed to recognize that strong families governed by loving and firm parents, <u>work to everyone's best interest by creating healthy and productive, self-governing individuals</u>. To Jesus, this commandment also included caring for elderly parents when they can no longer care for themselves. (Also read Mark 7:9-13.)

The last five commandments God set in place give a sense of peace within a community when one realizes there is an authority to prevent anyone from inflicting harm to life, property, marriage and reputation.

6. <u>Respect Human Life</u> – *You shall not murder* (Exodus 20:13). In God's eyes, right to life is more important than personal freedom. Protecting life was God's first priority. When a person stands on the side of abortion, assisted suicide, and euthanasia, they are assuming the authority of God. By making decisions that obviously belong solely to Him, a person not only breaks the sixth commandment but the first commandment as well. When human life has no value, society becomes lawless and no one is safe. Jesus took this commandment a step further by including our thoughts and words as potentially being murderous. God judges our thoughts! (Read Matthew 5:21-22.)

7. <u>Maintain Sexual Purity</u> – *You shall not commit adultery* (Exodus 20:14). Next to life, our second most precious possession is marriage. During this very spiritual experience and commitment, one spouse becomes part of the other – one

flesh. God established marriage in Genesis 2:24 and then showed its importance in Abraham's life in Genesis 20. Even the heathen king in this passage considered adultery a great sin. Marriage is the vehicle that God created to uphold society. His chosen mechanism brings forth life and is essential for the care (provided by the father) and nurturing (provided by the mother) of the young. If the family is strong, society is strong. If the family structure is weak, society will ultimately collapse. Obeying the seventh commandment brings blessings personally, emotionally and spiritually.

8. Respect Other's Property – *You shall not steal* (Exodus 20:15). Today, stealing occurs in more ways than commonly imagined. Thefts by corporate officers, burglary, armed robbery, shoplifting, embezzlement, petty thefts by employees, downloading unauthorized music via the internet, cheating to obtain a grade in school, identity theft, default of loans, false claims on expense reports, and wages (doing personal things when you are being paid to work) are running rampant.

   The destructive concept of "entitlement" promotes the idea that we should receive remuneration we have not earned. This idea of entitlement (taking from the productive rich by force of law and giving to the poor) has its foundation in Marxism. Established on the Biblical worldview, American life promotes diligence and hard work as the road to success. By prohibiting us from stealing, God is pointing us in the direction of work. Work is a gift from God that allows us to be productive contributing members of society. *If a man will not work, he shall not eat* (II Thessalonians 3:10). (Also read Ecclesiastes 9:10 and Colossians 3:23.)

9. Tell the Truth – *You shall not give false testimony against your neighbor* (Exodus 20:16). When we bear false witness (lie), we hurt God as well as other people. God is declaring that He will hold us accountable for ruining the reputation and integrity of innocent people especially in a judicial proceeding that could take away their life, freedom or property. It also applies to lying in general. Gossip damages reputations. As a Christian, our word should be our bond. Truthfulness paves

our public dealings and personal relationships with stability. In Matthew 5:37, Jesus instructed, *Let your "yes" be "yes," and your "no" "no."* According to Proverbs 22:1, *A good name is more desirable than great riches, to be esteemed is better than silver or gold.* (See also Ecclesiastes 7:1, Ephesians 4:29 and James 5:12.)

10. <u>Be Content with What You Have</u> – *You shall not covet your neighbors house* or anything else that belongs to your neighbor (Exodus 20:17). Coveting in and of itself is not sinful. Paul instructs the church in Corinth to *covet earnestly the best gifts* (I Corinthians 12:31 KJV). Coveting something can be good or bad. As Christians with God as top priority in our lives, we should and will seek (covet) His attributes as well as His gifts. Our infinite God is enough for everyone.

When we put ourselves first, we seek to fill the "God void" in our lives with "things." Our society actually promotes the bad aspect of coveting by its obsession with riches, fame, success and getting ahead at all costs. Many are never satisfied with the status quo and believe happiness lies in obtaining more. Politicians use envy to create division between the rich and the poor. They want to increase taxing the rich to provide more services to the poor or middle income groups. Politicians utilize this tactic to entice winning votes for their elections.

Most wars begin because one group covets what another possesses. Saddam Hussein looked across his border in 1991 and wanted Kuwait. In his day, Hitler had his eyes on all of Europe. These are just two examples of dictators who desired what belonged to others. In everyday life, we are often tempted to covet what we do not have. Christians must listen to God's command to be content with His provision in each season of their lives.

> Read Romans 7:7-9, 22-25 NLT. Discuss ways to protect yourself from these temptations.

The world's attempt to eliminate absolutes from our vocabulary and lives affects our decisions by invading our thinking in very subtle ways. Unaware of these effects, a person may find they are not obeying any of the Ten Commandments.

> *Woe to those who call evil good and good evil…*
> (Isaiah 5:20a)

In Conclusion

Now that we understand that God instituted human government, we will look at the development of a Biblical worldview, America's Christian heritage, the founding documents, the constitution, the separation of powers, and the political process within the next few lessons. Only by understanding your heritage will you be able to protect and defend it. In addition, this reflection helps to prevent man from repeating mistakes of the past.

Most Christians are aware of the legal battles waged over the Ten Commandments posted on public property. Those who are against this public display actually oppose God and do not want to be reminded that there are absolutes in His eyes. The truth of the matter is that scripture and the Ten Commandments are etched in stone all over Washington, DC. The Ten Commandments are inscribed both on and inside the Capitol Building, on the doors leading into the Supreme Court courtroom, and on the wall above the chairs where the Supreme Court judges sit. Indeed, scripture verses etched in stone are displayed throughout our nation's capital.

The following quotes from two founding fathers confirm the general thinking of those great men who formed this union called the United States of America.

"No truth is more evident to my mind than that the Christian religion must be the basis of any government intended to secure the rights and privileges of a free people." Noah Webster [2]

"The Christian religion is, above all the Religions that ever prevailed or existed in ancient or modern times, the religion of Wisdom, Virtue,

Equity, and Humanity…it is Resignation to God, it is Goodness itself to Man." John Adams [3]

Since 1777, every session of Congress has opened with a prayer from a man of God, a chaplain, with a salary paid by taxpayers. In addition, each Supreme Court session begins with a simple prayer acknowledging God.

As you go through the next week, pay attention to what is happening within your city, your state, and this nation. Are there important issues not making headlines in favor of more tabloid gossip? What subjects are being ignored? What truths are being overshadowed by secular lies? How can you make a difference? Pay attention to the issues that make the headlines and consider alternate solutions to the issues. Take the problems to God in prayer. Seek His solutions to our societal problems.

PATRIOTIC PORTRAIT

Rev. John Witherspoon (1723-1794), a signer of the Declaration of Independence, a member of the Continental Congress who served on over 100 Congressional committees. He was an American Revolutionary patriot of Scottish birth who became a famous educator, clergyman, and the President of the College of New Jersey (Princeton University).

Rev. Witherspoon's emphasis of Biblical principles affecting our government made a huge impact on the Colonies during the foundational days of America. His greatest contribution was his work as president of the college that shaped the future leaders of this new nation. During his tenure, 478 men graduated (about 18 students per year). Of those, 114 became ministers, 13 were state governors, 3 were U.S. Supreme Court judges, 20 were U.S. Senators, 33 were U.S. Congressmen; Aaron Burr, Jr. became Vice-President; and James Madison became President. Of the 55 delegates to the Constitutional Convention, (one-sixth) were College of New Jersey (Princeton) graduates, and 6 graduated while Witherspoon was president. He was a very strong believer of religious liberty, calling for fair and equal treatment for religious institutions. One man can really make a difference in a nation – John Witherspoon did.

John Witherspoon said: "It is in the man of piety and inward principle, that we may expect to find the uncorrupted patriot, the useful citizen, and the invincible soldier.—God grant that in America true religion and civil liberty may be inseparable and that the unjust attempts to destroy the one, may in the issue tend to the support and establishment of both."[4]

Reverend John Witherspoon, who lost two sons in the Revolutionary War, was a true patriot. Upon Witherspoon's death, John Adams said, "A true son of liberty. So he was. But first, he was a son of the Cross."[5]

RECOMMENDED READING

The Ten Offenses by Pat Robertson

What If Jesus was never Born? What if the Bible was never written?
By D.J. Kennedy & Jerry Newcome

QUESTIONS for THOUGHT and DISCUSSION

1. What is civic duty?

2. What is required of Christians in the public/civic arena?

3. Is the United States a Christian nation?

4. Can you think of good leaders (presidents, judges, religious leaders, etc.) this country has had? What made them good leaders?

5. Citizenship starts at the local level. What you allow in your local community impacts your life for good or bad. What are possible negative influences in your neighborhood and city?

6. What are possible positive influences in your neighborhood and city?

7. How can you as a citizen get involved in your neighborhood or city?

8. How can a local church get involved in their city?

9. How are the Ten Commandments viewed today by Christians?

10. Which commandments do we tend to ignore most?

11. List benefits of having absolutes versus no absolutes (see Judges 17:6; 21:25.). Start by defining absolutes.

Foundational Truth – Chapter 2

"In the final analysis, we, the people, are responsible for the corruption of our leaders by failing to demand a higher standard of conduct from our politicians. Increasingly, Americans have grown accustomed to a culture characterized by moral relativism and individualism. We have mocked Judeo-Christian values -- humility, virtue, honor -- and in the process, eroded restraints on social conduct. The results have become painfully obvious in the business arena and are becoming increasingly obvious in the political arena. When we do not demand honor, virtue, and accountability from ourselves, can we really expect more from our leaders? Have we merely gotten the leaders we deserve? The path to reform in the political arena runs straight through the people. We, the people, must first find a renewed appreciation for virtue, honesty, and humility in ourselves and our fellow man. If private virtue is reestablished in society, it will eventually become public and inevitably find its way back to the halls of government. Quite simply, it is up to us."

- Ken Connor, Author

Ken Connor founded the Center for a Just Society in 2005 with Colin Stewart and Genevieve Wood. He serves as the organization's Chairman and as one of its principal spokesmen.

Chapter 2

Biblical Worldview vs. Secular Worldview

Information taken from *Think Like Jesus* by George Barna

How Do You Make Decisions?

Now that we have established that this nation was founded on Biblical principles, it is time that we evaluate our thinking and decision making process. To do this I had to ask myself the following questions: Is my thinking and decision making process influenced more by the world or by the Bible? Do I ask myself, "What would Jesus do?" in most situations I encounter or only when it is convenient? Do I consistently pray about situations and issues, asking God for His solutions?

Chapter 1 laid a foundation for civic duty, citizenship and the Biblical role of government on earth. Citizenship in the United States has many privileges, but these come with added responsibilities. When you and I make the decision to be good citizens of this wonderful country we live in, we filter every decision through our personal ideology and theology as well as life experiences. At home, in relationships, at work, at play, on the highway, at church, and in political activities; we all filter every decision through our "life-lens," a combination of all that has influenced us plus life experiences of our past. These previous experiences and effects determine how we view the world or, in other words, our worldview (our individual life lens).

As Christians, we should reflect Jesus in all we think, speak, and do. We need to live a life that is congruent, a consistent life of faith at home, at work, at school, as voters and at church. To do this we must choose to develop a worldview that is pleasing to the Lord. According to the Christian researcher, George Barna, less than 10% of professing born again Christians have developed a worldview that is consistent with their faith.

If you are asking yourself how that percentage can be so low, look no further than your living room. Television, magazines, newspapers, and the internet are all prominent sources of information in our homes.

Television has been in American homes for over half a century as an invited guest.

At first, TV was fun and entertaining; but with each passing year, the subtle messages became bolder and standards of civility have lessened to the point of being downright base. If a friend or relative spewed forth vulgarities, put-down humor, anti-American views, and even anti-Christian views; we would ask them to refrain or they would not be welcome in our home.

Because we have gotten used to such television/entertainment, we allow its presence into our everyday life. As it slowly and subtly desensitizes us to accept violence, language and sexual content, we become immune to what has been happening to our precious environment.

For decades, the mass media through television, movies, music, magazines, and videos have bombarded us with their way of thinking. They tell us what to think, how to dress, how to look, what products to purchase, as well as what we should believe about our country, government, marriage, sex, homosexuality, adultery, and honesty.

If they were promoting high ideals that agreed with God's attributes, this would not be a bad thing. However, we know this is not the case. Every year these outlets lessen the standards of conduct, until we now see the results of this type of indoctrination acted out by fans as well as athletes at sporting events and in our everyday lives. Crude, rude, and violent behavior bombards us daily.

This secular behavior has even permeated the church. Compared to non-Christians, Christians are just as likely to get divorced, commit adultery, engage in pre-marital sex, and generally live and look just like the world. The Body of Christ, the Church, is influenced by society when it should be the other way around. I often ask myself why the church is not influencing society and how we, the church, can turn this around? Can this trend even be turned around? I believe we can make a difference. Christians can alter this path to destruction.

Why is a Worldview Important?

Your "life lens" or worldview will influence your personal life as well as those around you. It will determine the degree of success you experience in relationships, marriage, and career. There are many types of worldviews influencing us today. Choosing to develop a Biblical

> While my husband was in a store, the clerk commented on how good Ben and Jerry's ice cream was. He told her that he had never had any because Ben and Jerry's supported abortion rights, therefore he could not give them his money. When she said she wished she had that kind of strength, he encouraged her in that area. His comment got her thinking about the decisions she makes. He set a standard of living a life consistent with his Biblical beliefs.

worldview will probably mean changing your thinking about certain things. It is a commitment just like the commitment you made to Jesus when you were born again. Living your life according to a Biblical worldview will guarantee personal satisfaction, success and real intimacy with the Lord. It will also cause you to make a real impact on the world around you.

What is a Biblical Worldview?

Simply put, a Biblical worldview is thinking like Jesus. It is a way of making our faith practical in everyday situations. We will act like Jesus because we think like Jesus 24/7 as we deal with the world. This worldview is consistent with what the Bible teaches and influences our entire life. It helps us become the true reflection of God that He created us to be.

For instance:
- What do you do when a friend asks you to lie for them?
- Have you ever cheated on a test or helped someone else cheat?
- On a challenge, have you ever shoplifted?
- Have you made fun of others who are different from you?
- Have you spread gossip about someone?
- Have you lied on an application?

To think like Jesus is to see things from God's perspective, and then respond to each situation the way Jesus would. He is readily available to provide direct and personal revelation for each situation. He is always with us and never leaves us. We just have to ask for His help. Unfortunately, most of us are not listening to His direction or advice.

All too often, we fall into the trap of making decisions based on the situation. Situational ethics mentality has been creeping into American lifestyle for the past sixty years and is (when we stop to think about it) not in agreement with Biblical teachings. Having come from a social service background, I had to take a very serious look at my own worldview.

As we face everyday situations requiring decisions, we unconsciously run the process through a mental and emotional filter that allows us to make choices consistent with what we believe to be true, significant, and appropriate. This filtering process is how we have organized information to make sense of the world in which we live.

A Biblical worldview is a means of experiencing, interpreting and responding to reality in light of a Biblical perspective. In other words, simply put, it is asking the question, "What would Jesus do if He were in my shoes right now?" and applying the answer without compromising because of the world's possible reaction to our actions. Many ask the question but few seek the answer and follow through with it.

It is never appropriate to adopt a worldview simply because it produces positive outcomes. You should do it because it is right and the outcomes are a result of that "rightness." The Bible tells us to seek first His kingdom and then all the other blessings will come. That is the essence of a Biblical worldview. (See Matthew 6:33.)

While not the goal of a Biblical way of thinking, the outcomes of Biblical thinking found in scripture are:

- Physical Benefits   Protection, long life, vitality, sound sleep
- Emotional Benefits   Joy, fulfillment, happiness, no fear, self-control

- Decision Making Benefits   Wisdom, good plans, direction, discretion, insight
- Relational Benefits   Human acceptance, honor, good reputation, respect, justice
- Spiritual Benefits   God's approval, heavenly rewards, forgiveness, mercy
- Lifestyle Benefits   Success, wealth, blessings, abundant life

In addition to the benefits and rewards of thinking like Jesus, there are specific negative outcomes outlined in the Bible if we live in opposition to those principles. Read the first eight chapters of Proverbs. Take note of the negative outcomes.

As a Christian living for self in opposition to the principles of Jesus can produce the following outcomes:

- Unanswered prayer,
- Harsh judgment,
- Nagging guilt,
- Distorted perception,
- Anxiety and stress,
- Physical and emotional suffering, confusion, and lack of understanding.

When we are born again, our spirit becomes new. We become new creatures freed from the bondage of sin and are reconciled to God. However, our mind, will and emotions (soul) are not immediately renewed. We have to allow the necessary renewal of our minds by reading the Word of God and submitting our will and emotions to Jesus. He then enables us and helps us become that new creature renewed in the flesh, as evidenced by voluntary surrender to His Holy Spirit and a changed lifestyle. How do we manifest this new relationship?

When I surrendered all to Jesus and yielded to His Holy Spirit, I began to see things in a completely new way. Instead of seeing things through the world's eyes, I could see things as God sees them. His reality became my reality. Being able to interpret reality according to His eyes and truly hearing His words of profound wisdom enabled me to respond to my life in a more enduring way. This kind of spiritual renewal eventually transformed my life, making me whole.

Living and thinking like Jesus does not make life easier. Examine Jesus' life. He faced persecution, rejection, public ridicule, and rifts with family and friends. Those who fully commit to Him become targets for spiritual attacks because they threaten Satan's goals. Jesus told us life would not be easy, however He assured us we would never be alone because He was sending His Holy Spirit to help us, to comfort us.

He that is in you is greater than he that is in the world (I John 4:4).

What are the Other Worldviews?

As I studied some of the most prevalent worldviews, I was surprised to discover which ones had captured a portion of my thinking. As you consider the competing worldviews, you will also be surprised.

There are over a dozen competing worldviews. Americans have embraced most of these in part and, some, completely. Even believers who follow the guidelines of the Bible have unconsciously allowed these non-Biblical worldviews to seep into their belief systems. A competing worldview causes confusion and disruption between the faith and the lifestyle of a Christian believer.

Let's examine a few of the most prevalent non-Biblical worldviews:

- **Multiculturalism** – "What's right for you may not be right for me."
  Philosophy: All beliefs are equal.
- **Materialism** – "What you see is what you get."
  Philosophy: The theory that physical matter is the only reality and that everything, including thought, feeling, mind, and will, can be explained in terms of matter and physical phenomena. It is also the attitude that physical well-being and worldly possessions constitute the greatest good and highest value in life.

- **New Age Movement** – "You are God. Just follow your inner God."
  Philosophy: Type of Hinduism with many gods. It embraces the occult.

- **Secular Humanism (Naturalism)** – "Millions of years of evolution made you."
  Philosophy: Does not believe in God. Politically believes the state is all powerful. Humanism and Marxism best exemplify Naturalism's viewpoint. Many university and college professors espouse this viewpoint. The Humanist Manifesto expresses this viewpoint in detail. Politically, this ideology is against capitalism and for socialism, where the government controls all aspects of life and is the great provider from cradle to grave.

- **Hedonism** – "If it feels good, do it." Hedonists believe life is all about "me" and how "I" feel.

- **Postmodernism** – "There is no absolute truth." Truth can be whatever you say and believe at any given time.

How often have you heard any of the above statements used to explain away behavior that is morally or ethically in conflict with the Word of God?

Assignment:

Listen to the mainstream media (well known for its secular humanist agenda) as they try to argue their viewpoint. Notice how emotion/feeling–driven they are. They have no facts to argue their points. Feelings are everything. As a result, they often resort to "name calling".

What is the Most Prevailing Worldview?

Postmodernism is the mindset that declares that there is no absolute truth. It is a worldview born out of behavior rather than concept (philosophy and theology). It challenges much but answers little. If you are in the two youngest generations of Americans, you are influenced most by this worldview. It is widely taught in public schools, colleges, and universities throughout the nation. Examine the precepts that identify the worldview of the postmodern way of thinking:

- Choose to believe in God but will never compel anyone else to do so.
- Absolute moral truths do not exist or at least they cannot know them.
- There are no shared truths. A person's truth is based on their life experiences.
- Because each person's experiences are personal, they cannot be challenged; but neither can their experiences impact society because they simply belong within one person's life story.
- Moral behavior is a private matter. Right and wrong decisions are based on desire, emotion, and personal experience.
- Hyper-tolerance is one of the highest virtues.
- No external controls, established order, laws or limitations imposed by others.
- Life has no real purpose beyond survival and self-satisfaction.
- Feeling replaces reason, experience replaces logic, and contradiction replaces consistency.

What is Satan's Agenda?

Did you know that Satanist's have a 'bible'? In their bible, they have included the nine commandments to serve their god and evangelize the world. Do you recognize any of these principles?

- Satan represents indulgence instead of abstinence!
  "If it feels good, do it – it is no one's business but yours."

- Satan represents vital existence instead of spiritual pipe dreams! "Live for today, don't worry about tomorrow. My life experience is my truth. "
- Satan represents undefiled wisdom instead of hypocritical self-deceit! "Wisdom and truth are what I say they are."
- Satan represents kindness to those who deserve it instead of love wasted on ingrates! "Love is conditional only."
- Satan represents vengeance instead of turning the other cheek! "Get revenge at all costs, forgiveness is weakness."
- Satan represents responsibility to the responsible instead of concern for psychic vampires! "What is good for me may not be good for you so I won't waste my time on you."
- Satan represents man as just another animal, sometimes better, more often worse than those that walk on all fours, who, because of his "divine spiritual and intellectual development," has become the most vicious animal of all! "You are the same as the animals, no purpose but to survive."
- Satan represents all of the so-called sins, as they all lead to physical, mental, or emotional gratification! "No limits, no laws so indulge yourself as a true and complete expression of self."
- Satan has been the best friend the Church has ever had, as he has kept it in business all these years! "Tolerance of Satan's ways keeps the truth from succeeding."

The principles of postmodernism fit very nicely into the Satanic 9 Principles. It seems that the further away society gets from the truth of God, the more the worldviews reflect Satan.

The Biblical worldview believes:
- There is one true living God.
- There is evil – Satan, who opposes God.
- Man's ultimate authority is God and His word.
- Truth is found in God, Who is Who He says He is.
- There is a heaven and a place called hell.

Judeo-Christian Influence

Established on the Judeo-Christian worldview, our United States' Constitution, laws and style of government reflect the basic precepts of self-government and liberty that the Bible teaches. Americans believe that you can work hard and achieve your dreams. We have a far different work ethic from the other developed nations of the world. The European nations and Australia have mandated that companies give their employees a minimum of six weeks of paid vacation a year when hired. After a person has worked ten to fifteen years, they may enjoy up to twelve weeks of vacation. Europeans live for their time off. Their standard of living is lower as are their creative innovations compared to that of the United States because of the lack of incentive to work hard.

From birth to grave, the government cares for them. They have no need to trust in God to take care of them or lead them, because their trust is in the government. Those who do work hard and are productive (business owners) have extremely high taxes to pay to support those who are not productive. Businesses in those countries are not as productive and resourceful as those in America because of the emphasis on government entitlement, and all the disincentives to work hard and achieve economic rewards.

Practical Example:

When you were in school maintaining A's and B's on the honor role, how would you have felt if you were told you had to give a grade point to those students who were making D's and F's so they wouldn't feel bad about themselves? You worked hard for your grades and had to allow someone else reap the benefit without any effort.

Or perhaps the CEO of your company announced that all management would have to give up 20% of their income for those on the low-end of the pay-scale so they would feel better about themselves and be better able to pay their bills. You have worked hard to get where you are and have greater responsibilities on the job. Is this fair?

You would say, "That's not fair!." Yet most of our tax policies do exactly that – transfer wealth from hard workers and the productive to those who are not productive. This principle is the crux of socialism and big government. That is why conservatives, who believe in the Judeo-Christian view of limited government, support small government along with a free market society where opportunity to achieve is available to all who work hard.

Keys to Thinking Like Jesus

Our model in thinking like Jesus is Jesus, Himself. There are four interworking elements to facilitate His worldview.

1. He had a foundation in scripture that was clear, reliable and accessible.
2. He maintained a laser-beam focus on doing God's will.
3. He evaluated all information and life experiences through a filter that produced appropriate choices. (He thought outside the box with statements like *You have heard... but I say* (See Matthew 5:21-22).
4. He acted in faith.

Because Jesus was human while He was here on earth, He had to work hard to maintain a godly view of everything He encountered. If He could do this, we can do it also. God has provided us with all the tools – the foundation (His Word), the skills needed to focus and filter, and the means of faith that enable us to follow Jesus' example.

Where should you start? Know and commit to doing what God commands in the Bible. Obedience is the key. The Bible provides us with indisputable evidence that we are commanded to think like Jesus. Listed here are some examples from scripture to help you get started.

1. Seek God's Wisdom (Proverbs 2:2-7). God grants wisdom to those who truly seek it. We must pursue His wisdom as well as His will.
2. Make a commitment to develop a Biblical worldview (Deuteronomy 6: 2-9). God reminds us that it takes a commitment to what is important. Developing a Biblical worldview takes time, mental energy, diligence, and reliance on God's Word.
3. Allow God to transform your thinking and rely on His guidance (James 1:5-6). Romans 12:2 tells us to allow God to transform us into a new person by changing our thinking. God desires not just salvation for us, but that we would allow Him to transform our thinking and, thus, our lives.
4. Resist false teaching by being spiritually strong (1 Timothy 4:1, 7, 11). We must become spiritually equipped so we can

resist false teaching and the temptation to reject God's Word.

5. <u>Seek to know God's thoughts</u> (Isaiah 55:8). God's thoughts are completely different from ours. We must work hard to know, understand and accommodate His mind and heart so our worldview honors Him.

6. <u>Anything apart from God is insignificant</u> (Ecclesiastes 12:13-14). Solomon's final conclusion on the meaning of life is that we must respect God and obey Him fully.

7. <u>Trust God alone</u> (Proverbs 3:5-7). We must understand we cannot accomplish anything on our own. Finding His will and direction alone enables us to be successful. If we do not learn this, we will be victims of our own arrogance.

These passages make it very clear that what we think, how we think, and what we do as a result of those thoughts matters to God. Therefore, it should matter to us as well. The future of our country depends upon each generation carrying out the mission God has had for this nation from the beginning. Having a true Biblical worldview is the only way to maintain the nation and culture that God has given us. He expects us to be good stewards of all He has given us (our freedoms, our nation, the earth, etc.).

Few Americans currently possess a Biblical worldview. Most are immersed in the world's training via the mass media, public law, public school education, the internet, and conversations with peers. It will take an **intentional** process designed to develop, integrate, and apply a Biblical life lens in order to protect us from the savage mental and spiritual assault that occurs around us every day. If we fail in this task, we will be living lives that contradict God's perfect and eternal moral and spiritual code. That code was originally designed by our Creator to foster our relationship with Him, each other, and the world He has entrusted to us.

God has given us a great nation – different from all others. As a nation, we are the most blessed in the world. It is up to each one of us to make sure the American Covenant is not broken.

Characteristics of Those
Who Reflect a Biblical Worldview

Those who live out a consistent Biblical worldview are more likely to:

- Intentionally boycott a company or products due to that company's values that conflict with the Biblical worldview.

- Volunteer more than an hour of time to assist an organization in serving needy people.

- Choose not to watch a particular movie or video because the rating indicates it contains objectionable material.

- Not view adult-only graphics or visual content on the internet.

- Not download music off the internet to their mp3 player without paying for it.

- Pray for the President and other governmental leaders.

- Have a consistent devotional time with prayer and Bible study.

- Be involved at church through regular attendance and volunteering to serve.

- Believe that God is the all-powerful, all-knowing, perfect Creator of the universe Who rules the world today.

- Believe the Bible is truly God's Word and embrace its truth and principles daily.

- Support life issues, purity and traditional marriage.

If the Church in America had a consistent Biblical worldview that affected their daily lives; our communities, states and nation would be completely different. Why? Because we would be living lives that actually had influence on those around us and our culture. More importantly, we would be unified. Good would be good, and evil would be evil. Today's reality calls good evil while evil is called good. The following are examples of this upside down world.

- God says sex outside of marriage is sin.
  - Society says if it feels good, do it.

- God says homosexual sex is sin.
  - Society says it is a viable lifestyle.

- God hates divorce.

- o Society says if you are unhappy, then marriage is disposable.
- God says murder is a sin.
  - o Society embraces abortion and is moving towards embracing euthanasia.
- God respects life.
  - o Society devalues life.
- God says lying is a sin.
  - o Society says truth is whatever you say it is.

How Do We Develop a Biblical Worldview?

Addressed in the next chapter, the following seven questions will facilitate a practical and comprehensive understanding of God's truths and principles as well as foster the development of a Biblical worldview.

1. Does God exist?
2. What is the character and nature of God?
3. How and why was the world created?
4. What is the nature and purpose of humanity?
5. What happens after we die on earth?
6. What spiritual authorities exist?
7. What is truth?

These seven questions address the crucial persons who must be included in whatever worldview you develop: God, Satan and humankind. The ultimate objective of these questions is to provide a clear, comprehensive, and unified understanding of both spiritual and physical reality that will enable us to live like genuine Christians, as originally designed by God.

If we are to live a congruent lifestyle that honors God, each of us must answer these seven questions. According to scripture, the Bible is the foundation for living. Therefore, it is important to look in the foundational document for satisfying answers to these core questions.

However, if you do not have the desire to live a life in harmony with Jesus' thinking, this exercise is pointless. You and I must first decide for ourselves whether we live life haphazardly, or live life intentionally

> For some, the answers to these questions are a matter of innate faith and a basic Biblical understanding; but many others have not reached that level of spiritual maturity. But for all, they require a decision to live what we believe in our daily lives in spite of the influence of an out of control culture.

and in harmony with God's Word? Do we live a life influenced by the world or do we live life influencing the world toward God's ideals and principles.

PATRIOTIC PORTRAIT

Ronald Wilson Reagan (1911-2004), the fortieth President of the United States was born in Tampico, Illinois. His mother's commitment to her faith and Ronald's involvement at the First Christian Church in Dixon, IL had a profound influence on his life of faith. Growing up at the beginning of the Communist takeover of Russia influenced him and his view of the world. However, his faith was the complete opposite of the Marxist worldview.

His mother, Nelle, had an enormous impact on his spiritual life and belief in the power of prayer. Ronald Reagan had a call on his life to do great things and he lived up to his call. He started out in radio, moved to movies, television, and then into politics as the president of the screen actors guild. He first registered as a Democrat, and eventually, when the Democrat Party began to ignore the evils of communism, he switched parties. As a Republican, he became governor of California and then ran for president of the United States.

Ronald Reagan described his belief in limited government in this quote: "...man is not free unless government is limited. There's a clear cause and effect here that is as neat and predictable as a law of physics: As government expands, liberty contracts."[1]

When elected President in 1980, he said: "The time has come to turn to God and reassert our trust in Him for the healing of America...our country is in need of and ready for a spiritual renewal..." [2]

He designated 1983 as the "Year of the Bible." For a complete text of the resolution see "America's God and Country" by William J. Federer. On January 25, 1984, President Ronald Reagan explained:

> "America was founded by people who believed that God was their rock of safety. I recognize we must be cautious in claiming that God is on our side, but I think it's all right to keep asking if we're on His side." [3]

On August 23, 1984, following the enactment of the "Equal Access Bill of 1984," President Ronald Reagan, speaking at the Ecumenical Prayer Breakfast at Reunion Arena in Dallas, Texas said:

> "Without God there is no virtue because there is no prompting of the conscience...without God there is a coarsening of the society; without God democracy will not and cannot long endure...If we ever forget that we are One Nation Under God, then we will be a Nation gone under." [4]

President Ronald W. Reagan will be remembered as one of the best presidents of the twentieth century. He was a man of faith and conviction who always believed the best of America and her citizens.

RECOMMENDED READING

Evidence That Demands a Verdict, Josh McDowell, 2001

Thinking Like a Christian, Teacher's Edition, Noebel and Edwards, 2002

So What's the Difference?, Fritz Ridenour, 2001

QUESTIONS for THOUGHT and DISCUSSION

1. Are you living a life that is in agreement with the life of Jesus (the Word of God)? If you answered No or Sometimes, explain why and what holds you back:

2. Why is the church not influencing society?

3. Does your response to everyday situations/decisions vary based on the situation?

4. What term does the Bible use to describe compromising because of a perceived reaction to us?

5. Scan the first eight chapters of Proverbs. What are some of the undesirable outcomes listed in these chapters?

6. Does living a life transformed by God make our lives easier? Explain how or how not:

7. What characteristics do you think reflect a lifestyle of someone with a Biblical worldview?

8. What precepts of postmodernism or any of the other worldviews have crept into your life?

9. What will American society be like when the generation that embraces the postmodern worldview is in charge of our schools, businesses, churches and government?

10. What will this mean for your children and grandchildren?

11. Have the nations that have embraced Marxism/Socialism been successful? _____ Yes _____ No Describe the result.

12. Which, if any, of the seven worldview traits can you identify in your thinking and life? Be Honest!

Foundational Truths – Chapter 3

"Religion and good morals are the only solid foundation of public liberty and happiness."

> - Samuel Adams, letter to John Trumbull, 16 October 1778

"We have duties, for the discharge of which we are accountable to our Creator and benefactor, which no human power can cancel. What those duties are, is determinable by right reason, which may be, and is called, a well informed conscience."

> - Theophilus Parsons, the Essex Result, 1778

"If men of wisdom and knowledge, of moderation and temperance, of patience, fortitude and perseverance, of sobriety and true republican simplicity of manners, of zeal for the honour of the Supreme Being and the welfare of the commonwealth; if men possessed of these other excellent qualities are chosen to fill the seats of government, we may expect that our affairs will rest on a solid and permanent foundation."

> - Samuel Adams, letter to Elbridge Gerry, November 27, 1780

Chapter 3

Keys to Forming a Biblical Worldview

What Do You Believe – 7 Key Questions

The answers to the following questions will be brief summaries only. For a complete examination of these questions and their answers read *Think Like Jesus* by George Barna.

Does God Really Exist?

In reading scripture, I have noticed it does not present a strong case for God's existence. Instead, it seems to assume that any thinking person will recognize His existence. Therefore, the Bible focuses on matters implied by His existence, such as God's purpose, commands, and expectations.

When you think about it, there is no way to prove God exists. Of course, there are some people that do not believe God exists (atheists), and others who do not know or care if God exists (agnostics). So maybe it is more important to answer these questions:

- What do **you** believe about God's existence?
- **Why** do you believe that?
- And what **difference** does that belief make to how you think and behave?

Most people in America today believe in God and many would say they are Christians. However, what they believe about God varies. Christians believe that God has always, does presently, and will always exist because that is what the Bible teaches. However, for the most part, our knowledge and confidence regarding the existence of God is based on our faith in God and His words to us. Our belief in God's existence is an aspect of our trust in the Bible as a reliable source of truth.

As we will see, the Bible is a more reliable source of knowledge than many of the sources we rely upon every day for an understanding of life. Keep in mind that it is our faith that pleases God (Hebrews 11:6).

There are three ways to consider God's being: through …
    1.) Biblical statements,
    2.) logic and human reasoning,
    3.) personal experience.

The *scriptures* proclaim that God created the universe and provides tangible evidence of His existence. (Read Psalm 19:1 and Romans 1:20.)

Through *human logic*, we are able to confirm the validity of the scriptural inference that God's existence is undeniable because we can see and experience what He has made (the trees, flowers, mountains, seas, clouds, stars etc.). Therefore, our logic and our *personal experience* with creation bear witness that there is a Creator and we acknowledge His existence.

Those who refuse to believe are blinded by their rebellion. Unfortunately, many feel it is their duty to undermine Christians' belief in God's existence as often as possible. They do this by their relentless attacks on the Bible and on everything relating to God in public schools and their defense of Darwinism (evolution) as fact. It is not a big leap from doubting God's Word to doubting there is a God.

What is the Character and Nature of God?

To simplify the qualities of God, we will break it down to three distinct categories of His person: His essence, His greatness, and His goodness.

1. The Essence of God

God's essence is two-dimensional. *First*, He is spiritual in nature (we can't see Him). Because the concept of God being a spirit is outside our realm of experience, we have difficulty fully understanding Him. *Second*, God is very much alive and has affirmed His existence through the name He chose as His identity: I AM. He is not only the giver of life, He is life. He always has been, is, and always will be. He is relational and personal. This fact alone should affect our worldview. Therefore, we must learn to filter our life decisions through the lens of God's invisible but real existence. The ball is in our court. The choice is ours.

2. The Greatness of God

Because God is so great, man has always had difficulty relating to Him. Let's look at some of the aspects of His greatness.

He knows everything that ever has been or will be. He is all wisdom. Fortunately, the Bible says this wisdom is also available to those of us who seek it. (See Proverbs 15:3; Isaiah 40:28, 46:9-10, 48:5; Matthew 10:29-30; Acts 15:18; Romans 11:33; Hebrews 4:13; Job 20-28; Proverbs 3:18-19; Jeremiah 10:12, 23:5, 51:15; 1 Kings 3:10-11.)

He has unmatched power and authority over all created things as long as it does not contradict His nature (e.g. sinning since that would contradict His holiness, or lying since that would undermine His integrity). His attributes emphasize the perfection, consistency, reliability, and unity of His character and capabilities. (See Genesis 1; Isaiah 50:2; Jeremiah 32:17; Daniel 4; Matthew 19:26; Mark 14:36, Luke 1:37; Acts 9.)

He is anywhere He wants or needs to be, whenever He so chooses. This quality is referred to by theologians as omnipresence or "infiniteness" – no limits and no boundaries to His presence. (See Psalm 90:1-2, 139:7-12: Isaiah 44:6; Jeremiah 23:23-24; Ephesians 3:21; Jude 25; Revelation 1:8, 21:6, 22:13.)

He is personal – in fact, He is "tri-personal". Put simply, He is one deity whose fullness can best be understood in three distinct personalities – known to us as God the Father, God the Son (Jesus Christ), and God the Holy Spirit. (See Isaiah 63:10-11; John 16:13-14, 17:3; Romans 8:9; 1 Corinthians8:6; Ephesians 4:6, 30; I John 5:7.)

We are created in the image and likeness of God as a triune being. We have a spirit, a soul, and a body. Being created in the image and likeness of God indicates that God's attributes – power, authority, knowledge, wisdom, presence, and personality – are also available to us. Because He knows all and is present everywhere, He is always present to comfort or guide us when we need Him. Therefore, we can feel secure in the knowledge that what He has promised will be fulfilled.

3. The Goodness of God

- God is holy. (See Leviticus 11:44-45, 19:2; Exodus 15:11; Isaiah 6:1-4.) God alone is morally pure – completely devoid of sin and wrong motives.

- God always exhibits love. God showed His amazing love for us from the very beginning. His defining act of love was sending Jesus to earth as the ultimate sacrifice for our sins. (See 1 John 4:8, 16 and John 15:3.)

- God's faithfulness is unfailing in its consistency and availability; and best of all, it is not contingent on our behavior or emotions. He is more dependable than any friend we could find on earth. (See Psalm 8:4 and Psalm144:3.)

- God is righteous. God is always right and does what is right all the time. Righteousness is not just knowing what is proper, but acting on that knowledge. Therefore, the Bible declares, *"The Lord is righteous in everything he does"* (Psalm 145:17).

- God is completely reliable. He is predictable in His ways, but not always in His methods. God's character never changes and neither does our experience of the essence of that character. (See Numbers 23:19; Psalm 102:26-27; Malachi 3:6; James 1:17; and I John 1:9.)

In summary, His love cannot be fully experienced without the presence of Jesus Christ in our lives. God provided the means through Jesus' sacrifice for us to regain the relationship and access to Him that Adam had in the garden – being one with Him.

How And Why Was The World Created?

- The answer to this question will reveal how you view scripture. Our view of the sustenance of the earth/universe also affects our understanding of sin, forgiveness, truth, morality, and the purposes and outcomes of humankind. Therefore, it is important to know exactly what we believe about the beginning of life on earth as well as why. It appears that the whole purpose of Darwinism (the theory of evolution) was to undermine the authority of the Bible. If the Bible is not true, then why believe it?

  When I was in high school and college, it was hard for me to fully understand evolution vs. creation. I thought I believed the Bible, but questioned how evolution figured into the equation. This caused me to further question the truth of the Bible and, thus, God. If Satan can cause us to doubt the validity of the Bible and the existence of God, then he can gain the upper hand in our lives.

- It is important for us to know what we believe and how to articulate our beliefs to our children, grandchildren, and those around us so they will know and understand God's design both for the world and for their lives.

- How did the universe come about? Who or what was responsible? Read Genesis 1 & 2 and think about God's creative genius. He imagined what He wanted to create, one-step at a time, and then spoke it into existence. Because He created us in His likeness and image, our words have the same creative ability. What God did at the beginning of creation is so important, it is the first account recorded in the Bible. God literally imagined the universe and everything in it. He spoke and it appeared. (See Genesis 1:6-7, 9, 11, 14-15, 24, 26-30.) Notice God's pattern. Each day started with *God said.....* followed by *.....and so it was.*

- The Bible was not intended to be a scientific textbook. It was designed to allow us to know God and understand His nature and character. Therefore, it does not defend God as the creator. Today, the continual archaeological and anthropological discoveries are confirming the Biblical account. If the Bible did not call for at least a minimal measure of faith, then our entire relationship with Him would be radically different and less significant. Faith pleases God (See Hebrews 11: 6).

- It actually takes more faith to believe the theory of evolution than Biblical creation. The evolution theory suggests that the single-cell entity not only evolved in complexity, but also somehow mutated beneficial characteristics until a human being developed. However, fossil records do not produce an unbroken evolutionary chain to support the theory. In addition, there is the question of where the single-cell organism came from and what created it. A single cell alone has a code with hundreds of thousands of bits of information, which functions like a carefully designed factory. All of this information is necessary in order for the cell to reproduce itself.

There are a growing number of scientists (both religious and non-religious) who are putting forth the theory of intelligent design. This theory questions whether the universe exists by chance or by design. The intelligent design advocates contend that the more we study and understand the universe, the more we realize that the incredible complexity of the universe could not possibly have happened by chance; there has to be some grand design behind it (i.e. a designer).

Also, we must recognize that God has entrusted us with stewardship responsibilities over His creation. We are not only the inhabitants of His creation but also the managers of it. Our responsibility is to not only use and enjoy what God has made, but also to wisely protect it so that generations to come will experience the same awe and intimacy with Him (through His works) as we have been privileged to experience.

What Is The Nature And Purpose Of Humanity?

We can find the purpose of human life spelled out clearly in scripture. Deuteronomy10:12-13 asks the question *What does the Lord your God require of you?* Quite simply, this scripture can be narrowed down to two ultimate challenges: to love God and obey His commands. According to Matthew 22:37-40, we are called to love Him first and then to love people, because He wants us to treat others in the same fashion He regards and treats us.

We are to love and fear Him so dearly that what He thinks about us is all that matters. Then we are to obey Him and the guidelines He has provided to us through His Word. Obedience is more than just following the letter of the law; it is discerning what God would want – His will for us – and choosing to seek that outcome. We are to love and obey.

> Humans were created to know God intimately and have a loving relationship with Him.

"Why does He want that?" His nature is love. He is pure love. We love Him through a full appreciation of who He is and what He has done. Then we exhibit this love by submitting our lives to Him with undying loyalty and commitment. An essential element in loving God is to have sufficient faith in Him to trust Him completely. We face a daily battle with a relentless enemy. If we falter and give up, we could miss an opportunity to be completely transformed by His love.

Is the Nature of Man Good or Bad?

When Adam turned away from God in the garden, the nature of man became inherently selfish, stubborn, rebellious, and evil (Jeremiah 5:23, 17:9). We can be taught right from wrong; but when we are under pressure, our true nature and character will determine our behavior. In other words, the choices we make come from who we are: Character always determines behavior.

Ultimately, it is the power of God that changes our nature. His grace and transforming presence in us develops the fruit of the spirit: love, joy, peace, patience, kindness, goodness, faithfulness, gentleness, and self-control. Without the transforming presence of Christ in us, we remain obnoxious, selfish, evil-inclined adversaries of God (whether we think of ourselves in that manner or not.). This transformation is a process and does not occur overnight. The more of His Word we absorb into our hearts and the more time spent in His presence, the quicker the transformation.

Knowing God's Word is the number one thing that will give us the foundation to resist temptation and overcome the obstacles in every

> **Practical Example:**
>
> Lions have a different way of seeing than humans. Safari guides take groups out to see the animals in large open humvees after instructing everyone to stay seated and not stand up suddenly. They can drive right up to a colony of lions feeding after a kill, and the lions barely acknowledge their presence. Lions only see the vehicle and have learned it will not hurt them.
>
> However, if a person stands up in the vehicle, the lion will see the person and get agitated. If that person were to step outside the vehicle, the lion would consider them a threat and attack. When we are in unity with a group of fellow believers, the enemy, Satan, sees us unified as one, and we are protected. However, if we isolate ourselves, we are open prey for Satan to devour us.

situation. Belonging to a body of believers offers us a place to best know, love, serve and obey God. It is a place of refining and a place of protection. The Bible speaks of Satan as a roaring lion who goes about seeking whom he may devour. When we separate ourselves from the body of fellow believers / the church, we are left alone and become a likely target for Satan.

What Happens After We Die On Earth?

There is an American paradox regarding life after death. Most assume, with typical American optimism, that if we mean well and try hard, everything will work out for the best. While many have not confessed their sins and accepted Jesus Christ as their personal Savior, more than nine out of ten adults believe that they will experience eternal life in heaven when they die. (See John 3:3; 1 John 2:18-27, 5:13.)

According to the Bible, God created us with a body, a soul, and a spirit. The body is our physical being that eventually wears out, the soul is our mind, will, and emotions, and our spirit is that part of us that relates to God. When we are born again, our spirit comes alive and is instantly born into God's kingdom. (See I John 2:3-6, 3:4-10, 14.) We must renew our minds with the Word of God in order to get our mind, will, emotions, and body to come into agreement with God.

Because God is love, pure, and true, He cannot put up with that which is evil and impure. Because He loves us and wants a voluntary love-based relationship with the people He created, He allows us to choose between seeking to honor and love Him, or grasping for self-fulfillment and personal glory. Satan was a beautiful archangel until he decided to rebel against God, thinking he was better suited for the job than his Creator. Satan is devoted to two ends: undermining God and destroying God's highest creation, mankind.

Adam and Eve were Satan's first targets. Because of their sin, we are all born with a nature predisposed to sin continually tempted to reject God and His ways until the end of time. At the end of time, Satan and his followers will then be condemned to a "lake of fire" where they will be tormented for the duration of eternity. Until that time, we are the primary objects of Satan's unwavering attention and evil designs.

Those who love, worship, serve, and obey God, by believing in Jesus as their Savior will spend eternity in Heaven. Heaven was created by God and is the home of all three persons of God (the Father, the Son, and the Holy Spirit) and His angels, and is ruled by Him. It is a holy place, and is a reward for those who are faithful to God through their relationship with His risen Son.

> Salvation introduces radical changes into our earthly experience. The evidence of this change of heart is seen in the "fruit" of repentance, visible in our very countenance as well as in our lifestyle. This does not mean that we will not be tempted. However, His redemptive love is always there to pick us up and set us back on the correct path.

When we die, the Bible says we go instantly to heaven or hell (a real place in the bowels of the earth God created for the fallen angels or demons) based upon the choice we make regarding the role of Jesus Christ in our life. Those who choose to reject Jesus wind up in hell. This error in judgment will cause them to endure everlasting punishment, suffering, and personal destruction. (See Job 31:12; Matthew 5:22, 10:28, 23:33, 25:46; and Revelation 20:14.)

God gives us our choice. He clearly states in His Word that we are to choose life and not death. (See Deuteronomy 30:19.)

What Spiritual Authorities Exist?

Contrary to our perceptions, our lives are all about engagement in the eternal struggle between good and evil. It is a no-holds-barred confrontation between holiness and sin. Every moment of every day, we are at war. It is an invisible war but just as real as any war in the physical world. (See Romans 7:8-25 and I Peter 5:8.)

Those who refuse to acknowledge that there is evil in the world attempt to convince us that this is just a fantasy conflict conjured up by those who fear their own shadow and are uneducated. Those who believe this seductive reasoning are walking into a trap that is a recipe for destruction. The reality is that we are warriors in the most inclusive, longest-running, continuous battle of all time: the battle for people's spiritual affections.

On one side, we have God and His angels and on the other, we have Satan and all his demons (fallen angels). Humanity lies between the two, right in the middle of this age-old war. Satan specifically targets believers with his demonic frustrations and attacks as his way of getting back at God. Paul tells us in Ephesians 6 that we wrestle not with flesh and blood, but with wicked spiritual forces. The good news? God wins!

Fortunately, as believers we have been given authority (Luke 10:19), the Holy Spirit and His angels to guide and assist us by exposing Satan's plans and revealing strategies to defeat this foe. Since we are soldiers in His army, fighting His battle, we must fight with His plans and weapons totally relying on Him for direction and provision. (See II Corinthians 10:3 and Ephesians 6:10-18.)

Paul tells us to put on the full armor of God every day of our lives. We are in a daily battle and we must be equipped with the armor of God to stand our ground and defeat the enemy in our life. The Belt of Truth is our foundation. The Breastplate of Righteousness keeps our heart from a division in loyalties. The Helmet of Salvation protects our minds from the lying doctrines of demons. Our feet are shod with the Gospel of Peace, which helps us hold our ground and take peace into every situation. The Sword of the Spirit, His Word, is ever present for hand to hand combat. Last but far from least, prayer is our Lance. Thank God, we, as believers, have been given the power and authority to resist and rebuke Satan and his host of fallen angels known as demons.

Having a Biblical worldview, knowing God's Word, hiding it in your heart, praying and relying on the Holy Spirit in your life, gives you the authority to detect intrusions from Satan and resist the attacks quickly. The final question is "What is truth?" Understanding the concept of truth in a relative world is the foundation that helps us live a life consistent with the teachings of Jesus.

What is Truth?

Every worldview hinges on the understanding of moral truth. To postmodernists, all truth is relative to the individual and circumstances, resulting in self-absorbed attitudes and selfish behavior. To new agers, each individual is a unique and complete embodiment of truth, leading to a life characterized by overconfidence and outlandish self-centeredness. However, to the Christian, there are absolute moral truths that should not be violated. To do so attacks the character and purposes of God, who is the source and judge of all moral truth. To adopt God's truths leads to a life of significance; to reject His truths can only result in punishment and unwelcome consequences.

Because truth reflects what we believe to be indisputably accurate, our notion of truth is at the core of our understanding of and response to reality. In other words, a worldview must specify what truth is (or isn't) in order to help us make sense of reality and lay a foundation for our understanding of meaning, purpose, value, and righteousness.

Our education system, reinforced daily through magazines, television, movies, music, and even newspapers, leads students (and everyone who is exposed to mass media) to conclude that absolute moral truth does not exist. Consequently, many are seduced into such thinking. The progression of this thinking leads one to question whether right and wrong truly exists and makes the idea of sin seem baseless. If sin does not exist, then is there really a need for a savior if we have nothing to be saved from and no consequences to face? The notion of judgment and condemnation are eliminated with this mindset.

How can a person know what is true? As believers in Christ, our worldview is based on the Bible. God's Word, while powerful and true, must be interpreted within its intended context. Indeed, if the Bible contains truth, there is no need to embellish the information because it will speak and stand up for itself as God sees fit. Some voice the concern that we do not have the original manuscripts therefore how can they trust the text we today call the Bible? Scholars who have studied the preservation process emerge with little doubt that what survived throughout the centuries provides little reason to question the accuracy of the content.

One of the most impressive substantiations of the authority of the Bible, however, is that it possesses the attributes of that which scholars have agreed are the elements of truth. For instance:

- The Bible is internally consistent and unified in its principles and claims.

- There is also tremendous consistency across the many authors and centuries during which the various books were written and in which its stories unfold.

- The fact that the information remains so compelling, dignified, and relevant to all the cultures of the world many centuries after it was written speaks volumes to the timeless and universal wisdom of its Author.

God chose the written word because He wanted people of all races and regions to have access to His thoughts and principles. In His omniscience, He recognized that having written documentation of His laws, commands, and principles would be far superior, and more permanent than relying upon the preferred method of the day (oral communication) or other means uniquely available to Him (dreams, visions, and so on).

His truth is timeless and universal. So what does the Bible have to say about truth? The most important and fundamental principle conveyed in the Bible is that God is the essence of truth (Romans 3:4). Everything that comes from Him—words, plans, laws, judgment, blessings—is a manifestation of moral truth. He is the source of truth, the definition of truth, and the gauge of truth. (Read John 14:6.) The laws, rules, and commands listed in the Bible give us the guidelines we need to comprehend and carry out moral truth.

The Nature of Truth - God's truth does not change. It is what it is and it will always be the same. This attribute makes His truth completely reliable and comforting for us. (See Jude 1:3 and I John 1:6.)

Benefits and Impact of Truth - Truth does not exist in a vacuum; it influences our reality. Most importantly, God's truth sets us free. Moral law does not limit us. It allows us the freedom to achieve the full potential (destiny) that God placed within us. We must know and apply God's Truth in order for it to do us any good.

Attaining Truth - God has made His truth abundantly accessible. He sent Jesus to teach and emphasize what matters to Him. Then He protected the information and sealed the information through the work of His Holy Spirit. He then set in place pastors, teachers, prophets, and apostles to teach and reveal His truth. We are to study the Word for ourselves and take advantage of all the Christian resources provided through churches, books, magazines, radio, television, and internet.

The Challenge of Truth

The challenge for believers is to love His truth, to obey it in all circumstances, to promote it whenever possible and defend it whenever necessary. Contrary to public opinion, moral truth is not a private matter to be decided by every person according to each new set of individual circumstances. God's Truth is absolute, authoritative, and accessible. If we live by it, we will thrive; but in its absence, we will suffer. (See John 10:35 and II Timothy 3:16.) Our choices have consequences. The failure to recognize or acknowledge His truth does not change the fact that His truth exists, it is always right. It cannot be altered or ignored without peril.

Every moral issue and choice is addressed in the Bible, and may therefore be acted upon with wisdom and purity - if we draw upon the truth of scripture. Thinking like Jesus is not natural for us, so we must incorporate purposeful Bible study into our regular life regimen, and diligently apply what we learn from that effort. As politically incorrect as it sounds, moral truth is black and white. You are either with God or against Him on every moral issue of the day. Knowing the content of His Word will enable us to make the right choice every time.

> ### Remember this important point:
> Never accept a truth at face value. Always filter it through the grid of scripture, prayer, and counsel. Our enemy is clever and takes perverse pleasure when we

Now that we understand what a Biblical worldview is and how necessary it is to possess, we are ready to view America's Christian heritage in light of the founder's Judeo-Christian worldview.

PATRIOTIC PORTRAIT

George Washington Carver (1864-1943), an agricultural chemist of international fame, introduced hundreds of uses for the peanut, sweet potato, soybean, and pecan. This revolutionized the economy of the South since these crops replenished the soil, which had been depleted through the years of cotton growth.

As an infant, his mother was kidnapped, and he was raised by his aunt and uncle. Due to poor health as a child, he spent much time around the house and in the woods. He let the woods and nature be his teacher in his early years. He later went to schools in Missouri and Kansas. He graduated from Iowa State College of Agriculture and Mechanical Arts. George Washington Carver was also an accomplished artist and even received an Honorable Mention at the 1893 Chicago World's Fair. In 1896 he left his faculty position at the Iowa State College of Agriculture to join Booker T. Washington, President of the newly founded Tuskegee Institute in Alabama. While there he made many medical contributions, including Penol (a mixture of creosote and peanuts as a patent medicine for respiratory diseases such as tuberculosis) and a cure for infantile paralysis.

His discoveries from the peanut (over 300), the sweet potato (over 118), as well as from the soybean, etc., included cosmetics, face powder, lotion, shaving cream, vinegar, cold cream, printer's ink, salad oil, rubbing oil, instant coffee, leather stains from mahogany to blue, synthetic tapioca and egg yolk, flour, paints, non-toxic colors (from which crayons were later created). What a resume of discoveries. In spite of all of his accomplishments, he remained humble and turned down numerous opportunities that would have made him rich. Carver was committed to helping people and the South.

As a committed Christian, Carver gave all the credit for his discoveries to God as the Creator Who instructed him in his work. Carver named his laboratory God's Little Workshop and never took any scientific textbooks into it. He merely asked God how to perform his experiments. While speaking before the Women's Board of Domestic Missions in 1924, he told the 500 people assembled:

"God is going to reveal to us things He never revealed before if we put our hands in His. No books ever go into my laboratory. The thing I am to do and the way of doing it are revealed to me. I never have to grope for methods. The method is revealed to me the moment I am inspired to create something new. Without God to draw aside the curtain, I would be helpless." [1]

In order to be sure he would be undisturbed in his laboratory, he would lock the door. He confided: "Only alone can I draw close enough to God to discover His secrets." [2] He shared these observations about God in 1928: "Man, who needed a purpose, a mission, to keep him alive, had one. He could be…God's co-worker…" [3]   and then added, "By nature I am a conserver. I have found nature to be a conserver. Nothing is wasted or permanently lost in nature. Things change their form, but they do not cease to exist." [4]

In 1939, George Washington Carver was awarded the Roosevelt Medal, with the declaration: "To a scientist humbly seeking the guidance of God and a liberator to men of the white race as well as the black."[5]

George Washington Carver remarked: "The secret of my success? It is simple. It is found in the Bible, *In all thy ways acknowledge Him and He shall direct thy paths.* [6] George Washington Carver was a man of godly character who was used mightily by God for the good of all mankind. He served his God first and his nation second. (See Proverbs 3:6.)

(For more detailed information on the life of George Washington Carver, see *America's God and Country, Encyclopedia of Quotations* by William J. Federer.)

RECOMMENDED READING / MEDIA

Think Like Jesus, George Barna

Rocks, Fossils and Dinosaurs, G. Thomas Sharp, Ph.D.

Expelled – Documentary that exposes Darwinism v. Creationism bias in academics

QUESTIONS for THOUGHT and DISCUSSION

1. What characteristics do you think reflect a lifestyle of someone with a Biblical worldview? How many actually live out the Biblical worldview?

2. Did you ever have a time when you doubted the existence of God? What changed your mind?

3. Think about the goodness of God and list all His benefits.

4. How has the teaching of evolution affected your faith?

5. What is the difference between "pure" science and "junk" science? What is the influence behind each?

6. Do you remember the first time you allowed God's influence to shape your response to a specific situation? Explain.

7. Take a moment to evaluate your motivation for the things that you do. Be honest! Is your motivation to please others or to please God?

8. How does God develop our character?

9. What is the number one thing that will give us the foundation we need to live a life of victory over temptations?

10. What is sin? Who decides whether we sin or not?

11. What is "hell" and who is sent there and who lives in Heaven?

12. Why is it important for us to understand sin, surrender, salvation, and the soul?

13. Is evil present in our world? Is good? Explain.

14. How do you view the Bible? How do you properly interpret scripture?

15. Think about and discuss how following God's moral laws actually protect you and free you at the same time.

17. How many of our civil laws reflect God's truth.

18. How important is God's truth to you? Do you hunger to know the truth, even when it hurts?

Foundational Truths – Chapter 4

"The Hand of providence has been so conspicuous in all this, that he must be worse than an infidel that lacks faith, and more than wicked, that has not gratitude enough to acknowledge his obligations."

> \- George Washington, letter to Thomas Nelson, August 20, 1778

"[T]here is a degree of depravity in mankind which requires a certain degree of circumspection and distrust."

> \- James Madison, Patriotpost.us – Founder's Quote

Chapter 4

The Spread of Christianity to New Worlds

God Directs Early Explorers

Just as God formed each one of us (Jeremiah 1:5), He also formed nations. God called Abraham (Genesis 17:1-8) to become a nation set apart for Him. The nation of Israel became an unusual nation whose Lord was and is God Almighty. He also set the United States into being and set it apart to be a light of the Gospel to the nations ("a city on a hill"). A beacon of hope to the nations, America's system of government is one of self-government with roots strongly imbedded in Christianity. Until the founding of the United States, all other nations had kings who ruled over them. It was unheard of to allow a people to govern themselves through elected representatives who answered to the people.

This idea of people governing themselves came from the Word of God. I imagine this concept was as foreign as Columbus' belief that the world was round instead of flat! It literally took the Spirit of God planting a desire in the hearts of His servants to see the Gospel spread to unknown lands that brought about the discovery of the New World.

In the mid 1400's, God began to move on the hearts of various groups of people to relocate to lands yet unknown … places to which they believed God was sending them. Throughout the Bible, we can see how God relocated people to fulfill His plan in the earth and he still moves people throughout the world today. God knows what is happening everywhere and He has a master plan. He is in control even when it may not feel like it. However, God's plan does not just happen. He needs willing, believing people to work through. He needs you and He needs me to take our place in His Kingdom to achieve His goals. We are His hands upon this earth.

Who were the first explorers?

What do you know about the men who discovered the North American Continent and went on to explore it? Who were they and where were they from? Can you name any of them? What prompted their explorations?

God chooses ordinary people like you and me to do great exploits for Him, even though we are flesh and blood and never will be perfect. Only Jesus was perfect. Some of us have more weaknesses than others.

Christopher Columbus was one such ordinary person. Columbus was a Christian who loved the Lord and wanted to be used by Him. Even though his first name means "Christ Bearer," Columbus was not trained in religion. He was simply a businessman skilled in map making. He loved God and wanted to claim unknown lands in the name of Christ.

God will use all areas of a man's ability for His glory. God used Christopher's desire to serve Him and his expertise in navigation to discover the continents of South and North America. Unfortunately, he never fully submitted his life to the lordship of Christ but instead, allowed his weaknesses of pride and greed to take control. He allowed terrible maltreatment of the Indians and set a poor example for his men. He could have been a great leader if he had only listened to and obeyed God.

> Spiritual lesson:
> When we refuse to surrender all to God's control,
> we become slaves to our weaknesses.

The next explorers were men called to ministry and trained in self-discipline. They were true missionary explorers.

The Spanish Conquistadors brought Franciscan and Dominican Monks / Friars to the New World (South and Central America) to minister to the Spanish military. Many of them felt compelled by God to reach out and evangelize the Indians. This took them farther and farther north into North America. As they traveled, they made maps of the areas they were discovering. They set up missions in New Mexico, Arizona, Baja California, and California.

The French sent Jesuit monks to explore and chart new territory along the U.S. - Canadian border. Wherever they went, they worked one on one with the Indians, teaching them the Gospels. The best and brightest scholars that France had to offer, these men were from well-educated wealthy families, most with linguistic gifts that helped them learn the native languages. All of them loved God. They gave up their lives of luxury to give their very existence to His service. Some were martyred for Christ as they endeavored to spread the Gospel across North America.

Columbus, Franciscan Fray Junipero Serra, Jesuit Father Jacques Marquette and other missionary explorers loved and trusted God. They trusted Him when they did not know where they were or what to do next. They trusted God for provision and safety. They sacrificed everything so God could use them for His glory. These men of God planted the first spiritual roots in the New World and prepared the way for the first English settlers.

The First English Settlers

In 1585, England decided it was time to expand their world power by establishing colonies in America. Their motives under Queen Elizabeth were purely materialistic. They wanted more power and gold. Rumors abounded that there was not only gold in the new world, but also precious jewels. Since it was not fashionable to believe in God during that era in England, the first settlers' motives were not to promote Christ but to gain wealth.

Sir Walter Raleigh's first effort to send a group of settlers to establish a colony on Roanoke Island off the coast of North Carolina failed when the starving colonists gave up and returned to England. His second attempt of 115 people struggled to survive because few were prepared for the hardships in the wilderness.

> Imagine yourself in this scenario.
> How would you handle such a situation?

Finally, when they were nearly out of supplies, they decided to send their Governor, John White, back to England to replenish their stores. In going, he left behind his daughter and newborn granddaughter, Virginia Dare, the first white child born in America. Due to events in England, it took two years before he was able to return. Upon reaching American soil, he found the village destroyed and all inhabitants gone. They had vanished without a trace. To this day, no one knows what happened to them.

Meanwhile stories continued to circulate throughout England that the Indians used chamber pots of gold, encrusted with rubies and diamonds. Thus deceived, many people ignored their own personal safety to come to the New World.

Twenty years later, the newly formed Virginia Company sent more settlers to colonize the American coast. Motivated primarily by financial interests, they had only a moderate desire to spread the gospel. They raised money for the founding of a colony by stating that their goal was to save the souls of the Indians. They framed their venture in missionary terms. The men who put money into this colonization of the New World did it as an investment, expecting to make money on the venture.

The Virginia Company recruited 144 men for this trip… no families or women, only men. Most of those chosen were gentlemen down on their luck and not used to working with their hands. They were looking for quick money. They recruited one minister, Rev. Robert Hunt, specifically to evangelize the natives and minister to the colony. The expedition leaders were not truly submitted to God and thought having a minister amongst them would guarantee success. The Rev. Hunt was truly a man of God.

Upon landing in America, they knelt down and planted a cross in the sand of Virginia and Reverend Hunt dedicated the land to the Lord. Even though this historic event marked the first dedication of the New World to the Lord, the hearts of most of these men were hardened towards God.

Jamestown was established in May 1607, and did not prosper as the northern colonies did. They did not look to God as their provider and did not seek His guidance as the Pilgrims and Puritans who followed them did. The site of the settlement was an issue of great debate. Bartholomew Gosnold (founder of the Virginia Company) voted for moving to higher ground but the other men on the council did not want to move. The Jamestown site was in a low-lying, swampy area where summers were miserably hot and humid and the standing water was a breeding ground for diseases such as malaria. In addition, there was no easily accessible fresh water. Could it be that these men were too lazy to move?

These men could not get along with each other much less the friendly Indians that surrounded the colony. There was no unity, no leadership and each man was out for himself. Captain John Smith was their most capable leader but, like Columbus, he had a big ego and was arrogant and full of pride. Therefore, he used his leadership gift poorly. He caused most of their problems with the Indians since he had no patience with them and would sometimes shoot first, rather than take time to understand their ways.

The only person who took his job seriously was Rev. Hunt. He truly cared for this flock of self-centered men. The first years were filled with sickness and death. Rev. Hunt did more than his share of tending the sick, working to build the first structures, planting crops, as well as burying the dead. He set the example of a true Christian servant. He also conducted mandatory church services every Sunday. Unfortunately, only when these men were sick and believed they were dying were they willing to listen to Rev. Hunt's message of God's love. The first church built in America was in Jamestown.

Nine months after arriving in this new land there were only 30 of the 144 settlers still alive. Rev. Hunt did not survive past the first year or so. Eventually other colonists arrived along with a replacement minister for the church in Jamestown. These godly men who risked their lives to promote the gospel in this new land were true heroes. More and more colonists arrived to settle the area surrounding Jamestown. However, it still took this colony twenty years to become productive. Because of its poor location, Jamestown was eventually abandoned.

God's Chosen People

In the early 1600's the Spirit of God began to move within the Church of England. This movement caused friction within the church leadership. The Church of England was the official "church" of England and other sects were not tolerated. A House of Bishops governed the Church and did not like the new believers (on fire for God) who wanted to change the way the Church of England worshiped. Even though it was a purifying move of God, the House of Bishops did not take kindly to change and felt the church did not need "purifying". Out of this movement emerged two groups. The "Puritans" wanted to see a purer form of worship with more prayer and Bible reading. They believed in changing the Church of England from within. The second group of believers did not believe the church could change so they formed their own church. They were referred to as "Separatists" because they "separated" from the Church of England.

The House of Bishops did not like either group and called them both fanatics. They refused to appoint "Puritans" to any position of authority and generally ignored them. The Separatists, who would become known as Pilgrims, were not ignored but treated more harshly because the government did not recognize their churches. The Bishops wanted to stop the Pilgrims because they challenged the Bishops' authority. Therefore, feeling their power was threatened, the Bishops decided to make an example of the Pilgrims so that others would not follow their beliefs.

> This scenario seems familiar. Jesus faced this type of attitude from the spiritual leaders of his day.

Even though they had withdrawn their memberships from the Church of England, the Separatists were still forced to pay taxes to the church. In addition, they were bullied and arrested on false charges. Under the threat of imprisonment, the Separatists finally decided to flee England. Pastored by John Robinson, William Bradford's congregation of Separatists sought religious asylum in Leyden, Holland where they became a close-knit family.

As poor immigrants in Holland, they were not able to qualify for good paying jobs. Working two or three jobs to provide for their families, they sacrificed everything they had to commit themselves to God and His will. After twelve years in Holland, they were no better off financially. They were aging prematurely because of the hard work. Not only that, their children were learning Dutch ways and forgetting their English heritage while being drawn more and more to the ways of the world. They began to pray for God's direction on where they should go. Soon it became evident that the Lord wanted them to go to America.

They believed they were to build a new nation based on Biblical principles that would become a light to the world for Jesus Christ. Even though they knew the risks, they also knew that being in God's will was all that mattered. They could endure anything and go anywhere if they stayed within God's perfect will. The question now was how they would get there. They wrote to the Virginia Company looking for funding for their trip. Their petition was denied because the Virginia Company was nearly bankrupt.

A London businessman named Thomas Weston approached them unexpectedly with a proposal to help them. He had investors who would back their venture, enabling them to use the Virginia Company's Charter. This was their only open door, but they were reluctant. It was possible God was using their reluctance to warn them not to go through this door; however, they accepted the offer and began making their preparations.

They decided to send a third (41) of their congregation to America to start the new colony. The chosen families sold their houses and all unmovable possessions. They needed the money to pay for their shares in the American Plantation. Each person sixteen years and older would have one share and had to pay ten pound sterling (about $700 in modern terms). Those with extra funds could purchase extra shares. They would be in a partnership for seven years (Standard time for indenture.) At the end of seven years all land and profits would be divided according to the number of shares they each owned. Personal property such as houses, land and gardens would remain their personal property.

In all, there were 16 men, 11 women and 14 children moving to America. Since Pastor Robinson was not going, they appointed their elder, William Brewster, as their teacher and acting pastor until Robinson could follow later. At the last minute, Thomas Weston brought them a revised contract that demanded more money. Now they understood their reluctance to trust this man. They had to sell much needed supplies and extend their period of indenture to pay the added charges.

On August 6, 1620, the two ships, the Speedwell and the Mayflower, set sail for the New World. However, when they left the Speedwell at Plymouth, England for necessary repairs, the passengers crowded on to the Mayflower. Twenty Separatists decided not to continue on this journey. Fully trusting in God, the rest left Plymouth, England on September 16, 1620. Of the 102 passengers on the Mayflower, there were twenty-one Separatists and eighty-one "strangers". Most were sympathetic to the Separatists' cause, but a few were adventurers looking for riches.

Because of bad weather, it was impossible for the passengers to go up on deck during the entire journey, a journey that lasted almost two months. They could not even open the hatches for fresh air. They had no bathrooms, no running water, no fresh food (only dried food), no baths, and no fresh air. Many were seasick. I do not know of many today who could endure those circumstances. Because their trust was in God, they endured without complaining. Even the children did not complain. Now that is impressive!

Have you ever seen a life-size replica of the Mayflower? Surprisingly small, it is hard to imagine 102 people surviving in such cramped quarters for so long. Can you think of any movies you have seen that depicted sailors on ships that were dirty and nasty looking? Well, the sailors on the Mayflower were no different and some treated the Pilgrims with contempt. However, when the leader, a mean spirited man, took sick suddenly and died within one day, the rest of the crew stopped mocking them.

God truly protected them during this rough sea journey. God also used the time on the Mayflower to unite the Separatists and the "strangers", forming them into one company.

Since the storms blew them off course, they tried to sail south along the coastline but the headwinds prevented their progress. Apparently, God had other plans for them. When the Pilgrims realized they were not going to land in northern Virginia as planned, they knew they needed to draw up a governing compact to form their own government. Without some type of agreed upon laws for behavior, they knew everyone would do what was right in their own eyes and chaos would ensue.

The Mayflower Compact marked the first time free and equal men voluntarily entered into a covenant to create a civil society based on the Biblical principles of self-government. Next to the Ten Commandments, the Mayflower Compact became the second of our founding documents, the basis for all law and order in the new colony and the new nation. William Bradford, John Carver, Miles Standish, Elder William Brewster and Edward Winslow were the authors of the Mayflower Compact.

Mayflower Compact, November 11, 1620

"In the name of God, amen. We whose names are under-written, the loyal subjects of our dread sovereign Lord King James by the Grace of God of Great Britain, France, Ireland, King, Defender of the Faith, etc.

"Having undertaken, for the glory of God and advancement of the Christian Faith and honor of our King and country, a voyage to plant the first colony in the northern parts of Virginia, do by these presents solemnly and mutually in the presence of God and one of another, covenant and combine ourselves together into a civil body politic, for our better ordering and preservation and furtherance of the ends aforesaid, and by virtue hereof to enact, constitute and frame such just and equal laws, ordinances, acts, constitutions and offices from time to time, as shall be thought most meet and convenient for the general good of the colony.

"Unto which we promise all due submission and obedience. In witness whereof we have hereunder subscribed our names at

Cape Cod, the 11th of November, in the year of the reign of our sovereign King James of England...Anno Domini 1620."

When they set foot on this Promised Land, they knelt and gave thanks to God for a safe passage. They had begun their long journey by kneeling on the dock at Delftshaven to ask God's blessing; they ended it on the sands of Cape Cod, kneeling to thank Him for that blessing. Only then did they send out a search party to find a suitable location for their plantation. The search party came back safe, after a frightful encounter with unfriendly Indians, having achieved their goal of finding the best location for their plantation.

Plymouth is located on a perfect bay and slopes up to a plateau, a great place for their safe house. Orchestrated by God, they had a perfect site that met their every need.

The Indian tribe that had lived on this site was fiercely hostile. About nine months prior to the Pilgrims' arrival every man, woman and child had been killed by a plague. Historians to this day do not know why this plague destroyed this tribe (Patuxet Indians). The surrounding tribes felt that evil spirits killed the Patuxet tribe; therefore, they kept their distance from this spot. This enabled the Pilgrims to settle in the area safely. Fortunately, the other tribes in the region were peaceful.

The Captain of the ship agreed to stay with them until they had built some shelters for protection from the oncoming winter weather. The spot God had prepared for them was perfect. Land was already cleared at the top of the hill for planting, fresh water streams flowed nearby, and a buried stash of corn provided seed to plant in the spring.

After searching out the land, William Bradford returned to the ship to receive the news that his wife had fallen overboard and drowned. Bradford, at the age of thirty, had to make a decision between self-pity and bitterness, or throwing himself into leading the new settlement. He chose a productive life moving forward to a new life with new choices and opportunities. They named the site Plymouth after the town in England from which they set sail.

By the end of December the "general sickness", brought about by weakened immune systems, started to spread throughout the

Plantation. The Pilgrims began to die. Six died in December and eight succumbed in January. During that first winter, over forty-seven died, nearly half of the original group. With all the trials that first winter, the group grew closer together in their trust in God. At one point there were only five men well enough to take care of the sick. Captain Miles Standish, Elder Brewster and several others served the company. They chopped wood, cleaned, clothed, cooked, and tended the sick. They buried the dead at night so the Indians would not realize their number was diminishing.

On Sunday, the highlight of their week, they would dress up in their best clothes, red capes, green waistcoats, with colorful plumes in their hats; not the drab and somber black and brown attire pictured in history books. Two generations later under Puritan influence, a philosophy that frivolous clothes would cause frivolous attitudes was adopted. Pilgrim worship services were held in the blockhouse at the top of the hill that was built as a fortress with a flat roof and trapdoor. They had two large cannons on the roof that Captain Jones had left with them.

William Brewster would preach and, according to Bradford's journal, he was a gifted teacher. His preaching brought about a "sweet" repentance to their hearts. Repentance was a lifestyle as they continually searched their hearts for hidden or secret sins.

> If these settlers arrived in America today, what would they think of the church and society as a whole?

By spring, only three families remained untouched by death. The children survived best. Of eighteen wives, thirteen died, of seven daughters, none died and of thirteen sons, only three died. However, no matter how things appeared, their hearts remained soft towards God.

One day in early spring, God sent an Indian named Samoset to them. He spoke English and was able to educate them about the surrounding Indian tribes. While he traveled up and down the coast with various sea captains, he had learned to speak English. Through Samoset, they met Chief Massasoit of the Wampanoag's tribe. As a result of that meeting, a forty-year peace treaty of mutual aid was forged. Samoset also introduced them to Squanto who was invaluable in preserving their existence.

Squanto was a Patuxet who had been kidnapped by English traders and taken to Europe where he learned English and became a Christian while living in a monastery. When he was finally freed and returned to the New World, he found his family was dead. He lived with the Wampanoags but had no zest for life due to his grief. When Samoset took him to the Englishmen, Squanto found a new purpose in life as a life-saving mentor to the settlers.

God had prepared and then used these two English-speaking Indians to bring about a peace treaty and to teach the ill-prepared settlers skills to survive in the wilderness. Because these ill-prepared Pilgrims to the new world had all grown up in a city, the Indians literally had to teach them everything about farming and survival in the New World. About the same time, God sent another Indian to them named Hobbamok. A good man, he remained faithful to the Pilgrims until the day he died. To find out more about the details of God's miraculous provision and the running of Plymouth Plantation, read "The Light and the Glory" by Peter Marshall and David Manuel. It is written as a very interesting novel.

> Meditation:
> Take a moment to reflect on the greatness of God. He prepared the way for this colony, and through them, this nation.

Governor John Carver fell ill and died that April. They elected William Bradford governor, a position he held for many years. His book "Of Plymouth Plantation" is a journal of all that happened to them. The first wedding in the new colony occurred in the summer and was quite a joyful event. The happy couple was Edward Winslow, who had lost his wife, and Susanna White, who had lost her husband.

The First Thanksgiving

In the fall, the settlers celebrated their first harvest with a day of Thanksgiving to God, inviting the Indians as their guests of honor. Chief Massasoit arrived the day before with 90 of his warriors carrying numerous deer and turkeys dressed to cook. They taught the Pilgrim women to make hoecakes and a tasty pudding from maple syrup and cornmeal. They even taught them to pop corn! The Pilgrims provided the vegetables and pies. The first Thanksgiving celebration lasted four days with an abundance of food, footraces, wrestling and shooting contests with guns and bows.

In November, a ship arrived with thirty-five more colonists. There were many joyful reunions; however, these newcomers came empty-handed. Because there was not enough food to last throughout the long cold winter, the leaders chose to go on half-rations to stretch their supplies. Their harvest was plentiful for the original group but not enough to feed the additional newcomers. By the end of the winter, they were allowed to eat only five kernels of corn a day per person. However, God was good and provided another ship that traded trinkets for their beaver pelts, which allowed them to buy additional corn. Not a single person died of starvation that winter.

The first year they shared everything and had all land in common. By the second year, there was little enthusiasm for planting. The people were listless and uninterested. Because they shared everything, those who worked hardest received the same amount as those who did not work. There was little incentive to work hard.

Governor Bradford prayed for insight into the problem and God answered. Bradford realized that the communal system was not God's plan for them. This first experiment in communism failed to produce enough food to live on during the first two years. Finally, Governor Bradford gave each family a piece of land of their own (private property). This breathed new life into the colony and abundantly increased food production. Each family had their own business. With each passing year, the colony grew and prospered. Capitalism / free enterprise was birthed

Their approach to each trial that came their way was to set aside days to fast and pray for the reason for the trial. Regardless of the cause, the sincere repentance of each person reached God's heart. Because they witnessed the answers to the settlers' prayers, the Indians began to take notice of the God of the Pilgrims.

By 1629, the incoming settlers had increased until none of their members were left in Leyden, Holland. Governor Bradford kept a journal to record the history and progress of the prosperous and growing Plymouth colony.

In his words, he wrote, "we have noted these things so that you might see their worth and not negligently lose what your fathers have obtained with so much hardship".[2] He also noted that "it was the Lord's doing, and it ought to be marvelous in our eyes".[3]

PATRIOTIC PORTRAIT

William Bradford (1590 – 1657) was born in the Yorkshire farming community of Austerfield, England. He lost both his parents as a very young child and was shuttled among several relatives, never staying long anywhere. When he was 12, he happened into the neighboring town of Scrooby, and there discovered a church service in progress. He was astonished by its fellowship and its lack of ritual. This drew him back to this congregation that was so full of fervor for reform. By the age of 17, Bradford was a fully committed member, sharing the radical idea of separating from the official Church of England. At that time, this was a very dangerous decision, for Separatist leaders were hunted down and imprisoned. They soon decided to flee to the Netherlands when King, James I threatened to force them from the land.

Besides barely being able to make ends meet in the Netherlands, the government gave in to pressure from their English ally and began harassing the refugees. With Pastor Robinson's encouragement, they decided to make a new home overseas. The rest of the story is history.

Bradford was 30 years old, married and had a young son when preparations were being made for this journey. He was one of the leaders of this effort. When it was decided that not everyone could go, he had the difficult decision of leaving his four-year-old son behind. Yet, as Bradford wrote, "they knew they were pilgrims, and looked not much on those things, but lifted up their eyes to the heavens, their dearest country, and quieted their spirits."[4]

Young Bradford spent the rest of his life serving the new colony called Plymouth Plantation. He was governor of Plymouth for a total of 36 years with only five brief one-year respites. In 1623, three years after the death of his dear wife, Dorothy, Bradford married a widow, Alice Carpenter Southworth, who had two small sons. This second marriage appears to have been a happy one. She provided a home in Plymouth for Bradford's son who had been left behind in Leiden, and she and William had three children of their own, two sons and a daughter.

As the colony grew, so did the responsibilities of the Governor and his Court of Assistants. They were charged with the financial management of the colony, acting as judges in disputes, negotiators with the Dutch in New York and the new Massachusetts Bay Colony. They also had to maintain friendly relations with the Indians.

Eventually, the colony began to break up as settlers moved away to gain access to additional land. Consequently, the church was divided and the old "comfortable fellowship" ended. This clearly distressed Bradford. He finished piecing together his journal in 1650, bringing the record up to 1646. He ended it with a current list of the Mayflower passengers and their status in the year 1650.

William Bradford's journal is the most complete picture of the Plymouth experience recorded. His remarkable ability to manage men and affairs was a large factor in the success of the Plymouth Colony. The Pilgrims "desperate adventure" was marked by Bradford's stamina, versatility and vision. He is just one of the extraordinary men that God raised up to lay the foundation for the nation.

RECOMMENDED READING

Of Plymouth Plantation, William Bradford, Boston: Wright and Potter, 1901

QUESTIONS for THOUGHT and DISCUSSION

1. Do you know anyone today who would be willing to step out in faith, giving up comfort for a primitive life among unreached people groups?

2. Do you know any missionaries personally? What impresses you most about today's missionaries?

3. If you were going into an unknown territory with indigenous peoples, what do you think would be important to know and why?

4. What sets the Pilgrims apart from Christian society today?

5. What countries or religions can you think of today that treat their people the same way the House of Bishops treated the Pilgrims?

6. Just as the Pilgrims were reluctant to accept Thomas Weston's proposal, have you ever felt reluctant about a decision you were making?

7. Did you still make the decision or decide to postpone making the decision until you had more information?

8. Did it occur to you that the Holy Spirit might be warning you?

9. What does indenture mean?

10. What are some possible reactions to the living situation on the Mayflower? How would you react?

11. How do you think the Pilgrims handled this? If today you found yourself in this situation, how would you handle it?

12. Did God prepare the land for the Pilgrims? If yes, how did He do it? Has God ever prepared a place for you like He did for the Pilgrims? Explain.

13. How would you keep from losing your faith when faced with the deaths of your family members like the Pilgrims did that first winter?

14. Why were they thankful to God? List the things for which they probably gave thanks.

15. Why did personal property ownership breathe new life into the colony? What did this create?

Foundational Truths – Chapter 5

"It should be your care, therefore, and mine, to elevate the minds of our children and exalt their courage; to accelerate and animate their industry and activity; to excite in them an habitual contempt of meanness, abhorrence of injustice and inhumanity, and an ambition to excel in every capacity, faculty, and virtue. If we suffer their minds to grovel and creep in infancy, they will grovel all their lives."

- John Adams, Dissertation on the Canon and Feudal Law, 1756

"The propitious smiles of Heaven can never be expected on a nation that disregards the eternal rules of order and right, which Heaven itself has ordained."

- George Washington, First Inaugural Address, April 30, 1789

Chapter 5

The Puritans and Covenant Love

Time to Leave England

Back in England, the Puritans were finding it more difficult than they thought to change the Church of England from the inside. This is true for many today who have stayed in dead churches hoping to light a fire in them. It rarely works because hearts are hardened to change (because they are comfortable) and those seeking to affect change usually end up leaving.

Therefore, twenty years after the first Pilgrims had left England for Holland and then moved to America, the Puritans were no closer to affecting change in the Church of England. In fact, the Church of England was persecuting the Puritans for their beliefs so much so that life had become difficult for them. Therefore, they became convinced they must leave England for America or ultimately face prison in England.

Life in Elizabethan England was anything but fun. London was a very dark and dangerous city with streets full of refuse. Muggers abounded, drunkards and twenty-four hour taverns were on every street, and prostitutes hung from windows overhead selling their wares. Among the wealthy, the love of money was rampant. England, at this time, was a Godless society. It was truly a nation without a soul. True believers were mocked, thought to be stupid, and were looked down upon.

> Does that sound familiar? Take a moment and think about the treatment of Christians in general by society's elitists. We are treated in much the same way, are we not?

The Puritans were a people of deep commitment to Jesus Christ and took their walk with God so seriously that many of them kept spiritual journals to record their prayers and petitions regarding their battle against sin and self. One of the most committed and influential Puritans in England was John Winthrop. He was Cambridge educated, the owner of a sizable estate in Suffolk, an attorney in the Court of Wards and a Justice of the Peace. He penned these lines in 1612 at the age of twenty-four:

> *"I desire to make it one of my chief petitions to have that grace to be poor in spirit. I will ever walk humbly before my God, and meekly, mildly, and gently towards all men....I do resolve first to give myself-my life, my wits, my health, my wealth - to the service of my God and Saviour who, by giving Himself for me and to me, deserves whatsoever I am or can be, to be at His commandment and for His glory."*[1]

Winthrop's covenant relationship with the Lord grew and deepened over the years. His faith can be compared to the French and Spanish missionaries before him who gave up wealth and comfort for a life of service to Christ. This move of God produced so many new Christians that there was sometimes a self-righteous attitude coming from the new believers. This only fed the Bishops resistance to the Puritans. The first twenty years of the seventeenth century was a time of testing that produced maturity in the Puritans as they began to grow in their understanding of submission. All they really wanted was to turn the Church of England back towards the scriptural worship of the New Testament Church, with a strong emphasis on the Word of God and scriptural worship.

By the end of 1620 the Puritan movement had attracted adherents from all social classes and walks of life, including Oxford and Cambridge-trained clergy and some of the most brilliant scholars and theologians of the age. The Puritans had more material possessions than the Pilgrims and were better educated. The main difference between the Pilgrims and the Puritans in 1620 was that God was still leading the Puritans gradually to the place where they would be willing to give up what the Pilgrims had already given up. For the Puritans had more than the Pilgrims did—more money, more servants, more friends in high places, more education, and more business experience. The one thing the Pilgrims had over the Puritans was compassion.

For the Pilgrims, compassion was the fruit of undergoing a persecution so severe that they had to leave their native land. It was the fruit of daily dying to self, daily repentance and in receiving forgiveness. As they received forgiveness, then they were more willing to forgive others. After their years in Holland and the trip to America, they knew they could do nothing save for the grace of God. This Christ like compassion and humility marked the difference between the Pilgrims and most of the Puritans.

This very knowledge is very humbling when I stop to ponder what these brave believers were willing to do in the face of persecution. It makes me wonder what we, as believers today, would do in the same situation. The Pilgrims followed by the Puritans gave up all they had to move to a wilderness land in quest of religious freedom and opportunity. I have to ask myself what would bring me to a place where I would be willing to give all that is comfortable and familiar for the cause of Christ.

God was bringing the Puritans to that place of compassion and humility through the mounting pressure of increased persecution. In 1628, after Charles I took the throne, William Laud was appointed Bishop of London. He presented the King a list of English clergy with an 'O' or a 'P' behind each name. If Orthodox (O) the clergy were in line for promotion, but if Puritan (P) the clergy were marked for suppression. This was the turning point as it became clear that reforming the Church of England from within would be impossible.

Separation went against everything they believed. What were they to do? A startling option soon came out of this dilemma. This alternative was so radical that it was hard to pray about it. But pray they did and it began to be evident that they could reform the Church of England from within by moving across the sea to America. In America, they would be far enough away from church leadership and free to worship as they desired. They began to see it as an opportunity to demonstrate what could happen when a group of believers lived wholly and totally unto God.

America was a wild untamed frontier with many dangers, but they believed if God was with them, all the powers of hell could not prevail against them. Some far-sighted Puritans could see God's hand in everything that had happened and knew that now was the time for this radical move. King Charles had dissolved Parliament and announced that he would run the country himself (1629) and London had sunk to a new level of depravity. It was no longer a question of if they should go but how soon.

In 1629, a group of two hundred Puritans on two ships left England for America. Their leader, the Reverend Francis Higginson, exclaimed to the passengers:

> *"We will not say, as the Separatists were wont to say at their leaving of England, 'Farewell Rome!' or 'Farewell Babylon!' But we will say, 'Farewell dear England! Farewell the Church of God in England, and all the Christian friends there! We do not go to New England as Separatists from the Church of England, though we cannot but separate from the corruptions in it, but we go to practice the positive part of church reformation, and propagate the Gospel in America!"*[2]

The Massachusetts Bay Company formerly known as the New England Company held the Charter for this new colony. The charter was miraculously signed by the king without so much as a blink of the eye. Now all they needed was a strong leader to organize this exodus. The partners wanted John Winthrop to take the lead but Winthrop, himself, was unsure if it was God's will for him to go. Therefore, he did what most of us do in making major decisions. He made a list of pros and cons. This list, later published, helped thousands of Puritans to clarify their own decisions. The pros consisted of the obvious advantages of leaving a depraved England, sensing that the desolation of the protestant churches in Europe by Cardinal Richelieu in France and Wallenstein in Germany was a sign of the times. The church in England was corrupt and materialism was god. An example of the cons follows:

> *Obj:* *The ill success of other plantations may tell us what will become of this.*
>
> *Ans:* *None of the former sustained any great damage but Virginia, which happened through their own sloth....There were great and fundamental errors in the*

> *former which are like to be avoided in this, for their*
> *main end was carnal and not religious; they used unfit*
> *instruments, a multitude of rude and misgoverned*
> *persons, the very scum of the land; and they did not*
> *establish a right form of government.*

> *Obj: It is attended with many and great difficulties.*

> *Ans: So is every good action....The way of God's Kingdom,*
> *which is the best way in the world, is accompanied with*
> *the most difficulties.*

Thus, Winthrop decided that it was God's will for him to go. He met
with the other principles at Cambridge, where many of them had
attended university together. It was August 26, 1629 when these men
covenanted together for this mission. They sincerely believed God
ordained the mission. Historian Perry Miller would say, "These
Puritans did not flee to America; they went in order to work out that
complete reformation which was not yet accomplished in England and
Europe".

Three days later the general membership unanimously elected
Winthrop Governor. It then became his task to arrange passage for
over 1,000 Puritans. Winthrop accomplished this task and every ship
was ready right on schedule. He was aboard one of the first, the
Arbella. By this time, a little over two hundred Puritans had already
gone and established a colony at Salem. John Endecott was their
temporary governor until Winthrop arrived.

Covenant Love

Gov. Winthrop's group set sail in March 1630. On the voyage to
Salem, Gov. Winthrop received a vision for the new colony from
which he wrote his famous essay, "A Model of Christian Charity".
This essay was to become as important as the Mayflower Compact
because he took it a step further in outlining covenant love. The main
message was:

> *"This love among Christians is a real thing. It is absolutely*
> *necessary to the well being of the Body of Christ...we are a*
> *company...knit together by this bond of love. We are entered*

into covenant with Him for this work...we must work as one man.

"Now the only way to avoid this shipwreck and to provide for our posterity is to follow the counsel of Micah, to do justly, to love mercy, to walk humbly with our God. For this end, we must be knit together in this work as one man...We must hold a familiar commerce together in all meekness, gentleness, patience, and liberality. We must delight in each other, make one another's condition our own, rejoice together, mourn together, labor and suffer together, always having before our eyes our Commission and Community in this work, as members of the same body. So shall we keep the unity of the Spirit in the bond of peace. . .

"We shall find that the God of Israel is among us, when ten of us shall be able to resist a thousand of our enemies, when He shall make us a praise and glory, that men of succeeding plantations shall say, "The Lord make it like that of New England." For we must consider that we shall be as a <u>City upon a Hill</u>..."[3]

> **Note**: When America won the war for independence, the above literally came to pass - for they defeated the greatest military power in the world!

He believed that in America they would build "God's Kingdom on earth" and it would serve as an example to the world.

I believe we could all look back on our lives and find a time when we experienced victory due to covenant relationships. The Puritans were on the verge of discovering the power of covenant relationships.

As the *Arbella* approached Salem, Gov. Winthrop could tell that things were not right in Salem. There were only a few huts and tents and the people looked thin and ragged. Their eyes lacked any luster. Their leader, John Endecott quickly briefed Gov. Winthrop on the effects of the first winter. Of the original 266 settlers, only 85 were left. The others were dead or had given up and returned to England. The same general sickness that struck the Pilgrims their first year struck these Puritans as well. Sea voyages weakened the immune system causing scurvy and the general sickness. The Plymouth settlers sent their doctor, Samuel Fuller to assist the Puritans. Fuller helped substantially and provided an example of pure Christian love, which changed Endecott's opinion of the Pilgrims.

Winthrop was puzzled by this turn of events and sought God for the reasons this colony was struggling. He soon realized that they had not lived out their commitment to love one another. There is a difference in knowing what the word of God says and actually living it out in your life. There are two parts to covenant. The people were doing the first part – loving God with all their hearts. But they were not doing the second part – loving each other. The Pilgrims had learned this and Endecott could testify that it works because of his observation of the Pilgrims.

Endecott then continued with his report of the state of the church in Salem. After spending the first winter with Dr. Fuller from Plymouth, he had become convinced that the church structure adopted at Plymouth would work for them. Dr. Fuller, who was also a deacon, explained that under the leadership of Elder Brewster, the church at Plymouth was organizationally separate from the civil authority under Governor Bradford. Yet it obviously exercised decisive moral influence over it. The Separatist church leadership was provided by a pastor, a teacher, and a ruling elder, but these were chosen by the membership of the church (unlike in England where the leadership was imposed by a presbytery or hierarchy of Bishops). They closely protected their right to choose freely their own spiritual leadership as one of the basic tenets of their Christian faith. Anyone could worship in the Separatist church but to become a member of the church, one had to convince the eldership of the church of ones' personal, saving relationship with Jesus Christ and of the orthodoxy of their faith.

The Pilgrim's model was at the basis of our Bill of Rights in protecting the church from civil government interference in worship practices. There was a separation between the church and civil government for the protection of religious freedom. However, the church itself exercised decisive moral influence over the civil government.

Regardless of any doubts that Gov. Winthrop may have had about this system that allowed non-landholders to vote, he could see that whatever Plymouth was doing God was blessing them more each year. They were without doubt primarily interested in doing God's will.

> **Reflection**: What would happen if we would do this before our elections?

Governor Bradford called for a day of prayer the day before their elections. The people were not to work but to pray for the Lords' will as to whom He wanted them to vote into office.

Endecott went on to explain that after fasting and praying they had elected their pastor and teacher. Afterwards, they made a covenant to devote themselves to God and to love Him with all their hearts. Gov. Winthrop noted that they had not completed the process and that was the reason the colony was struggling. They forgot their covenant to love each other enough to exhort, admonish, and rebuke.

Gov. Winthrop and Endecott committed to live out covenant love with each other and to give all they had for this colony. They set the example for everyone to follow. Then they set about putting everyone to work, even the wealthy gentlemen who brought servants to do their work for them. No one was exempt from work. They committed to build adequate housing for as many families as possible by the end of summer. Everyone was to give 100% to the group effort so the colony could succeed.

That first fall and winter was a real test of the Puritan's commitment. Because more and more Puritans were arriving from England at regular intervals, the food supply was low. Each new group of arrivals stressed the food shortage further. Finally, Gov. Winthrop sent the ship, the Lyon, to England to purchase food and supplies. He paid for this from his own pocket. When by February of 1631 there was still no sign of the Lyon and they had run out of food, Gov. Winthrop called for a day of prayer and fasting. He did this often during his term as Governor. However, before that day came the Lyon was spotted off shore. Once again, God provided for His people and instead of fasting and prayer, they had a special day of Thanksgiving to thank God for all He had done.

These Puritans had obeyed the call of God and He honored their obedience.

Three months after Governor Winthrop's arrival more than a thousand Puritans had come from England. They began to spread out and settle Massachusetts. From Salem the Puritans moved on to settle Boston and other New England towns. They established churches and practiced covenant love everywhere they went. Between 1630 and 1646 (16 years), twenty thousand Puritans came to New England. They came committed to God and one another as obedient servants of the Lord.

Family and Community Life

Covenant love was carried out in family life as well as in community life. We tend to think of the Puritans as very austere and serious because they were very serious about their walk with the Lord. They were also serious in their attitude about sin. They did not treat sin lightly, as we tend to do today. However, because life in the colonies was so difficult humor provided a healthy outlet for the soul. They enjoyed every God-given opportunity to relax and even be a bit silly with each other. Laughter brings healing and that is what they needed to keep going in this untamed land.

 Keep in mind that the heart of the Puritans' lives was their willingness to deal with sin in their own lives and the lives of others. They dealt with sin through constant repentance and forgiveness. Their relationship with God and with each other was at the center of their lives. They believed that if something good or bad happened to one it was felt by the whole community. Therefore, excommunications (banishment) were not uncommon.

> **Example**: "The Scarlet Letter" where the lead character is found to be with child.

83

Typical church services were 3-4 hours long because the people hungered for the Word of God and they didn't have children's church! Because the word was so important to them they paid a tithing man to keep them awake. The tithing man was an independent businessman who had a long rod with a feather attached to one end and a brass doorknob on the other. The feather was used for women to tickle them awake. The doorknob was used for men to give them a little thump on the head. All businesses in the community were closed during church services, even the Inns.

If the church was at the center of community life, the family was at the center of church life. Covenant love was carried out in their family lives and community lives. Because the Puritans were realists in life they were also realists in death as well. One example of their unwavering faith was the famous Puritan Pastor Cotton Mather. He endured the deaths of all but two of his thirteen children and his wife. He did it with grace and dignity never wavering in his faith and trust in God. This was how the Puritans as a whole faced the harsh realities of life in this new land.

Puritan parents took their responsibilities as parents very seriously. They were no more tolerant of sin in their children's lives than their own. They knew that their children did not belong to them but to God. Therefore, God had merely entrusted their children to their care and they were accountable to Him in the end.

The Puritan parents did not let their fear of losing their children's love cloud their ability to deal with sin in a child's life. As a result, they were very strict. Courtship (dating) and marriage were very important to the community as a whole. There was a firmly established code of conduct for courting couples. There were specified nights for "calling" and strict laws against "night-walking" (couples wandering down inviting country lanes). As a result, the premarital birthrate was practically non-existent and sensual temptations were minimized. Of course, they did not have all the media outlets we have today bombarding our children with all forms of sensual temptations.

As a result of courtship not being treated lightly, couples were able to show greater wisdom when considering marriage. The Puritans did not arrange marriages but both sets of parents had to be in agreement and give permission for a couple to marry. If they thought that one or the other of them was not quite mature enough they would extend the engagement time. Therefore, engagements could last as long as three years.

Because they realized they did not know everything and did not always hear the voice of the Lord, Puritan parents welcomed input from the community on important matters related to their children.

Yes, Puritans were serious about their relationship with God but as mentioned earlier, they also had their fun side. Life in the colonies was difficult and humor provided a healing balm for the soul. It is very stress relieving to have a hearty laugh and they took every God-given opportunity to relax and laugh with each other.

Civil Government and Church Leadership

New England was a "plantation of religion" and proud of it. Almost all laws were based on the Bible and the Magistrates/Judges were expected to use the full power of the state to promote the agenda of the church. They believed in a state church and suppressed opposing viewpoints. They seemed to have forgotten that their reason for leaving England was their own experiences of persecution. They routinely banished other religions, such as the Jews, the Presbyterians, Quakers and Baptists, from Massachusetts.

Roger Williams and Anne Hutchinson were two who felt this banishment. Just as God pruned the people, He also pruned their leaders. The Rev. Roger Williams did not believe the Puritan vision for God's kingdom. He did not believe God would use human beings to set up His kingdom on earth. He was a perfectionist and held firmly to the belief in "Liberty of Conscience" (the attitude that "nobody is going to tell me what I should do or believe".). He took this to such an extreme that he refused to submit to authority. The church leadership took every opportunity to work with him and allow him to change but he could not see that lack of submission was a problem.

Roger Williams was a talented and brilliant man and it grieved Winthrop and Bradford to see his stubbornness. Williams finally fled to Rhode Island and founded the city of Providence. There he attracted every misfit, independent and rebel. He could not keep order. It was a nightmare for him but he was merely reaping what he had sown. In his later years, Roger Williams did see that no one could achieve perfection and he began to embrace everyone. However, it was still important to him to always be right. Do you know anyone like this? Sadly, I think we all do.

His greatest work was as a missionary to the hostile Narragansett tribe. He became a trusted friend of the chief and led many of them to Christ. Because of his relationships, Rhode Island was the only colony spared from all Indian uprisings. He was also able to warn Massachusetts about pending surprise attacks.

Another branch that was pruned was that of Anne Hutchinson, a member of John Cotton's church. She held a women's Bible study to discuss the Pastor's sermons. Soon the Bible study became more about what she believed which did not line up with church doctrine. Ultimately she was tried for heresy and found guilty for proclaiming that she was the only one who knew what the Holy Spirit was saying. When she wouldn't repent, she was banished from the colony.

On the other side of the coin was the Rev. Thomas Hooker who when he had a policy dispute with Gov. Winthrop asked for permission to go to Connecticut. Hooker disagreed with Gov. Winthrop's policy that only those who were dedicated to God's work had the wisdom to elect good leaders. Hooker believed every man should be allowed to vote.

After many discussions, it became obvious that this disagreement could not be resolved. Rev. Hooker was a man who listened to God, trusted Him and obeyed Him. He was a man under submission. Therefore, he did not hesitate when God directed him to start a church in Connecticut. He went to Gov. Winthrop and asked permission to be released to go to Connecticut and Gov. Winthrop reluctantly granted him permission with his blessing.

God was blessing the colonists. Divine intervention occurred regularly in daily life as God protected his covenanted people. One such example was of a carpenter working up on a house where eight children were sitting in a circle playing below him. He accidentally dropped a big bulky piece of wood over these little children. He cried out in agony, "O Lord direct it!" and the Lord did direct it. It landed in such a way that not one child was hurt.

Another instance involved two ships in distress. One sprang a leak a thousand miles off the coast causing the crew to abandon ship. They had no water but plenty of food. The other ship was out of food but had plenty of water. The second ship spotted the raft with the crew of the sunken ship. The Captain made ready to rescue the sailors but some of his men objected because they did not want to share what little food they had left. The order to rescue stood. As it turned out they each had what the other needed and so God provided for both and saved them all.

It seemed that those with hearts that scorned the covenant way were subject to God's judgment instead of blessings. For example the chief sailor, who urged the Captain not to take on the extra men, was just such a man. He was later in a similar situation but died at sea without anyone to save him.

The Puritan colonists sought God daily during those first difficult years but when they began to prosper and move out of the townships into the countryside, they forgot "it was God who had enabled them to prosper". Puritan New England was beginning to lose interest in the Word of God. Those who lived farther out from the local churches found it increasingly difficult to get to church. As a result, just 40 years after the arrival of the first comers their hearts were growing cold towards God. They were forgetting the Covenant Way.

The second generation, those born on American soil, never knew what it meant to suffer persecution for their faith. They never knew the desperate starving time their parents had known. Most importantly, their parents forgot to teach them the need to first pray and then commit their ways to the Lord. Therefore, they developed into a generation of strong capable but **self**-reliant Yankees (instead of God-reliant.).

As they began to move out into new territories to make their own way, they built new settlements. Life in these remote settlements did not always revolve around the church as they did in the townships. If their homestead was within an hour's drive of church, they would attend. If farther, they would not. Their minds were more and more distracted away from the Word of God. The ministers could see what was happening but were unable to get the people to repent and turn back to God.

> What have modern generations taught their children about their faith?

As those with opposing religious views left, they established new colonies, which grew into the original 13 colonies. Many of them had state churches that were fully sponsored by the colonies. The colonies grew and prospered, and in that growth with each passing generation the hearts of the colonists were turning cool towards God. Even the preachers were not preaching with the fire of the original pastors. During these times, God would use wars with the Indians to turn the hearts of the people back to Him.

PATRIOTIC PORTRAIT

Thomas Hooker (1586-1647) was born in July of 1586 in Marfield, Leicestershire, England. His father was a yeoman (a farmer who cultivated his own land, below gentry). Thomas attended a grammar school established by Sir Wolstan Dixie at Market Bosworth, about 25 miles from Marfield. From there he went on to Queens College, Cambridge, and then to Emmanuel College, graduating with a BA in 1608 and an MA in 1611. He remained on at Emmanuel College until 1618 as a Dixie fellow and catechist. While at Emmanuel College, Hooker was genuinely converted after going through a lengthy time of spiritual soul searching. Cotton Mather tells us, *"It pleased the spirit of God very powerfully to break into the soul of this person with such a sense of his being exposed to the just wrath of Heaven, as filled him with most unusual degrees of horror and anguish, which broke not only his rest, but his heart also."*[4]

Rev. Thomas Hooker served in several churches, making quite a name for himself as a truly gifted minister with a strong anointing in the area of conversion. However, because of this, in 1629 he attracted the attention of Bishop William Laud who threatened him with arraignment before the High Commission for his non-conformity and Puritanism. Ultimately, Hooker had to flee to Holland where he served in two churches before deciding to go to New England. In 1633, he arrived in Boston and settled in Cambridge where a number of his flock from England had settled.

Thomas Hooker's genius and anointing as a true man of God left a profound influence on the pulpits of England for years to come. He was a devout man of prayer who set aside one day a month to fast and pray. *"Prayer is my chief work, and it is by means of it that I carry on the rest."*[5]

After three years in Massachusetts, he had a dispute with John Cotton regarding the strict theological rule in Massachusetts. In particular, regarding who was eligible to vote. After asking permission to move to Connecticut and receiving Governor Winthrop's blessing, he and many of his flock moved in 1636 to found Hartford, where he was pastor until his death.

Hooker was one of the drafters of the Fundamental Orders (Constitution) of Connecticut (1639), under which Connecticut was long governed and which represent his political views. It was so significant a document that it became a model for all the other constitutions in the colonies, including the United States Constitution. The essence of Hooker's Election Day sermon was as follows:

1. The choice of public magistrates belongs unto the people by God's own allowance.

2. The election must be conducted by the people, but votes should not be cast "in accord with their humors, but according to the will and law of God."

3. Those who "have the power to appoint officers and magistrates also have the power to set bounds and limitations on their power" so that "the foundation of authority is laid in the free consent of the people," because "by a free choice the hearts of the people will be more inclined to the love of the persons chosen, and more ready to yield obedience."

He also promoted a plan for the New England Confederation. Hooker had a Biblical view of the role of government. He believed that government, in order to dispose of the affairs of the people, should be orderly and decent established by God to maintain the peace and union of such people.

Thomas Hooker died a victim of an epidemic sickness on July 7, 1647. "When one that stood weeping by the bed-side said unto him, 'Sir, you are going to receive the reward of all your labours,' he replied, *'Brother, I am going to receive mercy!'*"[6] Cotton Mather called him "the Light of the Western Churches". Dr. Thomas Goodwin said of him, "if any of our late Preachers and Divines came in the Spirit and power of John the Baptist this man did."

RECOMMENDED READING / MEDIA

God and Government, A Biblical and Historical Study, Vol.1, Gary DeMar. American Vision Press

"The Crucible" This 1966movie depicts the Salem Witch trials and gives an idea of that period of time in history. As with all Hollywood movies it is not to be taken as factual but merely a representation of the period.

QUESTIONS for THOUGHT and DISCUSSION

1. What is the value of keeping a journal?

2. How does the moral decay in 1629 London compare to America today?

3. Explain the differences between the reasons the Pilgrims left

4. England versus the Puritans' reason for leaving.

5. In your own words describe covenant love.

6. What are the two greatest commandments?

7. How would you live out covenant love with your family?

8. If your (future) children belong to God, how will this affect your parenting? Do you believe today's parents see their responsibility as parents in the same way the Puritan parents did and why?

9. Why would the Puritans be so intolerant of other Christian sects?

10. How does God view rebellion and lack of submission to authority? [Hint: Read 1 Peter 2:13; James 4:7; Romans 13:1-6 and 1 Samuel 15:23]

11. What is the difference between Roger Williams and Thomas Hooker in their attitude towards authority?

12. Should the right to vote be withheld for any reason?

13. As the hearts of the Puritans grew cool towards God's word how does this compare to America today or does it?

Foundational Truths – Chapter 6

"It is the duty of all Nations to acknowledge the providence of Almighty God, to obey his will, to be grateful for his benefits, and humbly to implore his protection and favors."

> - George Washington, Thanksgiving Proclamation, 3 October 1789

"I think all the world would gain by setting commerce at perfect liberty."

> - Thomas Jefferson, letter to John Adams, 7 July 1785

"As a man is said to have a right to his property, he may be equally said to have a property in his rights. Where an excess of power prevails, property of no sort is duly respected. No man is safe in his opinions, his person, his faculties, or his possessions."

> - James Madison, National Gazette Essay, March 27, 1792

Chapter 6

Life in Colonial America

Repercussion of Hearts Grown Cold

Hard times have a way of drawing us both closer to God and each other. When times are tough, we are more diligent to seek God; but as things improve, we allow ourselves to grow complacent. We have all experienced this cycle. When the Israelites who had witnessed God's miracles in the wilderness were gone, the next generation settled in the Promised Land began slowly to forsake God. We do the same after a time of testing. As the hearts of the second generation Americans grew cool towards God, His hand of protection lifted. The forty-years of peace with the Indians came to an end. There are consequences to forsaking our first love.

Phillip, the Chief of the Wampanoag's, hated the Christian Indians and had their pastor killed. When the murderers were caught, tried, found guilty and hanged; Chief Phillip declared war. Thus began what is called "King Phillips War". Four settlements were attacked, and every man, woman and child were killed.

New England was not prepared. Massachusetts declared a day of fasting and prayer. However, the Rev. Cotton Mather warned that one day of fasting and prayer would not be sufficient to turn away God's wrath. God wanted true repentance as well as their whole hearts. The settlers did not heed this warning; but as the attacks grew worse, they began to listen and see that they did indeed need God in their lives.

In the midst of this war, God moved miraculously on behalf of the colonists numerous times. One such instance occurred in Brookfield, MA, when the whole town was miraculously spared. The Indians tried repeatedly to set fire to the blockhouse where the colonists had taken refuge. Every attempt failed. Hearing about this miracle, crowds began to pour into church for the first time in years and finally listened with their hearts, not just their ears. The Christian "praying" Indians came to their aid and taught them how to fight. Then Captain Benjamin

Church came up with a successful plan of attack that killed "King Phillip" and ended the war!

Even in times of God's judgment, God's mercy rested upon the colonists and is still available for us today. As the end of days approaches, I only hope we will draw close to Him and trust in His mercy as His righteous judgment is poured out upon the earth.

The next battle had to be won on the spiritual level. God began to expose witchcraft and occultism in New England. Again, this was brought on because some colonists allowed themselves to backslide in their relationship with God. They had become so spiritually weakened that the supernatural manifestations of Satan's power were coming out into the open. These manifestations were very real in the form of witchcraft, occultism, poltergeist phenomena (demons at mischief) and so on.

Witches began hanging out their shingles claiming they could cure warts, straighten toes and make love potions. White magic served the purpose of gaining public acceptance of witchcraft. Black magic would come later in the form of hexes, casting curses on people, and spellbinding. Soon more and more people were going to see these "knowing ones" for advice and counsel. The Reverend Cotton Mather, one of few who was strong enough in the faith to fight these infestations, kept the most complete record of these demonic events. When the witches loosed demonic activity over whole villages, the people were powerless to stop the destructive activity.

Because of this outbreak, 120 persons confessed openly to signing a pact with the devil. Twenty people were executed for practicing witchcraft. That same year, hundreds of witches were also put to death in Europe. The New England witch-hunts only lasted five months. Believing a spirit of vengeance gripped the whole land, the clergy finally put a stop to the trials. New England was finally released from this terrible ordeal when several years later one of the judges, Samuel Sewall, publicly repented for his role in the trials.

> Repentance is so good for the heart. From my own experience, I know that when I repent with all my heart, God hears and fills me with His peace and situations begin to turn around.

In addition to the Indian war, the onslaught of witchcraft, and occult activity; there were droughts and a plague of locusts. All of these trials and tribulations ended when the people turned their hearts back to God.

Unfortunately, the people of New England again closed their eyes and went back to sleep. Soon, all those ministers who had been committed to the Puritan Way died. The ministers of the next generation were more intellectual and did not have a personal relationship with the Lord. Therefore, they were content to let New England sleep.

One Nation Under God?

By 1695, thirteen colonies were established along the eastern seaboard with religion at their center even though they had grown away from God (lost their first love). Each of the thirteen colonies had their own civil government as well as an official church, or they favored one church sect over the others. Rhode Island and Pennsylvania had the most religious freedom. Christian sects who were being persecuted in Europe were invited to come to Pennsylvania. And many of them accepted the invitation.

Virginia installed the Anglican Church as its official church and even expelled Puritan preachers in the name of religious uniformity. Maryland became a safe place for Catholics while New York and Rhode Island became havens for persecuted Jews from Brazil. Each of these colonies' laws was based on the Bible. Favoring one religious sect over another by the civil government was a common practice.

The Founders of this nation believed religion promoted virtue and virtue promoted republicanism (citizens elect representatives to represent them in running the government with the power belonging to the people.) Therefore, religion was necessary for republicanism. Because each colony/state had its own civil government and official religion, there was no unity among the colonies. In fact, they were far from being united as "One Nation Under God." Each state was more interested in protecting their own self-interests, rather than in working together with other states for the common good. The South thought the North was too rigid in its religion and the North thought the South was too lax.

The Light is Rekindled

In 1734, God began to reawaken America to His love and sovereignty. It started in several different locations throughout the colonies and grew into what is now known as America's first spiritual "Great Awakening".

The "Awakening" started with Rev. Jonathan Edwards and spread to other churches in New England. Jonathan Edwards was the most respected theologian that America ever produced. For some time he had been crying out to God for revival and had been preaching bold sermons proclaiming that man on his own could not accomplish the purposes of God except by the grace of God. This concept was not preached from the pulpits of the day. Popular teaching was that man alone could accomplish the purposes of God.

One Sunday in December 1734, several young people were born again. One was a young woman with a bad reputation who was so changed that she influenced many other young people to come to the Lord. Soon the whole atmosphere of the town was changed, and by the spring and summer of 1735, the presence of God was very apparent in the whole area. As a result, their services were full to overflowing, and people were coming from long distances to partake of this blessing. Soon other churches began to experience the same refreshing presence of God.

God used a young British evangelist, George Whitefield, to spread the good news throughout the colonies. When he landed in Georgia in 1737, Whitefield discovered a hunger for the Word of God amongst the people. Soon he was preaching to large crowds. Upon returning to England to raise money for an orphanage in Georgia, he found the pulpits of England closed to him because of the preachers' jealousy. He took his message of the gospel out into the open air. Soon revival was breaking out in England, also. Between 1736 and 1770, George Whitefield preached more than eighteen thousand sermons in America and England. His desire was to reach those pastors whose hearts had grown cold to the things of God and bring them back to life. Some responded and some did not. Traveling up and down the east coast and inland to rural areas of the colonies, George Whitefield preached until the day he died. He would preach as many as 600 sermons in a six-week period, and still felt that he should have done more.

Whitefield's work was aided by faithful dedicated American preachers who sparked further revival in their own areas. The ministry of William Tennant and his four sons carried the word of the new birth to the Presbyterians in New Jersey and Pennsylvania. He also started a university to train evangelical preachers, Princeton University. His son, Gilbert, became the most famous American-born evangelist of the Great Awakening. There were others reaching other denominations such as Theodore Frelinghuysen in the Dutch Reform Church; David Brainerd, a Presbyterian missionary to the Indians while Samuel Davies reached the Presbyterians in Virginia.

Even though these men performed miracles in their denominations and geographic regions, it was through the preaching of George Whitefield that God brought unity to the thirteen colonies. The Gospel is a great equalizer and it broke through the denominational barriers bringing the budding nation together. It reminded each colony that they were

During his final missionary trip to America, Reverend Whitefield had a great impact on a young free Black American teenager named John Marrant, an accomplished musician. He and a friend happened on a Whitefield meeting. On a challenge, he went in with the intent of disrupting the preaching. Instead, Marrant gave his life to Christ and dedicated himself to gospel ministry. Marrant overcame rejection by his family, not once but twice, and became an evangelist to the Cherokees. Noted Black American historian Arthur Schonberg (1874-1938) said of Marrant, "...a Negro in America like the Jesuits of old who spread the seed of Christianity among American Indians before the birth of the American Republic." He went on to work on a Plantation where he began to evangelize the slaves.

Once the Revolutionary war started, he was forced into the British navy. Following the war, he settled in England, studied under Whitefield, and was ordained as a Christian minister by the Calvinistic Methodists in 1785. He traveled around preaching in England, Canada, and back to the United States. He became ill in America and quickly returned to England where he died at the young age of thirty-seven. Despite his brief life, Marrant accomplished much, and was among the first Black Americans to successfully evangelize and minister to the American Indians.

not "an island unto themselves" but that they were all connected – one family. What God was doing in one colony, He was also doing in all the others.

The Great Awakening continued into 1770, just six years before the Declaration of Independence. God truly used this revival to unite this fragmented group of colonies. Because all the churches in the colonies were receiving the same salvation message in the same way, the walls that divided them were broken down. Repeatedly, Americans in all thirteen colonies received the message that all men are created equal and precious in the sight of God. This truth was declared "self-evident" by 1776.

National identity was developing as a result of the Great Awakening. Most of the men and women of the American colonies were deeply religious and well educated. Education was considered as important as religious training. Yale, Harvard, Princeton, Dartmouth, Columbia, William and Mary, and other colleges in the colonies were started as Christian colleges and seminaries. These are the Ivy League schools of today.

Tensions with England –
Before, During, and After the Great Awakening.

As an English colony, America was bound to obey the laws passed by Parliament and to submit to the English monarchy. For the first 100 years, Parliament had allowed the colonies to run themselves, even though the English government had the ultimate power to rule over them. However, as the colonies began to prosper, Parliament began to look to America as a source of income. (This seems to correspond with how the American government has come to view its citizens.)

First, they passed the Navigation Acts of 1651 and 1663, which prohibited the colonies from trading with any other country except England. The colonies did not like this at all, but they had to obey. Then in 1684, King Charles ordered Massachusetts to swear allegiance to the Crown and allowed Episcopal Churches be established in that area. The Men of Massachusetts met in Boston's Old South Meetinghouse to decide on their future. Giving up their charter would be painful, but obeying King Charles would mean giving up their religious freedom. Reverend Increase Mather, the prominent Puritan minister, reminded them of their heritage. When the vote was counted, submission to England's mandate was unanimously defeated.

> Assignment: Research scripture passages pertaining to submitting to civil authority.

The king was furious and threatened to send Col. Percy Kirk ("Bloody Kirk") and five thousand troops to force them into submission. Rev. Mather went into his study and prayed for God to intervene and have mercy on them. After praying, the Lord spoke to his heart that the colony would be spared. Two months later, they received word that King Charles was dead and Col. Kirk would not be coming. They discovered later that King Charles died the very day that Rev. Mather fasted and prayed. Could this have been just a coincidence?

The new King sent Sir Edmund Andros to put down any resistance in the colonies, but he was unsuccessful. He finally revoked the charters of all the colonies. His agents went to collect the charter from the colony of Connecticut. Just as it was to be handed over, the candles were mysteriously snuffed out and the charter disappeared!

From 1689 until 1760, peace returned to the colonies during the reign of William and Mary. The colonies continued to prosper and thrive economically. However, when King George III took the crown in 1760, England had just fought an expensive war with France in which the English ended up with new territories in the New World. In order to recoup some of the lost finances, King George III decided to let the colonies pay for keeping his troops. England also started enacting taxes on the colonies. Since the American colonists had no representatives in Parliament, they could not protest the numerous additional tax laws enacted upon them. They had no voice. These taxes and tariffs were very punitive and hurt many of the colonial merchants.

First, the Molasses Act of 1733 required a three-cent tax on each gallon of molasses not purchased from the British West Indies. The custom officials were not honest men and kept much of the money for themselves. Thus, revenues that England anticipated did not materialize. The Navigation Acts had been repealed; however, under

King George, they were reinstated. Parliament instituted the Stamp Act in 1765 that required the colonists to pay for British stamps that they were required to put on all printed matter - from marriage certificates to newspapers.

After vigorous protests, some of the tax laws were finally repealed. In the end, the King was not just using the colonies to pay for keeping his troops in America, but was actually using them to fully fund and support his adventures around the world. This unified the small resistance movement in the colonies and inspired them to grow and become stronger. The Committees of Correspondence were formed to facilitate the flow of information throughout the colonies to keep everyone informed about what was happening. These committees were very important to the resistance movement.

Where were the first seeds of rebellion planted in the American colonies? Would you believe they first sprouted in the pulpits of some of the churches? Many of the religious leaders believed the King had set himself above the law and had become a tyrant. Thus, they preached, "Where the Spirit of the Lord is there is Liberty" and that "when a ruler opposes God's will, his subjects cannot follow God's will." They did not want to rebel, but if resistance were the only way, they would support it.

The Tea Act of 1773 caused tensions to increase even more. Even though it eliminated the tax on British teas, it imposed a tax on American tea which would put the American tea companies out of business. In December of 1773, the first act of rebellion occurred in protest of the new tax on tea. The Committees of Correspondence sent urgent letters saying "Don't let the East India Tea Company unload its tea." That protest, called "The Boston Tea Party," made King George irate.

In response, the King ordered the closing of the port of Boston. This act alone brought all the angered colonists into greater unity as they came together to help the people of Boston in their hour of need. They brought barrels of rice and sheep as well as money. The Committees of Correspondence proclaimed King George a tyrant and began proclaiming that they had "No king but King Jesus!"

The Founding Fathers

By March of 1775, tensions had escalated to the point that Patrick Henry addressed the Virginia House of Burgesses saying, "There is no longer room for hope. If we wish to be free, we must fight. An appeal to arms and to the God of Hosts is all that is left us! We are not weak. We shall not fight our battle alone. There is a just God who presides over the destinies of nations; and who will raise up friends to fight our battle for us. I know not what course others may take, but as for me, give me liberty or give me death!"[1]

Who were the Founders and what did they sacrifice to start this nation? Today some textbooks portray these men as unethical opportunists, slave owners etc. Is that an accurate portrayal of the Founders? What purpose is served by vilifying our Founding Fathers?

The men who founded the United States of America were well educated and hard working. The majority were honorable Christian men willing to sacrifice their lives and finances for liberty. These were men of uncommon intelligence and character. Many of them were handling both business and civic affairs when they were young teens. By age 14, they were doing the work of adults in the marketplace or in college. They used the Bible to learn to read, were well educated in the Word of God, and studied it intensely.

These young men were not shallow thinkers as are Americans today. They were deep thinkers and firmly committed to a Biblical worldview. I believe they were born at this particular time in history to fulfill God's purposes in establishing the United States of America.

They accomplished much at a very early age because they did not have the distractions that we have today. To them reading and educating themselves was relaxing. Think about what we could accomplish if we did not spend so much time watching TV, listening to music, playing computer games, or going to sporting events and movies. They did have time to relax and have fun, but not as much time as we have today. Consequently, they discovered their God-given purpose early and pursued it with excellence and joy. When I look at what they accomplished, I am shocked by how shallow we have become as a people. They had a sense of duty and followed it without complaining.

When was the last time you heard someone talk about duty and self-sacrifice?

The Founding Fathers were extraordinary men who lived in extraordinary times. Were the founding fathers Christian? To some, the question is "Were they 'born again' or 'saved'?" In other words, did they have a personal relationship with Jesus Christ and follow His teachings? It is a difficult question to ask because many of them believed it was a private matter between God and themselves. There is historical evidence of personal salvation for Patrick Henry and John Jay as well as many others. All we have to go on is their writings that recorded how they lived.

The term Christian is also loosely used to denote a person whose beliefs about God, the world, and man are generally in accord with those of the Christian religion, but who may not live life as a dedicated follower of Christ. In this sense, the founders as a whole can be referred to as Christian because their beliefs, actions, and/or demeanor (generous, decent, and moral) line up with the Christian faith. They also firmly believed that Christianity was necessary for a representative republic. Self-government is a Biblical concept. The book of Proverbs is filled with references to self-governing principles of personal responsibility, self-control, hard work, duty and kindness.

These men may have had commonality of faith, but they had differing ideas on government and how it should be instituted. Some of them were Federalists who favored a stronger central government. Alexander Hamilton, John Jay, and Governor Morris were strong Federalists. George Washington and John Adams were moderate Federalists. Republicans supported the Constitution but believed it gave the central government far less power than the Federalists thought it did. Thomas Jefferson, Samuel Adams and John Witherspoon held the Republican viewpoint. Roger Sherman feared government power, and for that reason, he could be called a Republican. However, on commercial matters he was more of a Federalist. James Madison was a moderate Federalist during the Convention and the ratification debates; afterward he gravitated toward Republicanism. Patrick Henry, the champion of liberty, opposed the Constitution because he felt it slanted toward monarchy, but later in life it appeared that he became a Federalist.

In spite of their differences politically, the founders had some very basic principles in which they almost all agreed. These principles are either derived from, or at least compatible with, Christianity and the Bible. They all had the following beliefs:

1. A belief in God and His providence by which He guides and controls the universe and the affairs of mankind.

2. A belief in and respect for revealed religion. They recognized that God has revealed His truth through the Holy Scriptures.

3. A belief in the God-given power of human reason to apprehend truth. While reason does not supersede revelation, it serves as an aid in the search for truth where the Scriptures are silent.

4. A belief that man is not perfect or a perfectible being, and governmental theories must consider that fact.

5. A belief that God has ordained human government to restrain the sinful nature of man.

6. A belief that God has established certain physical laws for the operation of the universe, as well as certain moral laws for the governance of mankind.

7. A belief that God has revealed his moral laws to man through the Scriptures (revealed or divine law) and through the law of nature, which is discoverable through human reason and the human conscience.

8. A belief that human law must correspond both to the divine law and the law of nature. Human laws that contradict the higher law are invalid, nonbinding, and are to be resisted.

9. A belief that the revealed law and the law of nature form the basis for the law of nations (international law) and that this law of nations includes the right of a nation to defend itself against aggressors (just warfare).

10. A belief that both the revealed law and the law of nature include natural God-given, unalienable human rights that include life, liberty, and property.

11. A belief that governments are formed by covenant or compact of the people in order to safeguard human rights.

12. A belief that governments have only such powers as are delegated to them by the people in the said covenants or compacts, and that when governments attempt to usurp powers not so delegated, they become illegitimate and are to be resisted.

13. A belief that, human nature being what it is, rulers tend to usurp more and more power if given the opportunity.

14. A belief that the best way to prevent governments from usurping power is to separate their powers and functions into legislative, executive and judicial branches.

15. A belief that, human nature being what it is, a free enterprise economy is the best way to give people an incentive to produce and develop national prosperity.[2]

PATRIOTIC PORTRAIT

Samuel Adams (1722-1803), the "Father of the American Revolution" is also referred to as the "last of the Puritans". Jefferson considered Adams to be the patriarch of liberty. Along with his cousin John Adams, Samuel Adams labored over 20 years as a patriot and leader. He never served as President or Vice President, but he served Massachusetts in the legislature, as a representative to the Continental Congress and the Massachusetts Constitutional Convention, as well as the convention to ratify the U.S. Constitution. He also signed the Declaration of Independence and served as Governor of Massachusetts.

His education at Harvard during the Great Awakening greatly influenced his life. Religion and Politics were his passions. Adams' brilliance at grassroots organization and propaganda was demonstrated through the establishment of the Committees of Correspondence, through the Sons of Liberty and many other activities. Samuel Adams formed the Committees of Correspondence, which were largely responsible for bringing unity to the Colonists prior to the Revolution. He also instigated the Boston Tea Party.

Samuel Adams stated: "Neither the wisest constitution nor the wisest laws will secure the liberty and happiness of a people whose manners are universally corrupt."[3]

And in a 1750 he wrote: "He therefore is the truest friend to liberty of his country who tries most to promote its virtue, and who, so far as his power and influence extend, will not suffer a man to be chosen into any office of power and trust who is not a wise and virtuous man … The sum of all is, if we would most truly enjoy this gift of Heaven, let us become a Virtuous people."[4]

He wanted to see New England turn back to the Puritan state it once had been and thought the revolution would accomplish that. He was not a wealthy man, and lived very frugally and looked down on the tendencies toward frivolity, luxury, and excess after the war. He was the last Puritan and a great patriot.

Samuel Adams remarked to the young man whom his daughter intended to marry: "...I cannot however help repeating piety, because I think it indispensable. Religion in a family is at once its brightest ornament and its best security."[5]

Samuel Adams wrote in his Will: "Principally, and first of all, I resign my soul to the Almighty Being who gave it, and my body I commit to the dust, relying on the merits of Jesus Christ for the pardon of my sins."[6]

RECOMMENDED READING

America's God and Country, William J. Federer. An excellent resource for quotes and short biographies of these awesome men.

QUESTIONS for THOUGHT and DISCUSSION

1. When are you most likely to seek God with your whole heart? In good times or bad times? What draws you to Him? Explain:

2. In America today, what examples of the occult and witchcraft can you identify?

3. What was the Puritan Way?

4. Can you think of a time when you became so busy that you let your relationship with the Lord slip? What were the consequences of letting your relationship slip?

5. What needed to happen to bring the thirteen independent colonies together in order to become "One Nation Under God"?

6. What is a spiritual awakening?

7. Is there unity among the American churches today? Explain.

8. How would you describe the Ivy League universities today?

9. Is it ever okay to rebel against civil authority?

10 Was this God's judgment on an unrighteous king?

11. How do you think the Colonists protested these outrageous taxes and tariffs?

12. What was the root cause of their grievances?

13. How strongly do you feel about liberty? Is it important enough to risk your life to defend it?

14. What is your purpose or calling? At what age were you made aware of that calling? What are you doing to prepare? Write out your answers.

15. Using the description of Christian in this chapter, would the United States be considered a Christian nation, or at least founded as a Christian nation? ___Yes ___No Explain.

Foundational Truths – Chapter 7

"[W]hen the resolution of enslaving America was formed in Great Britain, the British Parliament was advised by an artful man, - who was governor of Pennsylvania, to disarm the people; that it was the best and most effectual way to enslave them; but that they should not do it openly, but weaken them, and let them sink gradually, by totally disusing and neglecting the militia."

> - George Mason, speech at the Virginia Ratifying Convention, 14 June 1778

"Americans! Ask the Declaration of Independence and it will tell you that its authors held for self-evident truth that the right to life is the first of the unalienable rights of man, and that to secure and not to destroy that right, governments are instituted."

> - John Quincy Adams, President of the United States

Chapter 7

The Declaration of Independence and Battle for Freedom

The First Signs of War

As resentment grew towards England, tensions mounted in the colonies. Samuel Adams formed the Committees of Communication to keep all the colonies informed of latest developments and offenses by the British. He was quite talented in writing political brochures, designing posters, and grassroots organization. These communications helped organize opposition to England's abuses.

Before Patrick Henrys' famous remarks in May of 1775, the English Parliament declared the colony of Massachusetts to be in a state of rebellion. This meant that British soldiers could now shoot rebels. Lives were now at stake. The rebel forces were organized by townships and were called "Minutemen" because they could be ready in a minute's notice to bear arms. In addition, they had men who were expert horsemen who would ride from town to town warning of British troop movement.

Of those riders, Paul Revere was the most famous, because of his April 1775 midnight ride to warn Samuel Adams and John Hamilton that the British were coming to arrest them. He did not ride alone that night. One of the many black patriots of the day rode out with him but instead of heading to Lexington, he rode north and alerted all the farmers and villagers along the way. His call brought the farmers together to ambush the British at the North Bridge and chase them to Concord and, then, all the way to Charleston. There are so many nameless heroes of the American Revolution. Today, America has just as many nameless heroes doing extraordinary things that make a huge difference in our lives.

Besides seeking Adams and Hamilton, the British were also coming to take the weapons the Minutemen had stored in Concord. Just after Paul Revere warned Adams and Hamilton, the British captured him before he could get to Concord.

Within minutes, the Lexington Minutemen were ready to fight the British. As they waited, tensions rose but all were determined to stand strong. When the British came into sight, their captain, John Parker, quickly saw the Minutemen were far outnumbered and called for a retreat. He wanted to join other Minutemen forces in Concord where they would have a better chance to defeat the British. He ordered his men to retreat and not to fire on the British. The British broke rank and pursued but their commander ordered them to keep rank and not to shoot.

However, shots were fired, but to this day no one is sure who fired the first shot. The battle of Lexington lasted less than fifteen minutes, but it marked the beginning of the war for independence. Eight Minutemen were killed and ten were wounded. If you have ever been to Lexington, then you have seen the beautiful serene green where this first battle took place. If you have not had the opportunity to visit New England, I urge you to make it a vacation priority. There is no better way to make history come alive than to visit these historic sites.

The British pushed on and by late mid-morning, 700 British troops arrived in Concord, only to find that the powder, cannon, and weapons had all been removed. A squad of 100 men stayed to guard the North Bridge while search parties hunted for the Minutemen. What they did not know was that Minutemen were ready and waiting for their arrival. Every farmer from the surrounding area had answered the call to arms. This time when the British fired, the Minutemen fired back and stood their ground. These farmers knew how to shoot and were very good marksmen.

The British knew they were in trouble and retreated back to Concord where they then decided to head back to Charleston. The Minutemen set up ambushes all along the way back to Lexington where the Redcoats met up with reinforcements.

These were truly the "shots heard round the world" and the Americans celebrated their first victory over the greatest military men in the world at that time. They reminded themselves that "As long as we keep our hearts right, God will shower His blessings on us. It is the God of heaven and earth whom we must thank. We cannot take pride in our own strength." What humble hearts these men had!

The second victory was the fall of Fort Ticonderoga. Benedict Arnold, a young Captain from New Haven, Connecticut asked permission to take the fort, which controlled the waterways, the gateway to New York. Joining forces with him was Ethan Allen and the Green Mountain Boys from Vermont. When they arrived, the gate to the fort was wide open and they walked right in and demanded surrender. When asked by whose authority, Arnold answered, "In the name of the great Jehovah and the Continental Congress!" God had given the Americans the gateway to New York and control of those waterways!

> Side bar: God knew the army needed these small successes to develop confidence in Him and in themselves while they faced the greatest military men of that era.

Bunker Hill was the next battlefield. In the middle of June, 1775, Colonel William Prescott and his men learned that General Gage planned to occupy the Charleston Neck and Dorchester peninsulas. These crucial areas were to the north and south of Boston. The Americans knew they would have to move fast because the British already controlled Boston. The Rev. Langdon prayed for them, seeking divine protection and placing them in Gods' hands.

Prescott and his men moved into the Charleston Neck where they began to fortify Breed's Hill, one of two hills on the peninsula. It was closer to Boston than the other hill, known as Bunker Hill. They worked quietly through the night, building a large fortification on the hill. In the morning, the British discovered the colonial forces were there and General Gage ordered an attack. He appointed General William Howe as field commander and they proceeded to charge the hill.

What happened was no small feat for the Americans. Twice the British charged and both times fell back with many dead and wounded. The Americans were winning! However, they began to run out of ammunition (this was a problem throughout the Revolutionary War) on the third British charge. With the Americans near defeat, British commander Major John Pitcairn mounted the hill and shouted, "The day is ours!" whereupon he was shot by Peter Salem, a famous Black Massachusetts Minuteman. This sent the British troops into confusion and allowed the Americans to escape safely to Cambridge across the river. Peter Salem was honored before General Washington for his bravery. For some unknown reason (except to God) General Howe chose not to pursue Prescott and his men. He could easily have taken Cambridge and captured thousands of patriots.

This was the first of many opportunities the British would miss during the war. Obviously God was at work. The British won the battle of Bunker Hill, but they lost nearly half of their 2,200 soldiers while the Americans lost only 441 men out of their 3,000 soldiers. God seemed to be blessing the American cause. However, they needed an intelligent and skillful military leader.

In the summer of 1775, a very humble George Washington reluctantly accepted the call to be Commander-in-Chief over the American military. He was chosen by a unanimous vote of the Continental Congress. In accepting, Washington made it clear that he did not feel equal to the command with which he had been honored. However, it is very evident that Washington was God's chosen man for this job. He was a man of strong moral character and integrity. He was a selfless and humble man with a supernatural gift of wisdom. Ordinary people loved him which prompted jealousy from many of his colleagues in Congress and the military.

Most importantly, he was a deeply religious man with strong faith in the providence of God. He had been raised by a praying mother who taught him to trust God and value prayer. This discipline of daily prayer got him through the war, the Constitutional Convention and the presidency. The affection of the American people never wavered in all those years.

The Declaration of Independence

In the spring of 1776, the Continental Congress was meeting in Philadelphia. With the first battles of the revolution having already taken place, they debated the direction they should take - whether reconciliation with England or independence. With a majority of town meetings in the colonies voting for independence, Franklin, Adams, Sherman of Connecticut, Livingston of New York, and Jefferson of Virginia quickly drew up a draft of the proposed declaration. Jefferson did most of the final composing, borrowing heavily from the phraseology of popular sermons of the day.

They needed a unanimous vote for it to pass and not all members were in favor of Independence. In the end, it came down to one vote. That one vote came from Caesar Rodney, the third delegate from Delaware, who was not present because he had been called back to Delaware on urgent business. When he received the dispatch that he was needed to vote on this historic declaration, he rode all night through a terrible storm to get to Philadelphia to cast his vote for independence.

> One vote does make a difference! Don't let anyone tell you otherwise.

On July 2, 1776, the Continental Congress approved the wording of the Declaration of Independence. On July 4, 1776, the delegates voted to accept it and declare America's independence from Great Britain. It was read in public for the first time on July 8, 1776 accompanied by the ringing of the Liberty Bell. Congress signed the Declaration of Independence on August 2, 1776, after it was written in script on parchment. There is a wide range of complaints listed in the document. Contrary to modern revisionist thought, it wasn't just about taxation and money. The main text reads:

> *"When in the Course of human events, it becomes necessary for one people to dissolve the political bands which have connected them with another, and to assume among the powers of the earth, the separate and equal station to which the Laws of Nature and of Nature's God entitles them...*

> *"We hold these truths to be self-evident, that all men are created equal. That they are endowed by their Creator with certain inalienable Rights, that among these are Life, Liberty and the Pursuit of Happiness...*

> *"We, Therefore, the Representatives of the United States of America, in General Congress, Assembled, appealing to the Supreme Judge of the world for the rectitude of our intentions...*
>
> *"And for the support of this Declaration, with a firm reliance on the protection of Divine Providence, we mutually pledge to each other our Lives, our Fortunes, and our sacred Honor."*

The day following the approval by the delegates of the Declaration of Independence, John Adams wrote to his wife, Abigail: "I am apt to believe that it will be celebrated by succeeding generations as the great anniversary Festival. It ought to be commemorated, as the day of deliverance, by solemn acts of devotion to God Almighty."[1]

Samuel Adams declared upon the signing of the Declaration of Independence by the members of the Continental Congress: "We have this day restored the Sovereign to Whom all men ought to be obedient. He reigns in heaven and from the rising to the setting of the sun, let His kingdom come."[2]

These quotes certainly make it clear that the founders as a whole were religious men. These men knew they were facing the most powerful military in the world but were willing to take a stand, regardless of the consequences. They knew they were in personal jeopardy. However, they believed they had a righteous cause and God would see them through.

God's Divine Intervention in the War for Independence

The Revolutionary War actually began in 1775 before the Declaration of Independence was signed. The last major battle occurred in 1781, but the treaty between Great Britain and America was not signed until 1783. Therefore, this war actually lasted eight years. Considering the mainstream media's coverage of war today, do you think we would be able to be at war for eight years? Think about it. The war for independence was fought here on American soil, not in some foreign country.

114

The American Army was outnumbered and constantly lacked sufficient supplies to fight. They literally had to draw the enemy far away from their lines of supplies to get the upper hand. General Nathaniel Greene summed up the war from the American point of view when he said, *"We fight, get beat, rise and fight again."*[3] The Americans refusal to stay down finally broke the British will to win. American perseverance and the hand of God won the war.

The British military was the most powerful army in the world and yet they made numerous mistakes and misjudgments during the war. On June 28, 1776, the British attempted to seal off the port of Charleston, the South's principal seaport, just as they had done in New York City. Due to poor information and misjudgments, they were unable to succeed. At the end of the battle, the British had lost upwards of a hundred killed or wounded men, two ships had been sunk, and many other vessels had been severely damaged. By the grace of God, the Americans reported only 12 dead and 24 wounded.

The British fleet sailed north to join the rest of the fleet at Staten Island to fight the eight thousand soldiers defending Brooklyn. The British had a combined army of twenty thousand. In five days the British had nearly surrounded the Americans and it looked as if all was lost. But God... Amazingly, the great British General Howe delayed attacking for over 48 hours allowing General Washington to come up with a bold plan to evacuate his men and equipment by boat across the East River. The weather had turned overcast and it began raining. Using every available small boat in the area, they began floating artillery equipment across the wide expanse of the East River.

All of Washington's generals advised against this plan but General Washington had made up his mind. He knew their only hope was that God would literally blind the eyes of the British to what they were doing. Under cover of darkness, they labored all night, making the two-mile roundtrip back and forth delivering men, equipment, and supplies to safety. They kept men on the front lines so that the British would not suspect anything on that clear, moonlit night. When dawn broke, they still needed another three hours to finish the evacuation. Tensions were high. How would they do it safely on such a clear day?

Major Ben Tallmadge wrote in his journal of what occurred next. "…and when the dawn arrived there were several regiments still on duty. At this time a very dense fog began to rise (out of the ground and off the river), and it seemed to settle in a peculiar manner over both encampments. I recollect this peculiar providential occurrence perfectly well, and so very dense was the atmosphere that I could scarcely discern a man at six yards distance…we tarried until the sun had risen, but the fog remained as dense as ever."[4]

This supernatural fog remained intact until the last boat, with Washington in it, had departed. Then it lifted, and the shocked British ran to the shore and started firing after them, but they were well out of range. The Continental Army had suffered a severe defeat, with fifteen hundred casualties. However, thanks to God for providing a storm, a wind, a fog, and too many "coincidences" to number, there was still a Continental Army.

On July 9, 1776, the Continental Congress authorized the Continental Army to provide chaplains for their troops. General Washington then issued the order and appointed chaplains to every regiment.

On that same day, he issued this general order to his troops, stating: "The General hopes and trusts that every officer and man, will endeavor so to live, and act, as becomes a Christian Soldier defending the dearest Rights and Liberties of his country."[5]

There were many instances of divine intervention in the war, but this was the most miraculous example of God at work on behalf of the Continental Army. There were very few major battles during this eight-year war because they were short on supplies. General Washington was conserving every man, bullet and ounce of gunpowder. The Congress did not understand this, and became embarrassed by an army that would not fight man to man. Washington, referred to by the British as the "fox," was brilliant in his strategies and his stewardship of the men willing to fight in this small army. Keep in mind that there were never more than 13,000 soldiers at any time during that long war.

God again intervened at the surprise attack on Trenton by the Continental Army on Christmas night, 1776. As they were preparing for their pre-dawn attack and loading into their boats to cross the Delaware River, a violent snow and hailstorm suddenly came up. This successfully reduced visibility to near zero, thus forcing the Hessian sentries to enter the garrison and rendering their attackers invisible until it was too late. This bold and shrewd move on Washington's part proved quite successful. As a man of prayer, Washington was definitely led by what he, himself describes as Divine Providence.

The war slowly dragged on, with much of it being played out in a game of cat and mouse because Washington never had enough men to launch a major offensive. It was frustrating and demoralizing, but Washington never gave up. This was the state of the war as the famous winter at Valley Forge approached. The time spent in Valley Forge training, freezing, and starving would definitely be the true test of their commitment to freedom. One in four was lost that winter to flu, smallpox, typhus, or exposure. The Congress, now missing its most talented men, was jealous of Washington, and refused to believe his continual pleas for supplies of winter clothing and food for his men. It was a desperate situation, but Washington did the best he could. Daily, he walked amongst the men to encourage and comfort them.

The miracle of Valley Forge was that the army stayed together and did not mutiny. They believed in God's deliverance just as their General believed. He was seen praying regularly on his knees in the surrounding woodlands. Valley Forge actually brought about a more disciplined and united army. They passed the test and came out of it stronger and more determined to beat the British.

Religious services were provided for the soldiers and attendance was required of all recruits. Prayer and Bible reading were common among the soldiers. Neither cussing nor swearing was allowed. A number of ministers also enlisted to fight for freedom. Many of those who did not enlist were preaching separation from England and the importance of individual liberty from the pulpits of the nation's churches. In addition, the churches regularly held prayer meetings for the army. They recognized that the only hope of winning the war was their faith in God.

How far we have strayed from the founding principles of our country! In today's military, chaplains are very limited in what they can do and are constantly under assault by the anti-Christian lobbyists.

On August 20, 1778, General George Washington wrote to his friend, Brigadier General Thomas Nelson in Virginia: "The hand of Providence has been so conspicuous in all this (the course of the war) that he must be worse than an infidel that lacks faith, and more wicked that has not gratitude to acknowledge his obligations; but it will be time enough for me to turn Preacher when my present appointment ceases."[6]

God's hand was definitely on the course of the war. Without His intervention and divine wisdom, the colonies could never have defeated the most powerful military in the world.

The Battle of Yorktown was the final skirmish of the American Revolution. The Americans won this battle with the help of the French Fleet, General Lafayette and an American slave named James Armistead who asked his master to let him fight for the Americans under General Lafayette. Lafayette dispatched Armistead to the camp of the patriot-turned-traitor, Benedict Arnold (then a British general), to pose as an escaped slave looking for work. Armistead obtained much vital information about British plans and troop movements, which he daily sent to General Lafayette. He pretended to spy on the Americans for Lord Cornwallis but always gave false information. It was his information that tipped off the movement of troops and ships to Yorktown that brought about the surrender of Cornwallis.

Lafayette penned a certificate to Virginia leaders praising the work and important contributions of Armistead which helped to bring about his freedom from slavery on New Year's Day, 1787. Following his emancipation, Armistead adopted the name Lafayette and went by the name James Lafayette henceforth. He remained in Virginia as a farmer.

PATRIOTIC PORTRAIT

Born in 1732 to Augustine and Mary Ball Washington, **George Washington** was a distant descendant of King John of England. When he was eleven years old, his father died and he lived with his older half-brother until he was sixteen years old. George's education consisted of home schooling and tutoring. He received his surveyor's license in 1749 from William and Mary College. From 1788 until his death in 1799, he was the college's chancellor.

At age 15, George Washington wrote out in his own hand *110 Rules of Civility and Decent Behavior in Company and Conversation.* Among them were:

108:   When you speak of God, or His attributes, let it be seriously and with reverence. Honor and obey your natural parents although they be poor.

109:   Let your recreations be manful not sinful.

110:   Labour to keep alive in your breast that little spark of celestial fire called conscience. [7]

At age 20, he wrote a personal book of prayers in a 24-page manuscript entitled, "Daily Sacrifice." He wrote this in his field notebook, in his own handwriting:

> *"Monday Morning...O eternal and everlasting God, I presume to present myself this morning before Thy Divine Majesty, beseeching Thee to accept of my humble and hearty thanks...Direct my thoughts, words and work, wash away my sins in the immaculate Blood of the Lamb, and purge my heart by Thy Holy Spirit...Daily frame me more and more into the likeness of Thy Son, Jesus Christ, that living in Thy fear, and dying in Thy favor, I may in Thy appointed time attain the resurrection of the just unto eternal life. Bless my family, friends and kindred, and unite us all in praising and glorifying Thee in all our works.*

> *"Monday Evening...Most Gracious Lord God, from whom proceedeth every good and perfect gift, I offer to Thy Divine Majesty my unfeigned praise and thanksgiving for all Thy mercies*

> *towards me…I have sinned and done very wickedly, be merciful to*
> *me, O God, and pardon me for Jesus Christ sake…Thou gavest Thy*
> *Son to die for me; and hast given me assurance of salvation, upon*
> *my repentance and sincerely endeavoring to conform my life to His*
> *holy precepts and example…*
>
> *"Bless O Lord the whole race of mankind, and let the world be*
> *filled with the knowledge of Thee and Thy Son, Jesus Christ…I*
> *beseech Thee to defend me this night from all evil, and do more for*
> *me than I can think or ask, for Jesus Christ sake, in whose most*
> *holy Name and Words, I continue to pray, Our Father, who art in*
> *heaven, hallowed be Thy Name…"[8]*

For those who purport that Washington was not a Christian, this manuscript, along with many of his other writings and his personal journal refute that belief. He was known to spend his Sundays fasting after attending services and regularly took communion. There is no doubt to those who knew him that even though he was very private about his faith and preferred to pray in private, he was a true believer in Jesus Christ.

As a young man, he started his lifetime of public service by serving in the military during the French and Indian War. As he was leaving his mother, Mrs. Mary Washington said to him: "Remember that God is our only sure trust. To Him, I commend you…My son, neglect not the duty of secret prayer."[9]

It became clear at the Battle at the Monongahela that the hand of God was on his life. Washington was the only officer on horseback who survived. After the battle, he wrote to his brother these words: "But by the all-powerful dispensations of Providence, I have been protected beyond all human probability or expectation; for I had four bullets through my coat, and two horses shot under me, yet escaped unhurt, although death was leveling my companions on every side of me!"[10]

Fifteen years later a chance meeting with an old Indian chief revealed the other side of the story. The Indian chief had taken note that Washington was not fighting like the British trained soldiers, but with more Indian-like wisdom as did those whom Washington commanded. The chief instructed his men to point their rifles at Washington to kill him. He recounts, "Our rifles were leveled, rifles which, but for you, knew not how to miss (they were expert marksmen) – 'twas all in vain, a power far mightier than we, shielded you." When they perceived they could not kill him, they ceased firing. The old chief went on to prophesy over Washington: "Listen! The Great Spirit protects that man (pointing at Washington), and guides his destinies – he will become the chief of nations, and a people yet unborn will hail him as the founder of a mighty empire. I am come to pay homage to the man who is the particular favorite of Heaven, and who can never die in battle."[11] Our amazing God used an Indian Chief to prophesy the future concerning this humble leader. And the rest, as they say, is history.

Washington was appointed Commander-in-Chief of the Continental Army in 1775 and served until the Treaty of Paris was signed, marking the end of the war. He then resigned his commission and went back home to Mt. Vernon to resume private life as a planter. He had little more than three years before he was again called to public service as president of the Constitutional Convention. On Tuesday, April 14, 1789, George Washington received official word that he had been elected the first president of the United States. This uncommonly honorable man was truly God's chosen man for the hour during this time.

I challenge you to read more about the awesome man who lead this country through a terribly long and arduous war, and then served for eight years as its first president.

In a letter written from Mt. Vernon, to John F. Mercer dated September 9, 1786, George Washington wrote: "It being among my first wishes to see some plan adopted by which slavery in this country may be abolished by law."[12]

Washington never lived to see this wish come true. Keeping unity among the states during the initial tenuous years of the new country was more important than addressing the divisive issue of slavery.

The following statement is attributed to George Washington: "Religion and morality are the essential Pillars of civil society."

This was the sentiment of all the founders. They knew that in order for a people to be self-governed, they first had to be able to govern themselves. Knowing God and living according to the Bible was the way to guarantee the success of the nation. This is still true today.

One of President George Washington's prayers:

> *"Direct my thought, words and work, wash away my sins in the immaculate Blood of the Lamb, and purge my heart by the Holy Spirit.... Daily frame me more and more into the likeness of Thy Son Jesus Christ."*[13]

We would all do well to pray this prayer.

Henry "Light Horse Harry" Lee gave a most accurate description of George Washington when he said Washington was *"First in war, first in peace, first in the hearts of his countrymen."*

RECOMMENDED READING / MEDIA

1776, David McCullough

America's God and Country Encyclopedia of Quotations, William J. Federe

Christianity and the Constitution, John Eidsmoe

The Light and the Glory, Peter Marshall and David Manuel. Will help you find out more about the war and how God moved on behalf of the Continental Army

The Crossing Excellent movie made for PBS, ~2003

QUESTIONS for THOUGHT and DISCUSSION

1. Where were the first shots of the Revolution fired?

2. Who fired the first shots?

3. How involved were the clergy in the American Revolution?

4. As Commander-in-Chief, what was Washington's biggest challenge?

5. Was the Declaration of Independence signed at the time the delegates voted to accept it? When was it signed?

6. From the above quotes, what can you determine about the men who wrote and signed the Declaration of Independence?

7. What were the consequences of putting their name to this document?

8. Is there a cause for which you would be willing to die?
   If yes, list those things for which you would risk your life:

9. In what situations have you had a chance to stand up and be counted, but because of fear of the consequences, you remained silent or backed down? Be honest. We have all fallen short in this area.

10. What characteristics were the British lacking in this war?

11. Why was this war different to the British troops?

12. Who was the last person to be evacuated?

13. Do you think his men took note of that?

14. What Biblical instance of Divine Intervention does this remind you of?

15. Is Congress today still slow to understand wartime needs of the military?

16. Has Congress ever been influenced by their feelings for the Commander-in-Chief?

Foundational Truths – Chapter 8

"Liberty must at all hazards be supported. We have a right to it, derived from our Maker. But if we had not, our fathers have earned and bought it for us, at the expense of their ease, their estates, their pleasure, and their blood."

- John Adams, A Dissertation on the Canon and Feudal Law, 1765

"Proclaim liberty throughout the land unto all the inhabitants thereof."

- Leviticus 25:10, inscribed on the Liberty Bell

Chapter 8

A Republic is Born

The War Is Over – Now What?

When the war was finally over, Americans rejoiced that they were now the United States of America. However, the struggle to actually be united was just beginning. Many of the ministers preached victorious exuberant sermons on the great victory, but some took a cautionary tactic by preaching God's divine interventions actually determined the outcome of the war. These men of God knew the struggle for the future of the republic was just beginning. The young nation would have to recognize God's hand in their deliverance to fulfill His plan and not man's plan. They believed if the people kept this in perspective, then truly God's kingdom had come or was almost come. At least the seed was planted and would soon grow.

Indeed, it does seem that God has a purpose for America and that alone is one reason why there have been so many attacks on our Constitution and Christian Heritage. I believe we have been asleep at the wheel far too long. We now have a Constitution we barely recognize and a culture that has slid down the slippery slop toward Sodom and Gomorrah. Many of the pastors during the post revolutionary war era recognized this dangerous possibility could happen if the American pastors and churches ever lost sight of God's plan and purpose.

Unifying the States

The war with England brought the colonies together in unity for the common cause of life, liberty and the pursuit of happiness, as expressed in the Declaration of Independence. They knew their lives were worthless if the British won the battle. Even during the war when they were all sacrificing and praying for one another, the Congress had to plead with the states for financial support of the military. Once the fear of death diminished after the war, those states that had not contributed their fair share refused to pay at all.

Massachusetts ended up paying more of the war's expenses than any other state even though her population was only about thirteen percent of America's total. Unfortunately, Massachusetts' experience is fairly normal to the human condition. I can remember times in my church when adversity brought everyone together and many gave generously to God's work who normally would have been more hesitant to do so. When the time of adversity or great need passed, these more reserved givers went back to their old ways. In most churches, the percentage of those who tithe is sadly not much more than thirteen percent. It is amazing what God has done with this thirteen percent when you really think about it. The American church has sent the Gospel around the world and continues to be the first to show up to help after major disasters.

During this post war period, the states seemed to disagree about everything. The disputes deepened and even became vindictive. The future of the new republic looked bleak. A change in leadership proved to be only a part of the problem. After the war, America's ministers were no longer her most influential leaders. General George Washington recognized the situation and was concerned. He wrote a letter to the governor of each state stressing the need to imitate Christ in all things in order to have a happy nation.

> How do you bring thirteen independent states together to form some sort of national government, in order to unify them and ensure their security?

In 1781, at the end of the war, a temporary measure was needed to provide some form of unified legal government. The Articles of Confederation were drawn up and ratified by the majority of states. Congress was given the power to declare war, make peace, draft treaties, and maintain a postal service. Some states thought this was still too much power and refused to ratify the Articles.

With the arguments and infighting between the states increasing daily, the Articles of Confederation proved to be inadequate. By the end of 1786 and early 1787, the new republic was in disarray. Again, George Washington came to the aid of his countrymen. He started a letter writing campaign to the men who were in a position to shape and influence opinions in America, stating that something had to be done.

The Constitutional Convention

In May 1787, the Congress met with the intention of patching the holes in the Articles of Confederation. They quickly concluded that a completely new Constitution was necessary. By unanimous choice, they chose Washington to chair this convention. This historical event was the first time in history that men had the opportunity to write a constitution for their own government.

Today, we don't realize how important it was that our Constitution was the very first written by the people for the people. In 1787, it was completely inconceivable for a country to do this. In our generation, we have witnessed other countries around the world go through this process, something that would not have happened except for the United States' experience commonly referred to as the great "American Experiment."

Unfortunately, this historical event turned into the stormiest convention ever held in America. There were heated disagreements on how representation would be determined. The northern states wanted representation dependent on population, as they were the most populous states. The southern states wanted representation determined on land under cultivation. In addition, the small states feared being overpowered by the bigger states, northern and southern. It was not a civil convention, and there was very little Christian charity exhibited. According to most historians, only the dignity of Washington's presence and demeanor preserved the convention at all. He said little, just listened. His ability to endure the emotional ups and downs of this convention defies human ability.

Can you imagine chairing a convention of grown men who were acting like children and completely refusing to compromise on even the simplest of issues? Washington's restraint pulled them through and kept the convention from falling apart completely. In reflecting on Washington, historian Page Smith said that Washington's ability to restrain himself determined his greatness as Commander-in-Chief of the Continental Army and as the first President of the United States.

> Put yourself in George Washington's place. You are the chair
> of a convention in which you feel strongly about the issues
> discussed but you cannot freely express yourself. Would you
> be able to deny yourself the opportunity to speak your
> mind? Would you be able to remain impartial and calm? Or
> would you be biting your tongue, trying hard not to speak
> your mind but failing?

Regardless of George Washington's heroic efforts, the mood got ugly.
It became apparent that this convention was doomed, as was the union.
The Pilgrims had willingly given up their self-interests and individual
rights to preserve their communities, but the states were unwilling to
give up their self-interests in order to form a more perfect union, one
designed by God. What could be done to rectify this situation?

At this lowest point in the convention, eighty-one year old Ben
Franklin rose to speak. In a quiet voice, he said:

> *"In the beginning of the contest with Britain, when we were
> sensible of danger, we had daily prayers in this room for
> Divine protection. Our prayers, Sir, were heard, and they
> were graciously answered. All of us who were engaged in
> the struggle must have observed frequent instances of a
> superintending Providence in our favor.... And have we now
> forgotten this powerful Friend? Or do we imagine we no
> longer need His assistance?*
>
> *"I have lived, Sir, a long time, and the longer I live, the more
> convincing proofs I see of this truth: "that God governs in
> the affairs of man". And if a sparrow cannot fall to the
> ground without His notice, is it probable that an empire can
> rise without His aid?*
>
> *"We have been assured, Sir, in the Sacred Writings that
> except the Lord build the house, they labor in vain that build
> it. I firmly believe this. I also believe that, without His
> concurring aid, we shall succeed in this political building no
> better than the builders of Babel; we shall be divided by our*

little, partial local interests; our projects will be confounded;
and we ourselves shall become a reproach and a byword
down to future ages. And what is worse, mankind may
hereafter, from this unfortunate instance, despair of
establishing government by human wisdom and leave to
chance, war or conquest.

"I therefore, beg leave to move that, henceforth, prayers
imploring the assistance of Heaven and its blessing on our
deliberation be held in this assembly every morning before
we proceed to business."[1]

As you can imagine, the silence was deafening. This quiet sober reflection was the turning point in the convention. With their priorities thus rearranged, they set out to create a new constitution.

The United States' Constitution is the oldest written constitution still in effect today. The greatest legal minds of the last two centuries have marveled at this astounding document as being beyond the scope and dimension of human wisdom. Consider the enormous problems the constitution somehow anticipated and the challenges it foresaw. There can be no doubt that more than human genius had a hand in its creation. The proof is in how well it has functioned through the history of our country!

The Constitution was framed from the basis of two hundred years of Puritan thought that man is a fallen being, sinful in nature, and in which "dwells no good thing." The Constitution was designed to anticipate the possibility of the worst happening in the civil government, just as the Puritans anticipated the very worst happening in the churches of their day. Therefore, they planned contingencies accordingly. When the worst occasionally did occur, the obstacle, rather than the system, would be eliminated.

Drawing from the most balanced philosophical, legal and political thinkers of the 17th and 18th centuries (Baron Montesquieu, William Blackstone, John Locke and others) the founders wrote a Constitution that was truly genius in its checks and balances, separation of powers, equal rights under the law, property rights and protection of states' rights. The founders were against an unchecked, absolute majority rule (democracy). That is why the United States is not a democracy, as many today assert, but a representative republic. Their main concern regarding a total democracy was what they called a "factious spirit." They wanted to avoid a mob mentality, knowing that individual rights would get trampled, as indeed they did just two years later in the French Revolution.

Biblical Principles Found in the Constitution and Declaration of Independence [2]

The Declaration of Independence is the foundation of our government; the Constitution is the structure built on that foundation. In the Declaration, the founders framed a statement of the basic American values or principles: equality and God-given rights.

Equality is used frequently today as a way of bringing the weight of government to bear towards bringing equality to all. However, on a closer look at the use of equality in the Declaration of Independence, the meaning is far different than its understood meaning in today's society. The founders believed we should all have equal opportunities to succeed through hard work and ingenuity. Today, equality is used to mean equal in income, health care, housing, and anything else you can think of. When government enacts policies to bring about distribution of wealth to impose equality, you end up with a people that are equally poor and equally miserable. The result of government's involvement is over regulation which shuts down the true equal opportunity to succeed. The government should be working to allow the people to become successful and prosperous instead of shooting for mediocre with very few actually succeeding.

We want to be empowered to achieve all that we can be through hard work and creativity. The Pilgrims unsuccessfully attempted to follow the equality or collectivist path. They nearly starved before realizing that plan did not work. When each family was given their own parcel of land, the incentive to work hard took over and the colony prospered. Private property and free enterprise were created and have been the foundation of the American way since. The colonists were all equally endowed with opportunity. Based on their own talents and work ethic, they prospered.

130

Just as the Declaration is the statement of our values, the Constitution is the vehicle to secure these rights through a federal republic. This republic consists of a federal government and state governments, with certain powers delegated to the federal government and others reserved for the states. These powers are further separated into legislative, executive, and judicial branches. Where the Declaration embraces liberty, the Constitution looks to a representative government as the means of securing it.

The following Biblical principles are found when looking at the Declaration and Constitution together:

The Providence of God
Declaration of Independence

The founders believed in God and that He had a hand in the affairs of men.

The Law of God
"The Laws of Nature and of Nature's God"
Declaration of Independence

This is a higher law that carries a moral imperative that is higher than any law made by man. It was the "Laws of Nature and of Nature's God" that entitled the colonists to fight for independence and become an independent nation.

The Law of Nations
Constitution, Article I, Section 8, Clause 10

The founders developed the concept of "Law of Nations" as an extension of natural, God-given law. Through this principle, the United States established war tribunals to bring foreign officials to trial for atrocities committed in violation of the Law of Nations or international law. It implies a power and authority higher than man.

The Equality of Man
Declaration and Constitution, Art I, Section 9, Para. 8

Based on Acts 10:34, "God is no respecter of persons" and Gal.3:28 that in Christ "there is neither Jew nor Greek," and Exodus 23:6 which provides for equal protection under the law. "All men are created equal" was never intended by the founding fathers to mean that everyone be considered equal in ability, wealth, or achievement. They recognized that such leveling concepts would limit human freedom – for in a sense, free men are not equal and equal men are not free.

God-Given Human Rights
Declaration and Constitution, Article I, Sec. 9; 5th and 14th Amendments

The Declaration states "life, liberty and the pursuit of happiness." At that time, the pursuit of happiness was understood to be love of country and rigorous attention to the duty of making oneself as virtuous, moral and useful a member of society as possible. With the Constitution, God-given rights are defined as "life, liberty, and property."

Government Secured Rights
Declaration and Preamble of the Constitution

The founding fathers recognized that rights are granted by God, not by governments. Government's role is to secure those rights so that men may enjoy the rights God has given them.

Government by Consent of the Governed
Declaration and Preamble of the Constitution

The concept of the "consent of the governed" has its roots in John Locke's social compact, which is rooted in the Calvinist-Puritan concept of covenant. Covenant means men, in the presence of God, join themselves together into a body politic. Today, "consent of the governed" is falsely interpreted to mean majority rule. The scriptural basis for this concept is in Romans 13; Daniel 2; and 1 Peter 3. Scripture teaches that God usually ordains government through people.

Sinful Nature of Man/Limited and Delegated Powers
Declaration, Preamble and Constitution

Because of the founding fathers' belief in the sinful nature of man, they favored a republican form of government over a democracy, which they believed would turn into "mobocracy" and the abuse of individual rights. There are four differences between a democracy and a republic: First, a republic is government by representatives, versus a democracy that is direct majority rule. Second, a republic places restrictions on majority rule through the separation of powers. Third, a republic respects individual rights regardless of whether the majority agrees or not. <u>Fourth,</u> John Adams describes a republic as "an empire of laws and not of men". You have probably heard the term "rule of law." In John Adams' definition, "Law" is above men; above the subjects, above the rulers, and even above the majority. They created the system of checks and balances to protect the rule of law from turning into abuses of power. Now you know why we have the rule of law and why it is important to respect and uphold it. Read I Kings 12:6-19 for an example of the struggle between the ruler and the ruled. The rule of law protects against this.

Rights of Criminal Defendants
Constitution

The accused is presumed innocent until proven guilty in a free society. The founding fathers adapted the Old Testament Jewish system of justice in writing the Constitution. Read Exodus 18:13-16; Deut. 1:16-17; 17:6; 19:15-21. The Constitutional provisions for the rights of accused persons include: a grand jury indictment in serious cases, a speedy and public trial, the right to be informed of charges against oneself and to confront and cross-examine witnesses, a minimum of two witnesses for charges of treason, the right to counsel and subpoena witnesses, protection against unreasonable search and seizure, self-incrimination; excessive bail and cruel and unusual punishment.

Property Rights
Constitution, Fifth and Fourteenth Amendments

The Bible also puts a high value on property rights. Much of Mosaic law deals with property issues. Read Exodus 20:15, 17. These verses in the Ten Commandments clearly imply property rights.

The Sanctity of Contract
Constitution, Article I, Sec. 10, Para. (1)

The right to enter into a contract with another person, expect the contract be honored, and expect the courts enforcement of them if necessary is closely related to property rights. See Psalm 15:1, 4.

Sundays Excepted
Constitution, Article I, Section 7, Paragraph (2)

In regard to Presidential veto power, the President has ten days (Sundays excepted) to sign or veto a bill. Read Exodus 20:8-10.

Separation of Church and State
Constitution, First Amendment

Old Testament scripture tells us that God was the supreme ruler of Israel and all authority is derived from Him. However, it also makes it clear that the kings were not to perform the function of a priest. In other words, the kings were not to touch the church. (1 Sam. 13; 2 Chronicles 26:16-21) In Luke 20:25, Christ also recognized two kingdoms, the church and the state. Each derives its authority from God. The First Amendment religious clause simply says the federal government was to keep its hands off the church and not establish a national church such as The Church of England.

"Separation of Church and State" is not in the Constitution
The founding fathers felt it was vital for the federal government to "encourage religion", and not block its effects on the people. The trend today of stripping this country of everything in public view that is Judeo-Christian is not in keeping with the intent of the First Amendment. It is an attempt to re-write our history and heritage removing everything Christian that helped create this great nation. The phrase "Separation of Church and State" is found in the Communist manifesto.

The Declaration of Independence, Slavery and The Constitution
Information in this section is taken from the "The Founders' Key" By Dr. Larry Arnn, Thomas Nelson

It was the belief of many Colonial experts (especially those who wrote the Declaration) that this document itself, would press for the abolition of slavery. As a result the Founders began to act on that pressure in ways to substantially reduce and restrict the practice of slavery. Much like the pressure today to reduce and restrict abortion. Today we have critics of abortion who say laws restricting abortion don't go far enough; the Founders, even more so, have been criticized for not abolishing slavery. What these critics fail to acknowledge is what they did do. In 1776 slavery was legal in all thirteen colonies so the Founders, starting with the Declaration, then set a pattern to ultimately do away with it altogether. So what did they do specifically?

- They limited and eventually outlawed the importation of slaves from abroad;
- They abolished slavery in a majority of the original states;
- They forbade the expansion of slavery into areas where it had not been previously permitted.
- They made laws regulating slavery to be more humane;
- As a result individual owners in most states freed slaves in large numbers.

As Thomas G. West, points out in his book *Vindicating the Founders: Race, Sex, Class and Justice in the Origins of America*, "Freedom was secured for the large majority of Americans, and important actions were undertaken in the service of freedom for the rest."

John Jay, one of the three authors of the <u>Federalist</u>, a diplomat, a governor of New York and the first Chief Justice of the Supreme Court was an avid and tireless abolitionist. He believed that when the Revolution started the citizens were so used to slavery that few really questioned it. But after the war "liberal and conscientious men" began to draw the lawfulness of slavery into question. Their influence enabled all of the above measures to be implemented. He believed it was like a little lump of leaven which eventually takes over so that the principles of freedom and liberty would eventually apply to all. Therefore, there was good reason to hope and believe that when the natural process of truth is watched and assisted but not forced then abolition could be achieved.

Obviously, the Founders knew that the language used in the Declaration regarding "all men are created equal" and declaring unalienable rights given by God to "life, liberty and the pursuit of happiness" were going to be thrown back at them for their perceived hypocrisy in regards to slavery. So how did they justify slavery versus the words of the Declaration? First, they believed that slavery was in conflict with what government was supposed to do and second, they never tried to justify it. Most of them spoke of it in a condemning way. Their conundrum was in how to deal with a system they inherited from the British Colonial period that had so entrenched itself into Colonial life. Hearts would have to be changed in order to eliminate this dastardly system.

As expected the British were quick to point out their hypocrisy in their immediate response to the Declaration and they did it with very hurtful and stinging language. The Founder's knew in their hearts they would be subject to this hurt because they used the same language against themselves on a consistent basis.

> *Dr. Larry Arnn, President of Hillsdale College in his new book The Founder's Key, addresses these issues quite eloquently. He contends that if a hypocrite is a man who pretends to virtues he does not have, the Founders were not that.*

Jefferson, a slave owner, never tried to justify it but he did condemn it and worked to end the practice. Many of the Founders were avid abolitionists and spent their lives working to end slavery. Jefferson's influence can be seen in the Northwest Ordinance of 1778, which bans slavery in all those territories. The Northwest Ordinance was for many decades listed in the US Code as the third "Organic Law" of the United States. Article 6 of the Ordinance contains the following passage on slavery:

> *There shall be neither slavery nor involuntary servitude in the said territory, otherwise than in the punishment of crimes whereof the party shall have been duly convicted: Provide, always, That any person escaping into the same, from whom labor or service is lawfully claimed in any one of the original States, such fugitive may be lawfully reclaimed and conveyed to the person claiming his or her labor or service as aforesaid.*

In Lincoln's famous Peoria speech he appeals to this pattern that was established through the Northwest Ordinance and Jefferson's influence in stopping the spread of slavery into the territories and future states. Lincoln was arguing that the Founder's disapproved of slavery and pointed to Article 6 of the Northwest Ordinance as evidence that they opposed slavery.

In using words with such eternal meaning, the "Laws of Nature and of Nature's God" the contradiction between the beliefs of Jefferson verses his actions were exposed. It is not much different than when we say what we believe regarding certain things and then turn around and do what we say we shouldn't do. The flesh is weak and we are not always in agreement with our spiritual absolutes. So therefore, those laws (of Nature and Nature's God) are not always obeyed. These laws obviously drew many of the Founders but for some, who had slaves, the temptation was too hard to resist.

The Founders did all they could to start the process of banning slavery altogether and they truly believed with these strictures in place it would happen. It appears that something interrupted the movement to eventually abolish slavery. So what happened? They failed to anticipate that after they died a way of thinking would arise that was not based in Biblical truth. In 1830, John C. Calhoun became an advocate for states' rights and slavery. His writings, *Disquisition on Government*, became influential in the southern states and brought in a new progressive and developmental thinking of a scientific nature which for some revealed a "new" truth. It was at heart a racial truth justified through science and tied to religion. According to this new doctrine, not nature (and nature's God) but history is the determinant of all things, including the status and even the consciousness of human beings.

This thinking was a harbinger of what we see today in Europe and the United States. The old liberalism of the American Revolution respected in principle the liberty of all and that was leading our nation away from the practice of slavery. The new doctrines of history respect in principle the liberty of none and they led (and are leading) away from the practice of freedom. So the standard that the Founders wished to establish as a maxim for a free society was interrupted so that it was never perfectly attained as was their intention. The interruption of that movement has come not from service to the principles and institutions of the Revolution but from their abandonment.

Conclusion

For over two hundred years, the Declaration of Independence and the Constitution of the United States have served America well because these documents are consistent with the principles found in the Bible.

The Constitution was not intended to be a living breathing document that can be updated and changed as the times change (except in the rare instances where Congress and the States ratify an amendment). It was written with such wisdom that it is all we need or will ever need to sustain this country. Just as the Bible is not a living changeable document, neither is the Constitution of the United States. The Bible is the roadmap and rulebook for the game of life and the Constitution is the roadmap and rulebook for governing the nation.

Those who seek to change the Constitution with the reasoning that it must keep up with the times do so at the peril of destroying the United States of America and the very freedoms on which this nation was founded. Over the course of time, the Constitution has been trampled on and, at present, is in deadly threat of being totally changed into what it was never intended to be.

It is imperative on each generation to know and understand our true heritage and the intention of the original Constitution of the United States of America so that we can protect what God has given us. Unfortunately, this has not happened. Therefore, we are now in great risk of losing it all.

As I write this book, the American people are rising up in the form of the Tea Party movement. Over the past year people have come to see for the first time that we have an Administration that fundamentally dislikes America. We, the people have come to be viewed as subjects and not citizens and in the process we are disrespected and treated as servants who should quietly obey and willingly give up our incomes for the common good. This is not remotely the American way that has made us the most prosperous nation in the world.

The Tea Party movement has grown into a national political force which is leaderless by design and each group has it's own emphasis but all are breathing new life into a 223 year old document known as the United States Constitution. This is a very good thing. We have finally awakened to the fact that our politicians for years have been merely paying lip service to the words of our Founders and the Constitution. Sadly, it has taken us too long to come to this conclusion as we have been jolted out of our comfort zones since the last election.

Now we have realized the simple truth that respect for our Constitution does matter and there are consequences when disrespect for our national heritage becomes accepted political dogma and agents of change have been let loose on the American people. We now know that we have duties as American citizens to protect liberty and to pass those protections on to our children. We can no longer take the easy way and ignore what is happening by pulling the covers over our eyes.

There is much work to do to begin to restore our Constitution and it will take many years of diligence to dismantle all that has been put into place and there will certainly be obstacles and opposition to our efforts. We must push aside our weariness in order to say to our children and grandchildren that we have done our part to secure all the opportunities and blessings of liberty for them and their children. They in turn must do the same for their children.

It is apparent that most Americans do not have a working knowledge of our Constitution. Many have not even read it. Most of our elected officials who are sworn to uphold the Constitution have not read it either. Now is the time to apply ourselves to gaining an real understanding of the Declaration and Constitution that have been given us. The next chapter will attempt to overcome the lack of knowledge of our Constitution.

PATRIOTIC PORTRAIT

Benjamin Franklin (1706-1790). Printer, scientist, author, and statesman, he served as a diplomat to France and England; was the President (Governor) of Pennsylvania; founded the University of Pennsylvania; signed the Declaration of Independence, the Articles of Confederation and the Constitution. Benjamin Franklin was the 15th of 17 children born to a candle maker. Because there were no funds for a formal education, he started an apprenticeship as a printer at the age of twelve.

By his late twenties he attained wide acclaim as a literary genius through the annual publication of his book, *Poor Richard's Almanac* (1732-1757). This book contained innumerable proverbs, such as:

> *God heals, and the doctor takes the fees.*
>
> *God helps them that help themselves.*
>
> *Work as if you were to live 100 years; pray as if you were to die tomorrow.* [3]

Benjamin Franklin educated himself in five languages and the sciences. He was known as the "Newton of his Age." He made important discoveries in electricity, coining the terms "positive and negative charges," "conductor", "battery," and "electric shock." His invention of the lightning rod earned him the Royal Society's Copley Medal and honorary degrees from Harvard and Yale Universities in 1753. He also invented the Franklin stove, the rocking chair, and bi-focal glasses in addition to numerous other scientific discoveries. He organized the first postal system in America, the first volunteer fire department, a circulating public library, a city police force, and the lighting of streets.

> Question for thought: How many people in modern times have accomplished as much in their lifetimes? Just imagine what it would be like to have accomplished even a fourth of what Benjamin Franklin accomplished.

Benjamin Franklin was raised as a Puritan Calvinist. In his teens, he began to question some of the beliefs of the Calvinists and quit attending church. Instead, he spent his Sundays studying. He became a "deist," an influential belief of that century. Deists believed in God as the creator and author of nature's law but did not believe God involved himself in the daily lives of those He created. However, according to David Barton's research, deism of the 1700's allowed you to believe that God was involved in your personal and corporate life.

This explains how Franklin could call himself a deist, but still believed in prayer and scripture. There is indication that his beliefs changed over his life span of eighty-four years. As he matured, he grew to believe that deism did not give any incentive for men to live better lives. He became disgusted with the way deists lived and therefore began to support Christianity. He believed Christianity gave people an incentive to live better lives. He also took the Bible very seriously.

Whether Benjamin Franklin ever embraced Jesus as his Savior is not known; however, there is strong evidence that in his later years, he recognized the need for God's grace as opposed to good works as the means to eternal life. Benjamin Franklin definitely believed that republican government and Christianity were dependent on each other for success. He even believed that government should encourage religion to ensure the future of the nation. In his last few years, he expressed his belief that God had guided the Constitutional Convention.

He is quoted as stating: "A Bible and a newspaper in every house, a good school in every district-all studied and appreciated as they merit-are the principal support of virtue, morality, and civil liberty."[4]

Note: the schools at that time used the Bible as a textbook.

In a letter dated April 1787, Benjamin Franklin expounded: *"Only a virtuous people are capable of freedom. As nations become more corrupt and vicious, they have more need of masters."*[5]

Benjamin Franklin wrote his own epitaph:

> *THE BODY*
> *Of*
> *BENJAMIN FRANKLIN*
> *Printer*
> *Like the cover of an old book,*
> *Its contents torn out,*
> *And stripped of its lettering and gilding*
> *Lies here, food for worms;*
> *Yet the work itself shall not be lost,*
> *For it will (as he believed) appear once more,*
> *In a new,*
> *And more beautiful edition,*
> *Corrected and amended*
> *By the AUTHOR* [6]

RECOMMENDED READING / MEDIA

John Adams, David McCullough

The Patriot, Mel Gibson. This movie depicts the war for independence. Note that it does include intense violence.

QUESTIONS for THOUGHT and DISCUSSION

1. Is there still a struggle for the future of our republic? Why?

2. How much of this struggle is spiritual?

3. What is the difference between a republic and a direct democracy?

4. How do you bring thirteen independent states together to form some sort of national government, in order to unify them and ensure their security?

5. What important element was missing from these meetings?

6. What was Ben Franklin really pointing out to the delegates in his famous speech?

7. Is the Constitution a Christian document? Explain.

8. What does it mean that we are 'created equal'?

9. What is equal protection under the law?

10. Is there a trend today toward using public opinion to govern the nation? Would this make us a majority rule nation instead of a nation ruled by laws?

11. Where is this most noticeable?

12. What is the difference between public opinion and the will of the voters?

13. How is the "rule of law" viewed today?

14. What was it that motivated the Pilgrims to work hard at Plymouth Plantation and Why?

15. Does the government infringe on private property rights today? If yes, give examples.

16. In reading about Benjamin Franklin above, have you had a similar spiritual journey? Explain.

Foundational Truths – Chapter 9

"Enlightened statesmen will not always be at the helm."

- James Madison, Federalist No. 10

"The Constitution of the United States is to receive a reasonable interpretation of its language, and its powers, keeping in view the objects and purposes, for which those powers were conferred. By a reasonable interpretation, we mean, that in case the words are susceptible of two different senses, the one strict, the other more enlarged, that should be adopted, which is most consonant with the apparent objects and intent of the Constitution."

- Joseph Story, Commentaries on the Constitution, 1833

Chapter 9

The Gatekeeper of Liberty: The Constitution

The United States Constitution is not a lengthy document. Following the preamble or statement of purpose, it lists the seven articles that give power to the government and establish how it is to function. The wording of the Constitution is more general than specific because the writers knew that specifics would cause division among the delegates and the states. However, due to its general wording, it has been open to debate between those who are "strict constructionists" and those who are "loose constructionists." At times, it has been the subject of stormy controversies regarding the proper interpretation.

The Founders and authors never intended that the Constitution be loosely interpreted. Just as the official rules of football, basketball, baseball, and soccer are not subject to change on a whim, the Constitution was not meant to be rewritten or amended at will. The Founders did recognize that there needed to be a provision for adding to the Constitution as the times determined. Therefore, they provided for a rigorous amendment process to make additions to the Constitution only when absolutely necessary. The process for amending our Constitution (a stringent amendment process requiring 2/3 consensus) is outlined in Article 5 of the Constitution.

The Founders firmly believed the hand of God directed the writing of the Constitution and, therefore, they had complete confidence that it embodied everything this country would ever need to succeed. As indeed, it has served the United States well for over two hundred years.

Unfortunately, as I mentioned earlier, 'We the People' of the United States do not have a working knowledge and understanding of the Constitution. Therefore, our elected leaders are free to pass laws and resolutions that are not allowed by the Constitution. An example of this abuse is the federal government's charitable giving. Concerning government "charity," James Madison said in a January 1794 speech in the House of Representatives:

> *"The government of the United States is a definite*
> *government, confined to specified objects. It is not like state*
> *governments, whose powers are more general. Charity is no*
> *part of the legislative duty of the government."[1]*

Today, the U.S. government gives away millions of dollars in charity, but it is not an intended function of the federal government. The money they give is simply not theirs to give. Charity is when I reach into my own pocket to assist my fellow man in need. It is a voluntary action and works well in the private sector. In fact, it is far more efficient than the federal government.

We Americans are very generous. When the federal government engages in charity, they are taking money by force of tax laws to help others. I think of it as robbing one group of people to benefit another group. If someone comes in and takes money from you by force, it is called theft. This is just one example of how the federal government, through our elected officials, has overstepped the Constitution.

Because 'We the People' do not know the Constitution, there is no public outcry when our leaders ignore constitutional principles. As this happens, our Constitution is slowly diminished. It is our responsibility to know and understand what our Constitution says and to hold our representatives accountable for unconstitutional behavior.

Sadly, many of our elected officials do not have a working knowledge of the Constitution and, thus, out of ignorance, unconstitutional laws are passed. Other people, on the other hand, just simply ignore the Constitution, to promote their personal power and political ideology.

Immediately upon finishing the body of the Constitution, the delegates agreed that a Bill of Rights to protect individual liberties should be added as the first amendments. The first Congress of the United States voted on the final version of the first ten amendments on September 25, 1789, and two years later in December, 1791, they became law. The Founders wanted to make sure that the majority did not trample on the rights of the individual. It is important to note that protecting freedom of religion and speech was their first priority.

The Preamble

The Preamble is the statement of purpose, which was to establish the supreme law of the United States. It also describes by the words, "We the People of the United States," that the power of the federal government comes from the people and the consent of the governed.

Language as written: *"WE THE PEOPLE of the United States, in Order to form a more perfect union, establish Justice, insure domestic Tranquility, provide for the common defense, promote the general Welfare, and secure the Blessings of Liberty to ourselves and our Posterity, do ordain and establish this Constitution for the United States of America."*

Please note the phrase "promote the general Welfare". This little phrase is how the Congress began to justify granting federal charity to people in need. But does "general welfare" actually mean charity or does it simply mean promoting policies that bring about general prosperity for the well being of its citizens? There is a big difference.

The Articles

The first three articles set up the three branches of government or separation of powers.

Article I – The Legislative Branch

This article provides for the establishment of the Congress as the legislative branch of government which makes our laws. The Congress includes a Senate and a House of Representatives. Each member of the House of Representatives is elected to office every two years by the registered voters in their state district. House members must be 25 years old, a citizen of the United States for seven years, and live in the state that elects them. To replace a member who dies while in office or cannot complete his/her term, the Governor of their state calls a special election. Article I also explains how the number of representatives from each state is determined. Section 2 of the Fourteenth Amendment changed how people were counted and in 1842, the Congress imposed a district system on the United States. Each Congressman represents a specific district in his/her state. There are 435 members (districts) in the House of Representatives.

The members of the Senate face election every six years. They are on a staggered two-year basis so that not all Senators are first termers or freshmen at the same time. One-third of the Senators are up for re-election every two years. Each state has two Senators. Senators must be 30 years old, a citizen of the United States for nine years, and live in the state that elects them. Originally, Senators were appointed by their state legislatures.

The Seventeenth Amendment, 1913, changed the rules to allow for direct popular election of Senators. Each chamber (House and Senate) elects their own leaders and establishes their individual rules of order and conduct. The Vice President is the President of the Senate and only votes to break a tie. The Senate elects another person as President to preside over the group when the Vice President is not present. To replace a Senator who dies in office or cannot complete his/her term, the Governor of that state appoints a replacement to complete the term. The replacement then stands for election during the next voting cycle.

The process of removing somebody from office, known as impeachment, begins in the House of Representatives. Once they determine there is enough evidence to impeach, a trial is held in the Senate with a vote of the Senators as to whether to remove them or not. Two-thirds of the Senators must vote yes in order to remove the offending official from office.

Congress also has power over the conduct of federal elections and can alter such regulations at any time. The states actually draw up the Congressional district lines. The Supreme Court in 1962 dealt with proper apportionment of election districts in its decision in *Baker v. Carr,* which allowed voters to go into a federal court to force equitable representation. This decision was based on the equal protection clause of the Fourteenth Amendment.

Article I also establishes how members are to be paid and how many need to show up to conduct official business. It also institutes the Congressional Record where everything said and done during business in each chamber is officially documented. All bills for increasing taxes begin in the House of Representatives, but the Senate must also approve them, just like any other bill. All other types of bills can begin in either chamber but must be approved by both before going to the President for his approval. The President has ten days, excluding Sundays, in which to approve or veto a bill. If he takes no action within those ten days, that legislation automatically becomes law. If he vetoes a bill, it goes back to the Congress where further changes can be made. Or they can simply vote on it again. A two-thirds vote to approve the bill will over-ride the Presidential veto and the bill becomes law.

Article I also lists the stated powers of Congress such as:

- raising, spending, and borrowing money;
- providing for armed services, providing for organizing, arming and training of the military;
- setting rules for citizenship,
- establishing post offices, building roads and building post offices;
- regulating commerce,
- establishing federal courts to support the Supreme Court, etc.
- protecting the sanctity of contracts.

The "commerce clause" which gives Congress the right "to regulate commerce with foreign nations, and among the several states," has been used as a strong argument for the expansion of federal government power in the 20th century.

Besides its enumerated and inherent powers, the Congress has implied powers under Article I "to make all laws which shall be necessary and proper for carrying into execution the enumerated or expressed powers." In other words, they can make laws that would aid in carrying out the stated powers in the Constitution. Finally, Article I contains guarantees of the writ of habeas corpus, prohibits bills of attainder (laws passed to declare someone guilty of a crime) and ex post facto laws (criminal laws passed by Congress can be applied only from the time they are passed - not retroactively), and also improve certain limitations on state power.

Article II –The Executive Branch

This article establishes the Executive Branch of Government. The leader of the country is the President of the United States. The President and Vice-President are elected every four years. Each state Legislature decides how the "electors" (members of the Electoral College) from that state will be chosen. This process varies from state to state. For instance, Texas delegates at the state party conventions first elect two at large delegates. Later during their congressional caucus, they elect an "elector" to represent their district. The total number of electors will equal the number of Representatives and Senators of that state. If a state has eight Representatives and two Senators, there will be ten electors. Senators, Representatives or other elected officials may not be named electors to the Electoral College. The electors meet after the general election to place their votes which are then counted, certified and sent to the President of the U.S. Senate where all the states votes are counted and the election is finalized.

The Founders were concerned that the direct election by general vote of the populace would turn into a popularity contest that would favor the large states and discriminate against the small states. Therefore, they set up the Electoral College as the final word on elections. That explains how a President and Vice President can win the popular vote but lose the election in the Electoral College. The election of 2000 is an example of this.

Read Article II, Sections 2, 3 & 4 for the enumeration of presidential powers. (See the website for the Constitution at end of this chapter.)

The powers of the President are limited to those listed in Article II. However, there are those who believe the President is given executive power (through Executive Orders) not limited by the provisions of the rest of the article. Every President has had to make the choice of interpretations for himself. Some have used executive orders sparingly and others have used them abundantly. Executive Orders could be abused by an elected leader who does not govern, but rules. This could pose a serious problem to "We the People."

Article III – The Judiciary Branch

All the judicial power of the United States, including the courts of law and justice, will be headed by one Supreme Court. Congress can set up other courts as needed. Federal judges shall hold their offices during good behavior. Very few are removed for bad behavior and most consider these appointments for life. Besides listing the stated or enumerated powers, the judiciary interprets laws and the Constitution with an authority that must be deferred to. However, Congress can pass laws restricting the jurisdiction of the federal courts, such as prohibiting the courts from hearing cases regarding religious freedom or marriage. Congress can also eliminate the number of seats on the Appeals Courts, thus effectively firing some judges. Article III also defines treason, guarantees trial by jury in criminal cases, and lays the basis for federal jurisdiction.

The Definition of Treason: Betraying the United States is making war against the United States, being loyal to an enemy of the U.S., or giving that enemy help or comfort. No person shall be convicted of treason unless there is testimony of two witnesses to the same overt act (this is a basic Biblical principle), or by confession in open court.

The Eleventh Amendment (1798), which prohibits suits against any state by citizens of another state or foreigners, was passed in reaction to the Supreme Court accepting jurisdiction of a suit against a state by a citizen of another state.

Article IV – The States

Article IV deals with the relationship of the states in honoring each other's public acts, their records, and their legal reports. It provides for the return of criminals to the state where their crime was committed (extradition) and prohibits states discriminating against citizens of other states, or in favor of its own. The article guarantees a republican form of government for every state and provides for the admission of new states as well as the government of territories.

Article V – Amending the Constitution

Article V provides for amendments to the Constitution. To amend the Constitution, the proposed Amendment must receive two-thirds vote of the Representatives and Senators. It then goes to the states for ratification. Three-fourths of the states must pass it within the next seven years in order for the Amendment to be ratified. If the states fail to approve or ratify the proposed changes, the Amendment dies.

Article VI – Constitutional Supremacy

Article VI establishes the Constitution and federal law as the supreme law of the land, superseding the laws of the states. It also provides an oath of office for members of the three branches of federal government that requires each individual to swear to uphold the Constitution of the United States. It does not specify any religious qualifications or affiliation necessary for the person to hold the office. Early in US history, some of the states did have religious requirements or qualifications for those seeking local, state and federal office (U.S. Congressmen and U.S. Senators).

Article VII – Ratification of the Constitution

Article VII declares that the Constitution should go into force when ratified by nine states, the two-third vote margin needed since there were only thirteen states.

The Amendments

The Constitution has been changed gradually over the years through the Amendment process. Some of the twenty-seven amendments were a direct result of Supreme Court decisions. The first ten amendments, the Bill of Rights, were added within two years of the signing of the federal Constitution in order to ensure sufficient guarantees of individual and state liberties. George Mason (1725-1792), a member of the Virginia House of Burgesses, a lawyer, judge, political philosopher and planter is known as the "Father of the Bill of Rights." His influence is worldwide because all succeeding constitutions of other countries have incorporated the pattern he set forth for the US Bill of Rights.

Mason vehemently opposed a strong federal government because he feared it would usurp the sovereignty of the individual states. He practically wrote the first ten amendments to the United States Constitution to specifically limit the power of the federal government. These rights are expressed also in the Virginia Bill of Rights which he also wrote. His statement before the General Court of Virginia regarding the "Laws of Nature and Nature's God" was later incorporated into the Declaration of Independence.

Originally, the Bill of Rights applied only to the federal government. But since the passage of the Fourteenth Amendment (1868), many of the guarantees contained in the Bill of Rights have been extended to the states through the "due-process" clause of the Fourteenth Amendment.

The Bill of Rights – The First Ten Amendments

Amendment I - Guarantees the freedom of worship, of speech, of the press, of assembly, and of petition to the government for redress of grievances. The original text reads:

"Congress shall make no law respecting an establishment of religion (create an official national church), or prohibiting the free exercise thereof; or abridging the freedom of speech, or of the press; or the right of the people peaceably to assemble, and to petition the Government for a redress of grievances."

Notice what popular phrase is not mentioned in this Amendment. This Amendment is not to protect government from religion but to protect churches from government. As we have already discussed in previous chapters, the Founders felt the promotion of religion was important for a representative republic.

Because of this false interpretation of the Constitution, prayer, the Ten Commandments, and Bible reading have been removed from public schools. The ability to remove all symbols of Judeo/Christian beliefs from schools and other public places came through the Scopes Monkey Trial. At the end of this heated debate, the court ruled in favor of teaching Darwin's version of creation, which is better known as evolution. The authority of the Bible was stripped by that one court decision, allowing for the demise of truth in our government, schools, and society. Today, public/government schools teach the idea that right and wrong depends on the present situation (relativism) instead of the Ten Commandments and other Biblical principles. Therefore, everyone does what is right in his own eyes just like in the days of the Judges of Israel (Judges 17:6 and 21:25).

Amendment II – guarantees the right to bear arms openly. Americans were to be prepared to bear arms at a moment's notice to protect themselves, their state, and their country. The Founders believed that an unarmed public would be subject to tyranny.

Amendment III – guarantees freedom from quartering (housing) soldiers in a private home without the owner's consent.

Amendment IV – protects the people against unreasonable search and seizure, a safeguard only recently extended to the states. Authorities must have a warrant issued by a judge describing what will be looked at and what will be taken.

Amendment V – provides that no person shall be held for "a capital or otherwise infamous crime" without first being indicted or charged with an offense. It also guarantees protection against being held responsible for the same crime twice (double jeopardy), testifying against themselves, or "being deprived of life or limb or property without due process of law." The phrase "due process of law" also appears in the Fourteenth Amendment, which has caused an ongoing debate as to whether both these amendments guarantee the same rights.

Amendment VI – guarantees the right of a speedy and public trial by an impartial jury in all criminal proceedings, as well as the right to the assistance of counsel for his defense.

Amendment VII – allows for a jury trial in federal civil courts where someone sues another for more than $20.00.

Amendment VIII – prohibits excessive bail, fines, and "cruel and unusual" punishment.

Amendment IX – simply states that the list of rights guaranteed by the Constitution does not mean that the people do not have other rights that are not already listed or implied.

Amendment X – acknowledges that the powers not given to the United States by the Constitution, or denied by it to the States, belong to the States, or to the people themselves.

Example: The Supreme Court decision Roe v. Wade was based on the idea that there is a right to privacy in the Constitution, thus taking abortion laws away from the states where it belonged. Overturning this decision does not mean that abortion would be illegal, only that it would be up to each state to decide the issue of abortion.

The First Ten Amendments, The Bill of Rights, were crucial to the ratification of the Constitution as a whole. The Constitution was ratified on the assurance of a Bill of Rights protecting individual and states rights from being overrun by the federal government. The Bill of Rights was ratified on December 15, 1791.

The Other Amendments

Amendment XI (1798) – Only citizens of a given state can sue their own state.

Amendment XII (1804) – Revised the way the President and Vice-President are elected. In case of a tie vote within the Electoral College, the House of Representatives will determine the President through a state by state vote with each state delegation having a single vote. Amendment XII also decides what constitutes a quorum for this vote. A majority (50% plus one) of all the states will be required to make this decision before March 4th following the national election. (The twentieth Amendment gave them more time.) The Vice-President will automatically become President after the specified deadline. The Constitutional guidelines for the President and Vice-President are identical except that the Senate votes on the Vice-Presidential candidates.

Amendment XIII (1865) - This Amendment abolished slavery. No one can be forced to do work without compensation except convicted criminals.

Amendment XIV (1868) – Guarantees the rights of citizenship to all persons born in the United States, or given citizenship by the United States government. It also guarantees that they are citizens of the state where they live with equal protection under the law (every citizen is equal in the eyes of the law and is given the same protection under that law). It also states that the number of representatives from the states will be determined by counting all the people in the state, except Native Americans who are not taxed.

> NOTE: The 13th, 14th and 15th Amendments were all passed by Republican majorities in the period right after the Civil War. By 1875, ten years after the Civil War ended, Republicans had successfully passed almost two dozen civil rights laws. Black American legislators often played significant roles in the debates surrounding the passage of these laws. During the years following the Civil War, there were a total of 23 Black American Congressmen (13 were former slaves) and 3 Black American U.S. Senators – all Republicans. At the end of Reconstruction, the Democrats began to gain control of the Congress and many state Houses. Most of these civil rights laws were rescinded. It would be another 89 years before any other civil rights laws were passed.
>
> For a complete history of African Americans from the Constitution up to the present see: *American History in Black & White* by David Barton, Wallbuilder Press. (Wallbuilders.com)

Amendment XV (1868) – The United States or any State cannot deny anyone the right to vote based on their race, the color of their skin, or the fact that they were once slaves.

Amendment XVI (1913) – gives Congress the power to tax personal income. This is a controversial amendment because many believe this is an unconstitutional function of government.

Amendment XVII (1913) – institutes the direct popular election of Senators in each state. Prior to this amendment Senators were appointed by the State legislatures.

Amendment XVIII (1919) – prohibited the manufacture, sale or movement of beer, wine, or liquor anywhere in the United States or anywhere under the control of the United States. This Amendment was later repealed.

Amendment XIX (1920) – The right to vote cannot be denied because of sex. Women could now vote.

Amendment XX (1933) –abolished the so-called lame-duck Congress and alters the date of the presidential inauguration. The term "lame-duck" Congress refers to the period of time from the November election until the next year when the new Congress is sworn in.

Amendment XXI (1933) – repealed the Eighteenth Amendment but allows the states, territories, or other areas under the control of the United States to pass laws making it illegal to make, sell, move or drink beer, wine, or liquor. It gave the power back to the states.

Amendment XXII (1951) – limits the number of terms a President may serve to two terms.

Amendment XXIII (1961) – permits the residents of the District of Columbia to vote in the presidential election and pick electors to the Electoral College in the same way the states do.

Amendment XXIV (1964) – prohibits the poll tax and any other tax required as a condition for voting in primaries or general elections. Trying to suppress poor and black voters, southern states once charged an outrageous tax for the right to vote. Some also instituted literacy tests, making it difficult for certain individuals to pass, thus losing their right to vote.

Amendment XXV (1967) – established the procedure for filling the office of Vice President between elections, and for governing in the event of presidential disability.

Amendment XXVI (1971) – lowered the voting age in all elections to 18.

Amendment XXVII (1992) – set up Congressional pay raises to go into effect after the next election with the new Congress in place.

Because the issue of amending the Constitution is taken very seriously, not all proposed Amendments have received the required two-thirds states approval. The Constitution has worked well for over two hundred years and actually requires little to make it more effective. The courts, in forcing the issue of same-sex marriage on the American public, are making it necessary to push for a marriage amendment to the Constitution. This amendment would protect the Biblical concept of marriage between one man and one woman – an amendment that has not been deemed necessary until the present day.

Jean Yarbrough, professor of government and author of two books on Thomas Jefferson, said Jefferson believed the amendment process was necessary to keep pace with the times. However, if the people wished to alter their frame of government, say, to fund public improvements or education, they were free to do so by constitutional amendment and not by allowing their representatives to construe the powers of government broadly.

Link to the text of the Constitution of the United States:

www.earlyamerica.com/earlyamerica/freedom/constitution/

PATRIOTIC PORTRAIT

James Madison (1751-1836) is called the "Father of the Constitution", not because he wrote the Constitution – for he was just one of many – but more because of his role in getting it ratified by the states. Madison spent over a half century in public service. He was the youngest delegate to the Continental Congress, signer of the Declaration of Independence, member of the Constitutional Convention, leader of the pro-Constitution forces at the Virginia Ratifying Convention, champion of religious liberty in Virginia, contributing author (with Hamilton and Jay) to the Federalist Papers, Secretary of State and chief advisor to President Jefferson, two-term President of the United States, during which time he was Commander-in-Chief for the War of 1812, and Rector of the University of Virginia.

Madison was the first born of ten children to James and Eleanor Madison. His father was an Episcopal Church vestryman and lay delegate to the Episcopal Convention of 1776. Both parents were committed to the church and pious living. He was home-schooled until the age of 12, and then went to school for several years under the tutelage of a Scotsman named Donald Robertson, and later under the Rev. Thomas Martin, an Episcopal minister who lived in the Madison home.

At 18, he enrolled at the College of New Jersey (now known as Princeton) where he came under the influence of the college president, Rev. John Witherspoon, who stressed divinity and theology in addition to the usual curriculum of the classics, history, philosophy, and the writing and speaking of good clear English. They retained their close association as they served in Congress together years later. During his college years, Madison was inclined toward a career in the ministry, and, upon graduation, continued in graduate work – adding some Hebrew to his knowledge of classical languages and literature. He was an avid student of the Bible.

As things deteriorated with Great Britain, Madison soon felt drawn to a life of public service. After this point, his writings concerning his faith changed considerably as he became a firm believer in separating church and state. The Christian religion, particularly Rev. Witherspoon's Calvinism, influenced Madison's view of law and government. He believed in the innate depravity of man and knew there needed to be a system of checks and balances to keep one set of interests from dominating the whole.

From these beliefs, Madison contributed nine essential elements to American political thought according to *Christianity and The Constitution - The Faith of Our Founding Fathers* by John Eidsmoe.

1. Power must come from the people. Government must be responsive to the will of the people through popular elections, so would-be tyrants can be voted out of office.

2. The government has only such powers as the people delegate to it through the Constitution. Government must be limited.

3. The Constitution is required to respect natural law and natural rights, as are the institutions of government created by the Constitution.

4. He supported the separation of powers between the three branches of government to minimize the danger of abuse.

5. Madison and like-minded delegates supported a system of checks and balances for each branch of government.

6. Madison saw the strength of free government in the multiple interests that prevailed across America. Diversity of thought would protect against one person or group usurping too much power.

7. Madison advocated moderation, and he demonstrated this in his own life.

8. He opposed slavery, even though he owned slaves. He believed emancipation should take place as a gradual process.

9. He showed an undying defense of religious liberty. He witnessed Baptists being persecuted in his home state of Virginia and felt it was wrong for one Protestant religion to persecute another.

James Madison, "The Father of the Constitution", gave the United States a legacy that lasts to this day. His contributions to the Constitution are those sections involving the separation of powers with accompanying checks and balances, and influenced the First Amendment through his firm belief there should be no "national religion" but his choice of words (which would have saved today's misinterpretation of the First Amendment) did not make the final version of the First Amendment.

- - - - -

PATRIOTIC PORTRAIT

Frederick Douglass (1818-1895) was born into slavery on the Eastern Shore of Maryland in 1818, and was given the name Frederick Augustus Washington Bailey (Baly), after his mother, Harriet Bailey. During the course of his remarkable life, he escaped from slavery, became internationally renowned for his eloquence in the cause of liberty, and went on to serve the national government in several official capacities. Through his work, he came into contact with many of the leaders of his time.

His early work in the cause of freedom brought him into contact with a wide array of abolitionists and social reformers, including William Lloyd Garrison, Elizabeth Cady Stanton, John Brown, Gerrit Smith and many others. Garrison mentored the young Douglass, and taught him that the Constitution was a pro-slavery document. Douglass accepted this claim until a later time when he decided to study the Constitution and the writings of the framers for himself. What he discovered was that the Constitution was actually an anti-slavery document. He concluded:

"The Constitution is a glorious liberty document. Read its preamble; consider its purposes. Is slavery among them? Is it at the gateway? Or is it in the temple? It is neither. If the Constitution were intended to be, by its framers and adopters, a slaveholding instrument, why neither slavery, slaveholding, nor slave can anywhere be found in it? Now, take the Constitution according to its plain reading and I defy the presentation of a single pro-slavery clause in it. On the other hand, it will be found to contain principles and purposes entirely hostile to the existence to slavery."[2]

As a major stationmaster on the Underground Railroad, he directly helped hundreds on their way to freedom through his adopted home city of Rochester, NY. Renowned for his eloquence, he lectured throughout the U.S. and England on the brutality and immorality of slavery. As a publisher, his *North Star* and *Frederick Douglass' Paper* brought news of the anti-slavery movement to thousands. He helped recruit African American troops for the Union Army, and his personal relationship with Lincoln helped persuade the President to make emancipation a cause of the Civil War. Two of Douglass' sons served in the 54th Massachusetts Regiment, which was made up entirely of African American volunteers. The storming of Fort Wagner by this regiment was dramatically portrayed in the film *Glory!* A painting of this event hangs in the front hall at Cedar Hill.

In 1872, Douglass moved to Washington, D.C., where he initially served as publisher of the *New National Era*, a publication intended to carry forward the work of elevating the position of African Americans in the post-Emancipation period. This enterprise failed when the promised financial backing failed to materialize. During this period, Douglass also served briefly as president of the Freedmen's National Bank, and subsequently, in various national service positions. He received presidential appointments from Republican Presidents Ulysses S. Grant, Rutherford B. Hayes, and James A. Garfield. Democrat President Grover Cleveland removed Frederick Douglass from office, but Republican Benjamin Harrison reappointed him.

RECOMMENDED READING

The Constitution of the United States
> www.earlyamerica.com/earlyamerica/freedom/constitution/

QUESTIONS for THOUGHT and DISCUSSION

1. How would you compare the interpretation of the Constitution with the interpretation of scripture?

2. Who should be responsible for charity - Government or Individuals? Why?

3. What is it called when districts are drawn to favor incumbents?

4. Besides making laws, what are some specific powers the Constitution gives to Congress? [See complete list in Section 8 of Article I.]

5. What are the two ways a bill becomes law?

6. Trivia question: How many states are in the United States? What was the last state admitted into statehood?

7. How many times has the Constitution been amended? Can you name a proposed Constitutional Amendment that failed to be ratified in the last thirty years?

8. How did the Founders feel about government promotion of religion versus what we see happening in our civil society today?

9. Should Christians have guns?

10. Why is protection from unreasonable search and seizure important?

11. What is "due process of law"?

12. How long does it take to bring criminals to trial today? Define "speedy":

13. What is "cruel and unusual" punishment? How are prisoners treated today?

14. The 14th amendment has produced what is called the "anchor baby" syndrome. What is an "anchor baby" and why is it a controversial subject?

15. If you were a legislator today, what would cause you (issues, circumstances, etc.) to favor passing a Constitutional Amendment? Do we need one to protect traditional marriage and family?

Foundational Truths – Chapter 10

"There are more instances of the abridgment of the freedom of the people by gradual and silent encroachments of those in power than by violent and sudden usurpations."

> - James Madison (speech to the Virginia Ratifying Convention,16 June 1788) Reference: Bartlett's Quotations (352)

"No man can well doubt the propriety of placing a president of the United States under the most solemn obligations to preserve, protect, and defend the constitution. It is a suitable pledge of his fidelity and responsibility to his country; and creates upon his conscience a deep sense of duty, by an appeal, at once in the presence of God and man, to the most sacred and solemn sanctions, which can operate upon the human mind."

> - Joseph Story, Commentaries on the Constitution, 1833

"One single object ... [will merit] the endless gratitude of the society: that of restraining the judges from usurping legislation."

> - Thomas Jefferson, letter to Edward Livingston, March 25, 1825

Chapter 10

Separation of Power - Who Has the Most Power?

The Legislative Branch

As we saw in the last lesson, the legislative branch of the government makes our laws. The stated powers of the Congress include raising, spending and borrowing money; providing for armed services, providing for organizing, arming and training of the military; the power to declare war; setting rules for citizenship, establishing post offices, building roads, post offices and federal buildings; regulating commerce, establishing federal courts to support the Supreme Court, along with a host of other duties.

Congress is charged with oversight of the military and the federal courts. They have the power to impcach judges who misbehave. They also have the power to limit the types of cases federal courts can hear. In the last thirty years, the federal courts have stepped into the arena of actually making laws, instead of judging cases and ruling simply on their constitutionality. Because of this abuse of power, there is a move in Congress to prohibit federal courts from hearing cases regarding religion.

Sadly, Congress in the past fifty years or so has been hesitant to limit the jurisdiction of the courts even though doing so is within their power. This may be a result of elected officials who do not understand the Constitution as they should or they are willingly allowing the judiciary to unconstitutionally "legislate" from the bench – unpopular laws that would be difficult for Congress to pass. By doing the latter, they do not have to go on record with a vote for "bad" legislation that could cost them their job by making their constituents angry.

What started out as temporary part-time public service has turned into full time and lifetime jobs in Congress. Too many are driven by job protection / getting re-elected and not by what is best for the nation as a whole. This mindset prevents them from taking courageous and righteous stands for liberty. Power is now the name of the game in Congress.

Therefore, allowing the courts to deal with controversial issues protects the elected politicians from the voters because Congress would not be able to pass these issues into law without loud protests from the public. Despite what we hear in the media, a wide majority of citizens support traditional values; and each year a greater percentage of the population opposes abortion. As the percentage of pro-abortion population has decreased, some in Congress who support this unpopular issue have used the courts to force these things upon the nation. And not just abortion but the homosexual agenda as well.

Each house of Congress has committees that oversee almost every facet of government, and these committees can have two or more sub-committees. Each committee has its own staff. There are thousands of staffers who work in Congress, moving from Congressman to Congressman, Senator to Senator and from committee to committee within this very large bureaucracy.

Keep in mind that oversight is one of the main functions of the Congress. For example, it is the responsibility of Congress to monitor our intelligence agencies and make sure they have the funding and regulations they need to be effective and operate efficiently. Committee members on the House and Senate Intelligence Committees receive the same intelligence reports that the President receives. Therefore, they cannot claim they were not privy to the same report as the Executive Branch unless they were not actually reading all the reports (not doing their job) or are "playing politics." Unfortunately, there has always been much political playing in Washington, D.C.

Government has grown large – larger than the Founders could ever have imagined or intended. Therefore, Congressmen and their committees are stretched and sometimes fail to do their jobs, because there is no way they can read all the proposed bills. Some of the legislative bills, especially appropriations bills, can be so large that the elected official relies on staff to read it in total and report on it. They are also given a summary of the legislation that many rely on when making decisions to support or not support. However, it must be remembered that the "devil is in the details" and relying on a summary may cause the elected official to support legislation that they would not support if they understood those details. Even bills that have the best of intentions have all kinds of negative unintended consequences. The sad thing is once these have been passed and become law very few are rescinded or even fixed. Just like the Constitution many laws are broadly written which then allows the regulatory agencies to interpret them any way they want causing heavy burdens to be placed on businesses and individuals.

> The one enumerated responsibility of Congress that is most abused today is the "Commerce Clause". The Founder's intention was that Congress would make sure that commerce between the states remains open and free. Today this clause is used to grab ever increasing power over the people of the United States – thus infringing on our liberty!

When emergencies occur and politicians consider certain bills as urgent and feel they must be passed immediately with little or no discussions, "We the People" need to be suspicious. Emergency/crisis situations provide opportunities for those who view the Constitution as a changeable document to institute such changes in the Constitution that the American people would normally not tolerate. These changes always take away our freedoms and chip away at liberty.

Earmarks are another practice that has taken root in the past fifty years. One of the Democrat speakers of the House thought this system up as a way of buying votes for sweeping legislation that was proving hard to pass. Earmarks allow individual Congressmen and Senators to be given money for their pet projects in exchange for their support of legislation most of the people of this nation would never approve. These elected officials can then claim to be bringing home money and jobs to their districts – "bringing home the bacon."

Since Congressmen run for election every two years, they never cease to campaign even when they are new to the job. They are constantly concerned with raising money for the next election.

After each election and before taking office, all newly elected Congressmen and Senators go through an orientation to help them understand the system. Part of that system is learning how to write legislation or a bill. Each house of Congress can introduce bills which are identified by a specific number. House bills have HB before the number, indicating the House of origination. Senate bills have SB before the number. Once introduced, the bill goes to the appropriate committee for approval. Usually it will go to as many as three committees before presentation to the floor of the House or Senate for a vote.

All bills that require funding go through the Appropriations Committee, which is the most powerful committee in each of the Houses. When a House bill passes, it then moves to the Senate and starts the committee process again. If it passes the Senate, it goes to a joint committee of the House and Senate for any revisions or compromises. It is then voted on once again. If it passes, it moves to the White House for approval.

The President has ten days (excluding Sundays) in which to sign the bill into law or to exercise his veto. If the ten days passes without a signature, the bill automatically becomes law. If the bill is vetoed by the President, the Congress can override that veto with a two-thirds vote. This process is part of the built-in checks and balances that the Founders felt was the key to preventing any one group from attaining too much power.

The Executive Branch

The Executive Branch consists of the President, Vice President and all the cabinet members who advise the President on foreign affairs, national security, military issues, judicial issues, education, health and welfare, agricultural issues, national parks and forests, commerce, and environment issues.

Once the President appoints the cabinet members, they must be approved by the United States Senate. Each of the cabinet members appoints lower level undersecretaries who work under them to carry out the will of the President. Today, these departments have become so large; many require their own buildings to house all their employees. These employees are all a part of the huge government bureaucracy that continues from administration to administration. These are lifetime jobs little chance of getting fired or laid off since government never shrinks. In many instances, these government employees have their own agendas that do not particularly agree with that of the President.

The State Department is a prime example of this. They resist most presidents' agendas, and have been known to leak information to discredit and undermine the President's stance on the issues as well as his goals. Each department has hundreds of regulations that they enforce on the American people. Therefore, in addition to all our laws, there are hundreds of government regulations and fees (taxes) by which the populace must abide.

> **Note:** Only Congress has the authority to make laws. Agencies such as the FDA, EPA, DEA, or FBI cannot make laws; however, they do make regulations and enforce these regulations in accordance with federal law. However, this is being abused and Congress is not doing its job of oversight by reining in these abuses. For example: EPA is setting regulations to enforce Cap and Trade without the legislation being passed into federal law.

Some of these regulations are passed by law through Congress. However, some are put into place by the administration when Congress can't get it accomplished by passing the necessary legislation. One example of this is the energy tax/cap and trade legislation that is having trouble making its way through the Congressional approval process. The Energy Department is setting into place new regulations to essentially do what the Cap and Trade Bill would do, however the public is not able to voice their opinions or comments on the matter. These agencies can be driven by extremist viewpoints and resent being slowed down or hindered by "We the People".

When there are vacancies for federal judges at any level, the President has the authority to nominate qualified judges to fill those vacancies. As a check and balance, the Senate is charged with approving the nominee by a "simple majority floor vote" (advise and consent). A list of names is submitted to the Senate Judiciary Committee for consideration. This committee is charged with certifying that the person nominated is qualified. Once qualification is granted, the name of that person is submitted to the floor for an up or down vote. Until recent years, Presidents' nominees have been appointed readily with very few being rejected.

Sadly, today this process is often corrupted by politics and ideology; so at times, good qualified judges are not being sent to the floor for a vote or some choose not to put themselves and their families through this sometimes personally destructive process. Therefore, there are more vacancies on the federal bench than ever before. A qualified judicial candidate is one that is rated by the American Bar Association as qualified, has the required degrees and demonstrates understanding of Constitutional law. Each President has their own judicial philosophy and looks for judges who will uphold that philosophy.

In today's political climate, the use or threat of a filibuster has become more common in Congress. Using the filibuster in this way (advise and consent) is an unconstitutional abuse of the process (filibusters were never intended for this purpose), which then forces the nominee to attain sixty votes in order to be approved. The Constitution only requires a simple majority of the 100 U.S. Senators.

The President is allowed by the Constitution to make appointments during Congressional recesses. Sadly, sometimes a recess appointment is the only way a President can get his qualified nominees into office. The President is also allowed to enact Executive Orders as needed. Some argue that this gives the President too much power. The Constitution is vague on the use of these Executive Orders (EO), so it has been up to each President to decide how much or little to use this privilege. Most presidents have been frugal in their use of this privilege because abusing it could give undo power to the Presidency that the founders never intended. This abuse could lead to excessive Presidential power circumventing the Legislative process. At this writing, President Obama is on track to using Executive Orders more than any other President in history and has crossed over into bypassing Congress.

The President is the Commander-in-Chief of the military during times of war, but he cannot declare war. Only Congress can declare war and authorize funding of war. Since WWII, we have not declared war on any nation. Korea, Vietnam, Gulf War I, Bosnia, and the Iraq War are considered military conflicts. Due to political concerns, declarations of war are almost impossible to attain from Congress.

The Judicial Branch

The United States Supreme Court was created under Article III, Section 1 of the Constitution and the Judiciary Act of 1798. This Act organized the Supreme Court, the federal circuit courts and the federal district courts. It also established the Office of Attorney General, and reserved the president's right to nominate justices for appointment to the United States Supreme Court with the advice and consent of the Senate.

When first created, the judicial branch was by far the weakest and most timid of the three branches, restraining itself from strongly upholding and deciding controversial issues. However, in 1801, in Marbury v. Madison, Chief Justice John Marshall asserted that the doctrine of judicial review permitted the Court to review the constitutionality of congressional legislation. In his 34 years as Chief Justice, he succeeded in strengthening the central government and making the Judiciary branch, in some respects, the strongest branch of the national government.

The Framers considered the rule of law essential to the safekeeping of social order and civil liberties. The rule of law holds that if our relationships with each other and the state are governed by a set of rules, rather than by a group of individuals, we are less likely to fall victim to authoritarian rule. The rule of law calls for both individuals and the government to submit to the law's supremacy. By doing this, the Framers formed another protective layer over individual rights and liberties. No one was above the law. However, we see today that the rule of law is being eroded by individuals with the consent of some of the judiciary.

> Note: The Constitution says nothing about using or citing international law as the basis for deciding cases before the court.

Thomas Jefferson cautioned that "The Constitution is a mere thing of wax in the hands of the Judiciary, which they may twist and shape into any form they please." He considered that having these justices be the ultimate arbiter of all constitutional questions was a very dangerous doctrine and one that would ultimately place us under the despotism of an oligarchy – the rule of few over many. Mr. Jefferson was prophetic, for today that is what is happening in our courts.

Federal Judiciary Facts:

The United States Supreme Court consists of the Chief Justice of the United States and eight associate justices. At its discretion, and within certain guidelines established by Congress, the Supreme Court hears a limited number of the cases it is asked to decide during the year. Those cases may begin in the federal or state courts and usually involve important questions about the Constitution or federal law.

The 94 U.S. judicial districts are organized into 12 regional circuits, each of which has a United States court of appeals. A court of appeals hears cases from the district courts located within its circuit, as well as appeals from decisions of federal administrative agencies. In addition, the Court of Appeals for the Federal Circuit has nationwide jurisdiction to hear appeals in specialized cases, such as those involving patent laws, and cases decided by the Court of International Trade and the Court of Federal Claims.

The United States district courts are the trial courts of the federal court system. Within limits set by Congress and the Constitution, the district courts have jurisdiction to hear nearly all categories of federal cases, including both civil and criminal matters. There are 94 federal judicial districts, including at least one district in each state, the District of Columbia and Puerto Rico. Three territories of the United States -- the Virgin Islands, Guam, and the Northern Mariana Islands -- have district courts that hear federal cases, including bankruptcy cases.

There are two special trial courts that have nationwide jurisdiction over certain types of cases. The Court of International Trade addresses cases involving international trade and customs issues. The United States Court of Federal Claims has jurisdiction over most claims for money damages against the United States, disputes over federal contracts, and unlawful seizure ("takings") of private property.

Today's Judicial Activism

In the last sixty years, many federal judges have subscribed to an activist mentality believing they have the power to tax and make laws based upon their own personal political/philosophical beliefs, regardless of whether they line up with the Constitution. This makes me wonder if I make decisions in a similar way without regard for God's Word.

The Constitution makes it clear the powers to tax and make laws are duties of the Congress and not the courts. Because of this, many groups in this country have used the courts to make laws that they knew would be unpopular and therefore, would not get passed through the legislature. In the last few years there was even a judge in Kansas who levied a tax on the people which was clearly a violation of the separation of powers.

Our Constitution is a document that defines individual rights in terms of what the government cannot do to you (The Bill of Rights). These are sometimes referred to as "negative rights". Those who have been using judicial activism are eroding the negative rights (the rights that protect us from the government) into "positive rights" wherein the Constitution is used to define what government 'must' do on your behalf. These would be rights to housing, education, food, clothing, jobs, or health care; rights that require the state to obtain the resources from other citizens to pay for them.

Thomas Jefferson said, "On every question of construction, carry ourselves back to the time when the Constitution was adopted, recollect the spirit manifested in the debates, and instead of trying what meaning may be squeezed out of the text, or invented against it, conform to the probable one in which it was passed."[1] In other words, judges should not invent ideas from the Constitution that simply are not there, but should adhere to the spirit in which the Constitution was originally written.

> It is important to remember that while judges and lawyers may be custodians of the Constitution, the Constitution itself is a document that is the heritage and responsibility of every American citizen.

Separation of Powers Today:

By distributing the essential business of government among three separate but interdependent branches, the Constitutional Framers ensured that the principal powers of government - legislative, executive, and judicial - were not concentrated in the hands of any single branch. This balancing of power was intended to ensure that no one branch grows too powerful and dominates the national government, possibly overpowering the individual state governments.

Today, however, our system of separation of powers has become a structure that encourages gridlock or stalemate. Therefore, what cannot be accomplished today legislatively is being accomplished by the court system. The judiciary are circumventing the legislative process, and in so doing, making a mockery of "we the people." They have also

> "The accumulation of all powers, legislative, executive, and judiciary, in the same hands, whether of one, a few, or many, and whether hereditary, self-appointed, or elective, may justly be pronounced the very definition of tyranny."
> -James Madison

become the most powerful branch of government, whereas originally, they were intended to be the weakest.

The greatest concern for our system of separation of powers is that all three would be controlled by the same ideological bent or one political party. The founder's went to great lengths to prevent this from happening. But when "We the People" are not as educated as we should be about our heritage and our wonderful miraculous Constitution, we can be easily led by deceivers who both look and sound good.

The price for liberty is eternal vigilance. When we have been lulled to sleep and not taught the basics of good government, vigilance takes a back seat to living our daily lives. Until the most recent elections, we the people have always been more comfortable with splitting the powers of the legislative and executive branches by voting in different parties and that is a good safeguard or check and balance. With the election of 2008, the Legislative branch, Executive branch and over one half of the judiciary are all of the same ideological bent.

> **Important perspective**: Michael Boldin, founder of The Tenth Amendment Center says regarding the Constitution, "The best way to look at it is that it does not apply to you. It doesn't apply to me. It doesn't apply to any person at all. It applies to the government, and it sets the boundaries of what government is supposed to do."

Electoral College

The Electoral College was created as an additional safeguard in our system of checks and balances. Hamilton and the other founders believed that the electors would be able to ensure that only a qualified person becomes President. They wanted a buffer between the population and the selection of a President. They feared a tyrant could manipulate public opinion and come to power (that is exactly what happened in Germany with Hitler). The founders also believed that the Electoral College had the advantage of being a group that met only once, and therefore could not be manipulated over time by foreign governments or others.

> Therefore, Americans actually do not have a direct election of the President by the population. The states elect the President.

The Electoral College was also part of a compromise made at the Constitutional convention to satisfy the small states. Under the Electoral College system, each state has the same number of electoral votes as they have representatives in Congress, thus no state could have less than three. The result of this system is that in less populated states such as Wyoming (3 electors) each elector represents far less number of voters than electors from more populated states such as California with 54 electors.

The Electoral College system is a "winner takes all system." The candidate that wins the popular vote of that state takes all the electoral votes. This makes it possible for a candidate to lose the popular vote, but win the electoral vote. The "winner takes all system" was not mandated in the Constitution but was decided by the states themselves during the course of the 19th century. Some states have unsuccessfully tried to change this system.

Some complain rightly because there are clear problems with the Electoral College. However, because there are more advantages to keeping it as is, making any changes is very unlikely. The smaller states would never agree to losing their advantage. Any change would mean changing our entire constitutional system. You change one element, and you affect them all. To eliminate the Electoral College means we would become a direct democracy instead of a republic.

Without the Electoral College, there would be no incentive for just two political parties. We would have to deal with multiple political parties and candidates for president – with the possibility of having minor party candidates end up as the top two vote getters. When this happened in a recent election in France, the electorate had a choice between right wing and a more extreme right wing candidate. In other words, they got two radical wild card candidates. With more candidates in the mix, no one gets a majority of the vote necessitating a run-off election between the top two or three vote getters. In this type of system, unfortunately, the best candidates can lose to the least qualified.

Very few democracies in the industrial world have a presidential system with direct election. In fact, France, Finland, and now Russia are the only examples. France adopted direct election in 1962 and Finland in the 1990's and they have had only one election since.

Has a presidential candidate ever lost the nationwide popular vote but been elected president in the Electoral College? The answer is yes, but it has only happened three times:

- **In 1876** there were a total of 369 electoral votes available with 185 needed to win. Republican Rutherford B. Hayes, with 4,036,298 popular votes won 185 electoral votes. His main opponent, Democrat Samuel J. Tilden, won the popular vote with 4,300,590 votes, but won only 184 electoral votes. Hayes was elected president.

- **In 1888** there were a total of 401 electoral votes available with 201 needed to win. Republican Benjamin Harrison, with 5,439,853 popular votes won 233 electoral votes. His main opponent, Democrat Grover Cleveland, won the popular vote with 5,540,309 votes, but won only 168 electoral votes. Harrison was elected president.

- **In 2000** there were a total of 538 electoral votes available with 270 needed to win. Republican George W. Bush, with 50,456,002 popular votes won 271 electoral votes. His Democratic opponent, Al Gore, won the popular vote with 50,999,897 votes, but won only 266 electoral votes. Bush was elected president.

Electoral College Facts

If the vote of the Electoral College results in a tie, the House of Representatives will pick the President by a state-by-state vote with each state delegation having one vote. One member from two-thirds of the states participating will be required to make a quorum. A majority (50% plus one) of all the states will be required to make this decision before March 4th. (The Twentieth Amendment gave them more time.) The Vice-President will automatically become President at this point. The Constitutional guidelines for the President are the same for the Vice-President, except that the Senate votes on the Vice-President candidates.

In conclusion, at each election cycle in recent years, the Electoral College has come under attack. The media elites consistently slight the Electoral College. Every four years, the reporters and pundits repeat the stock phrases about the Electoral College including "constitutional relic," "archaic", and "antiquated". Despite its odd and often criticized processes, the Electoral College has served the United States well.

Because of its efficiency and effectiveness, the Electoral College represents the model of representative government that current "reformers" are advocating. The electors meet for one day – not even in Washington – cast their two votes (one for president, one for vice president), then they disband. Some states don't even pay for their lunch on that day. If only the federal government could be so efficient and effective!

Ultimately, the states elect the President of the United States. The highest popularly elected officials in the United States are the states' governors, not the President. Any change toward a popular voting system undermines the states, and the very basis for the Federal system.

For more information, you can search online for the article: *Rethinking the Electoral College—Or Not* by Tara Rossor. Additional information can be found at: usgovinfo.about.com/od/thepoliticalsystem/a/electcollege.htm or at: En.wikipedia.org/wiki/U.S._Electoral_College. For dangers of the direct popular election see: Direct Election of the U.S. President: Unacknowledged Perils from the Electoral College Web Zine.

PATRIOTIC PORTRAIT

John Jay (1745-1829), was the first Chief Justice of the United States Supreme Court appointed by President George Washington. He was a Founding Father, a member of the First and Second Continental Congresses and served as the President of the Continental Congress. He also served as Governor of the State of New York (1795-1801). He has been referred to as the "father of American conservatism" and was one of the three granite pillars of America's political greatness along with Washington and Hamilton. This trio of brilliant and powerful men was unmatched in our history for accomplishments and influence. John Jay's son, William Jay, described him as, "a rare but interesting picture of the Christian patriot and statesman."

Jay did not attend the Constitutional Convention but strongly supported ratification. Along with Alexander Hamilton and James Madison, Jay wrote the Federalist papers which explained the principles of the Constitution. They were instrumental in securing the ratification of the Constitution.

On October 12, 1816, John Jay admonished: "Providence has given to our people the choice of their rulers, and it is the duty, as well as the privilege and interest of our Christian nation to select and prefer Christians for their rulers."[2] In addition to serving as the first Chief Justice of the United States Supreme Court, John Jay also served as president of the Westchester Bible Society in 1818 and president of the American Bible Society in 1821.

John Jay was a man of impeccable honesty and integrity. It is recorded that when asked as he lay near death, if he had any final words for his children he responded: "They have the Book."[3]

- - - - -

179

PATRIOTIC PORTRAIT

John Marshall (1755-1835) was the Chief Justice of the United States Supreme Court for 34 years after his appointment by President John Adams. He served with General Washington during the freezing winter of Valley Forge in 1777-78. He was a member of the Virginia House of Burgesses and strongly advocated the ratification of the Constitution. He turned down President Washington's offer to be the United States Attorney General, though he later served as U.S. Minister to France, where he gained a reputation for refusing to take French bribes. He also served
as a United States Congressman before being appointed Secretary of State, and then Chief Justice of the Supreme Court in 1801.

His influence helped form the judicial branch of the government, as in the 1833 case of *Barron v. Baltimore*. In that case, Marshall emphasized that the Bill of Rights restricted only the national government.

> And, in the case of *McCulloch v. Maryland*, John Marshall stated the profound truth: "The power to tax involves the power to destroy."[4]

During his last months of life, Marshall solidified his firm belief in the divinity of Jesus Christ according to his daughter, "He determined to apply to the communion of our Church, objecting to communion in private, because he thought it his duty to make a public confession of the Saviour He also thought highly of President George Washington's life of faith, and considered him a truly devout man."

The country mourned at his death. During his funeral in 1835, the Liberty Bell cracked.

RECOMMENDED READING

Men in Black, Mark R. Levin (Threshold Editions)

QUESTIONS for THOUGHT and DISCUSSION

1. Are presidential executive orders being abused today?

2. Since Congress has the power to prohibit federal judges from hearing certain cases should they put a prohibition on cases regarding religion? Why?

3. Can you think of any other types of cases that federal courts should be prohibited from hearing?

4. If we had term limits on Congressmen and Senators so that every six to twelve years there were constantly new people coming into these positions, who would hold all the power?

5. Why did the framers of the Constitution exempt Sundays from the time frame for signing or vetoing legislation?

6. What is the confirmation process for cabinet secretaries and Ambassadors, etc.?

7. Can this process be politicized? How? Why has this process become so controversial?

8. Discuss the pros and cons of recess appointments and why they would be necessary. Also, what is a qualified judicial candidate?

9. What would be a good reason to vote against a judicial nominee?

10. Did the Founders intend the Judiciary to be the strongest branch of government?

12. Do we, as Christians, make decisions without regard for the Word of God as many judges do without regard for the Constitution?

13. What can we do, as citizens, to prevent the runaway judiciary from abolishing our inalienable rights? It would only take five votes to do it.

Foundational Truths – Chapter 11

"Guard with jealous attention the public liberty. Suspect every one who approaches that jewel. Unfortunately, nothing will preserve it but downright force. Whenever you give up that force, you are inevitably ruined."

> - Patrick Henry, speech in the Virginia Ratifying Convention, 5 June 1778

"The accumulation of all powers, legislative, executive, and judiciary, in the same hands, whether of one, a few, or many, and whether hereditary, self-appointed, or elective, may justly be pronounced the very definition of tyranny."

> - James Madison

"If, from the more wretched parts of the old world, we look at those which are in an advanced stage of improvement, we still find the greedy hand of government thrusting itself into every corner and crevice of industry, and grasping the spoil of the multitude. Invention is continually exercised, to furnish new pretenses for revenues and taxation. It watches prosperity as its prey and permits none to escape without tribute."

> - Thomas Paine, Rights of Man, 1791

Chapter 11

The Political Process

The Two Party System

The political system of the United States is primarily based on a two-party system. In order for us to understand how the system works and our part in it, we must understand the parties involved. Each political party has its own political philosophy and values. Our job is to carefully examine each party's stance on issues regarding taxes, size of government, foreign policy, military, welfare reform, church-state issues, family values, and moral issues regarding respect for life, marriage, and children.

> Let me state emphatically that **God is not a Democrat or Republican!** He wants us to treat political issues with His perspective in mind, see them as He does and vote accordingly. Also, let me state my priority. I am a Christian first, conservative second, and then a Republican. I long for more statesmen and less politicians within both parties. No party is perfect and we will always have disagreements on public policy but if we discern God's viewpoint, our choices will produce correct results. After all, government is not our provider and if we ever look to government instead of God to meet all our needs, the United States is destined to become another Roman Empire.

Some people voice their dissatisfaction with both parties. No matter which party we associate with, there will be issues that we disagree with because neither of the two parties are perfect. However, they are all we have to work with in the USA right now.

The American system is a two party system. Yes, there are third party candidates; however, if elected, they would have to work with both of the other parties in Congress to pass laws. They will ultimately choose to caucus with one of the parties. Because they could not do anything by themselves, they would end up voting with one party more than the other.

We need to pray for our elected officials daily and then hold them accountable. They work for us and should not be allowed to ever forget that. Let your voice be heard through letters, emails, and phone calls. Let them know you are watching what they do, not what they say. What they do is more important than what they say to get elected.

Political Parties and What They Believe

Each party has a core set of beliefs and values from which they form their platform for public policy. These platforms are constantly changing with each presidential election cycle. Every four years (presidential election years) the state party organizations have conventions to formalize their individual state party platforms.

For example, in Texas, this process actually starts at the precinct level, with a precinct caucus following the closing of the polls in the primary election. At this caucus, individuals may present a formal resolution to be adopted as part of the state party platform. These resolutions are then forwarded to the Senatorial District/County Convention, where the resolutions committee will decide which resolutions will be voted on and ultimately be considered at the state convention. Also, delegates to the state convention are chosen at the District/County convention. The resolutions committee at the state convention prepares the state party platform to be considered by all the delegates. Delegates to the National Convention are chosen at the state convention.

Not all states operate this way. Texas, for example, is a bottom up, grassroots state whereas California is the opposite. It is top down from the leadership, and the grassroots are not as influential.

The national resolutions committee meets several days before the national convention to finalize a party platform that will be presented at the convention. The delegates then vote to accept them or not. Therefore, it is possible for a party to evolve and change over the years, depending on the worldviews of those who participate and make these decisions.

In the early days of the Democrat Party, the members were much more conservative, fought for the little guys, were anti-abortion, and supported a strong military. These attitudes started changing in the late sixties and early seventies, as radical liberals of the sixties revolution began to run for office and to slowly take control of the party.

Today, the Democrat Party is nothing like the party our grandparents knew. With each presidential election cycle, there is an internal struggle within each political party. The mainstream media feeds this struggle in an attempt to shift them further to the left of center on the political spectrum. This shift to the left within the Democrat Party draws the people further and further away from the principles of the Constitution. The Republicans have also ignored the Constitution on more than one occasion.

The Republican Party is now becoming the party that stands up for the little guys, protecting free markets and opportunity for all, protecting the life of the unborn, supporting a strong military and limited government. Whereas they were known as Country Club Republicans or the Party of the Rich, there has been a drastic shift in party demographics since 1980. In researching the history of civil rights, I discovered the Republican Party to be the party that has supported civil rights as far back as Abraham Lincoln. The Republicans were responsible for nearly two dozen civil rights bills and three civil rights Constitutional Amendments in the ten years after the Civil War.

When Reconstruction ended, the Democrats gained control of Congress and had most of the bills rescinded. It was 89 years before any civil rights laws were introduced again in Congress. The civil rights acts of the 1960 – 70's only passed because the Republicans supported them and the Democrats were divided.

So, political parties are subject to shifts which are determined by their constituent groups. Because of the shift away from the basic values on which this nation was founded, many southern Democrats switched parties. The south that used to be a Democrat stronghold has shifted to be more Republican. Just as the Democrat Party left their more conservative, pro-life, pro-military, and pro-America platform, the Republican Party is just as susceptible to leaving their core values. Shifts happen.

When we get involved in this process, we influence these shifts. When you make a decision to support a party, you must be diligent to make sure that party both remembers and governs with those core values in mind. If those elected by the parties are not voting in agreement with their party platform, the party platform is undermined. The party leaders need to be held accountable for how they vote.

> Justice at the Gate, a nonprofit organization dedicated to mobilizing Christians to pray and vote righteously, produces a good comparison of the Democrat & Republican Party Platforms on specific Biblical issues. *"In Their Own Words"* covers the issues of school prayer, abortion, homosexuality, and school choice & faith based education. It follows the party platforms of each party since 1972. Go online for more information to: www.justiceatthegate.org for information.

You must carefully and prayerfully filter each party's positions on the major issues of the day through basic Biblical principles. Seek God for His perspective. Many Christians do not use a Biblical model of filtering their decisions when choosing who to vote for at the city, county, state and national levels. Many do not even vote! Our right to vote is our basic responsibility as citizens and Christians. We will be held accountable for our stewardship of this nation. Therefore, we need to approach this responsibility as educated voters acting from God's perspective.

> Note: Remember that many brave men and women have sacrificed their lives and limbs in order to protect our freedoms. When we take time to educate ourselves and vote our conscience, we honor them.

The last page or so of this chapter compares the basic philosophy and core values of the Republican and Democratic Parties on the most basic of key issues. Examine them closely. Decide for yourself which party lines up Biblically and in agreement with the Founders' philosophy for good government. You can also check out the official party websites to read their platforms word for word.

The Republicans and Democrats are the main political parties in America today. Good or bad, anything accomplished within our government is done through these two groups. An elected official from the Libertarian Party or Independent Party has little power to affect the system. They will always line up with one side or the other.

Many citizens say they vote for the man, regardless of party affiliation. This is an idealistic view that does not reflect the reality of Washington, D.C. The truth of the matter is that, presently, no matter how honorable the man, he is under tremendous pressure to go along with his party on most measures, and definitely in choosing the leaders of the House (Speaker, etc.), Senate (Majority Leader, etc.), their respective committees and subcommittees. The best example we have on how arms are twisted is on the Health Care Reform bill of 2009-10. The leadership in the House and Senate are literally buying votes with taxpayer money!

If a representative does not go along with his/her party, that representative risks his office being moved to a closet in the basement and getting poor committee assignments. And they will never be chosen for any leadership positions in the future.

Therefore, it is important to decide which party represents your Biblical values. Even though neither party is perfect, there is usually one that upholds Biblical values more than the other. Notice where the parties line up with the founding fathers' belief in limited government and free market values and with the main responsibility of the Federal government being to protect its citizens from foreign attack, to protect individual liberty and private property rights. These God-given rights that the founder's believed in are currently being chipped away. They knew rights *given by* government are rights that can be *taken away by* government.

The bottom line is that if we, as believers, had all voted from God's perspective in unity and gotten behind one party (changing it from the inside), we would have a very different nation today.

Primary Elections

In most state and federal elections, there is first a primary election where members from the same party run against each other for the opportunity to be the Republican or Democrat candidate in the general election. Even though the primary election is the most important election, it has the smallest turnout of voters. The primary election is our best opportunity to pick the person that best represents our beliefs to run in the fall general election. If you and I wait until the general election, then we are stuck with the candidates chosen through the primary election.

Primary elections should not be taken lightly. Sadly, the majority of Americans do not even participate in the primary elections, choosing instead to wait until the general election in November. Not all states have a primary election choosing instead to hold caucuses where they select their candidates. Primaries make all the difference and I can't stress enough how important it is to make the sacrifice to know who the candidates are and to vote. Men and women have died so we can have the privilege of choosing our leaders.

Partisan Politics

Some elective positions are non-partisan – meaning the candidates do not run by party affiliation. In most communities, city council and school board elections are non-partisan. In some states, judges run without a party affiliation in a non-partisan race. It seems that we are hearing more and more about partisan versus bi-partisan in relation to specific votes on pieces of legislation. Presidential candidates are always asserting they will bring both parties together to accomplish more. Does this work? In the past, it has worked occasionally. Recent history shows it hasn't.

My understanding of bi-partisanship is when representatives from both sides of the aisle are willing to compromise to pass legislation for the benefit and good of all people. It used to work.
Since the 2000 election cycle, bi-partisan means that one party must fully agree with the other for the passage of bills. One side is more intent on grabbing more power instead of working together for the good of all the people. Some have even admitted that they vote for bad

bills just to get even with their opposition. In other words, they are not considering what is best for the people whom they represent but are willingly doing things that will harm this country to get back at their opponents – just because they can. Sounds like children in a school yard!

This not only harms the people, but it can result in a gridlock where little gets done. Remember these elected men/women work for us. In our private businesses, we would fire employees who purposely set out to hurt us. Given today's realities, gridlock does not always seem like a bad thing. I am a firm believer that if there is a doubt about something, especially something as important as public policy, it is better to do nothing than to do the wrong thing.

Unintended consequences sometimes develop when laws are passed in haste. One recent example is Congress' desire to protect our children from lead based content in toys and other kids' items. They very quickly came up with the Consumer Product Safety Act that was so loosely written that it is bankrupting many industries like the off-road vehicles manufacturers who make small vehicles for children 12 and under. Many families go out on weekends to ride off road. If they can no longer purchase child size bikes, the kids will end up riding adult size bikes resulting in more accidents. Also, charities that sell used clothing and toys, books etc. are being hurt tremendously. It would have been far better to let parents protect their children by shopping wisely instead of allowing the government to get involved. Mothers know best!

The Founders believed in personal responsibility, not having government control every person's safety every day of his life. When Congress considers "the people's" best interests and individual rights, bi-partisanship works well. Sadly, this rarely occurs today. Since 1940 there has been a movement to change the thinking of Americans from universal individual rights to "favored group" rights. The concept of group-think deviates from our Constitutional foundation and has brought about extreme polarization and partisanship.

Choosing a Candidate

When choosing candidates to run for office, Exodus 18:21 admonishes us to "select capable men from all the people – men who fear God, trustworthy men who hate dishonest gain – and appoint them as officials…". Colonial America had its own set of requirements regarding who could run for office in each area. Most of the states required the person to be a professing Christian and church member. Even after the war for independence and the ratification of the Constitution, some states still required candidates to hold to the Christian faith.

The Founders seemed to believe that having men in office that held a Biblical worldview with Judeo-Christian values would better protect individual liberties and opportunity for all.

So what do we look for in a good candidate and what are the key issues of the day? Since September 11, 2001, voting intelligently has taken on new importance. Voting today determines whether America as we know it will exist for our children and their children. In fact, choosing leaders in a time like this, where our very existence and way of life is threatened by terrorists without and runaway judges within, requires that we think in terms of choosing the right people in whose hands the destiny of the nation will be placed.

> "If men of wisdom and knowledge, of moderation and temperance, of patience, fortitude and perseverance, of sobriety and true republican simplicity of manners, of zeal for the honour of the Supreme Being and the welfare of the commonwealth; if men possessed of these other excellent qualities are chosen to fill the seats of government, we may expect that our affairs will rest on a solid and permanent foundation."
> - Samuel Adams, letter to Elbridge Gerry, Nov. 27, 1780
> [Patriotpost.us – Daily Founder's Quotes]

Voters must pay special attention when voting for the office of President. Presidents appoint judges. Since judges serve as long as they behave –they are essentially appointed for life, they will affect the nation far into the future. Therefore, we must know what type of judge each potential Presidential candidate would appoint to this very prestigious and influential position. There are two types of judges: those who think they can make law and rewrite the Constitution (activist judges) and those who respect our Constitution and will only interpret law (strict constructionists). At this time, we are seeing that "we the people" means little and is being replaced by "we the judges."

Why have "we the people" taken a backseat to "we the judges"? Could it be that "we the people" became complacent and have not diligently held our elected officials accountable? Could it be that you and I have not been voting intelligently or simply not voting at all? We seem to be so blinded by personality and "coolness" in our candidates for President that we fail to pay attention to what is actually being said.

Read everything the candidate has in writing and listen to them speak on radio or TV. Focus on what they are actually saying. They all have published websites containing their policy statements and beliefs. When all we consider is their appearance and personality, we run a great risk of voting for the wrong person. Listen to their words and discern what they say. When they use the word "change," find out what that actually means.

Some want to see more people vote, without regard for whether or not these voters will take the time to understand the issues. They truly believe more people exercising their right to vote will benefit America. They see voting as a form of self-expression. When voting is perceived to be simply a means of self-expression, attempts are made to make it easier for everyone (citizen and non-citizen) to vote, without regard for legal registration. This leads to fraud which then makes elections illegitimate.

These groups claim taking measures to ensure every vote is legitimate -like showing a photo ID - may disenfranchise minority groups. These groups may then be afraid to show their driver's license or other form of government ID and therefore not vote at all. If you are who you say you are and registered to vote legally, why should you be afraid to show your ID?

Every legal citizen 18 years and older has the right to vote, however, voters must know who and what they are voting for besides the candidate's looks, persona, humor, fancy words, or catchy commercials. This is not a popularity contest. The issues are crucial to the future of the nation and to our children, grandchildren and great grandchildren. As Christians, we need the Holy Spirit's discernment regarding the candidates and what they really stand for, if anything. One way to do this is to <u>listen</u> to what they say without looking at them or read their policy positions and speeches. Staged television events capitalizing on good looks, oratorical skills and vague promises can be deceiving.

Unfortunately, a winning at all costs mentality, whether legal or not, seems to be infiltrating our election process. It was most evident in the election of 2004. It was reported that union workers gathered to intimidate campaign workers, trash political party headquarters, and even harass voters at early voting locations. In 2008, Black Panthers intimidation at voting locations reduced the number of qualified voters who should have voted. Our nation has a proud history of honest and peaceful elections (and transfer of power). Ballot security is crucial to keep our elections from becoming that of third world countries with massive fraud and intimidation of voters.

Unfortunately, much of this trend is the result of thirty years of indoctrination into situational ethics, where the end justifies the means. Truth and honesty have become unimportant because they are dependent on what you want them to be at the time whether true or not.

When the teaching of creation science, prayer in school, and the Ten Commandments were banished from America's classrooms, the door was thrown wide open to reducing ethical conduct to the lowest common denominator. The reigning thought being that there are no absolutes (relativism), and no such thing as absolute truth. As Christians, we are to live our lives in agreement with God's Word and teachings, not on what is right in our own eyes. Our whole system of free elections is now threatened because of this culture of relativism. The hint of tyranny is creeping into our elections and many elected officials are resorting to bullying the American people.

This is not the time for self-indulgence, the essence of the "me" generation. We can no longer choose our leaders by their style, rhetoric, or personality. We are deciding who has what it takes to confront our enemies, and deter nations who would give aid and sanctuary to our enemies. Moreover, we are deciding who will pick judges to fill the next vacancies on the federal judiciary. It is important that we, as Christians, pray for wisdom on our choices, and not simply respond to the images, negative ads; news reports and talk (spin) of the campaigns and media. If this nation is to survive, we cannot succumb to past traditions but apply critical thinking to the issues, do our own research and pray.

When we lived in California, the choices for U.S. Senate were the very liberal, pro-choice Democrat or the more moderate Republican candidate (also pro-choice). Neither candidate was acceptable from a pro-life perspective. If I didn't vote for either, then the worse of the two would be elected. I had to vote for the better of the two. In the primary, I voted my conscience and supported the pro-life candidate who lost.

In our human understanding, sometimes the choices that are presented to us are both undesirable. We must trust God's sovereignty and vote for the person more acceptable. Not to vote is a vote for the worst candidate.

This is not just true about national presidential elections, but every election from your local city and county elections all the way up to the national level. At each level, elected officials are making decisions that affect your life.

Example of local election folly: A couple who lived in a coastal community voted for a local ordinance without taking the time to research all its implications. The ordinance passed. Later when they tried to build on their property, this ordinance prevented them from

> Reminder: It is our responsibility to pray, be engaged in the issues, and be diligent to do our own research in choosing candidates. Also, on Election Day, do not pay attention to exit polling. It only serves to suppress voter turnout.

doing so because it was beachfront property. They owned the land, but were prohibited from building on it and, therefore, couldn't even sell it. Local ordinances and local elected officials are important and can quite seriously affect you and your life.

God says we need to choose candidates who fear God and are trustworthy. This is a good guideline. Most of our elected officials are politicians and very few are true "statesmen."

A good definition of a politician is one who makes their decisions based upon current polling data, rather than on what is right for the constituents and the nation <u>long term</u>. On the other hand, a "statesman" is that person who makes their decisions and positions based upon what is good for all the people on an enduring basis. Statesmen are more concerned with securing what is best for the nation in the long term and are willing to make the hard decisions rather than popular decisions.

We need to find and support candidates who have a strong moral fiber and character. Their past moral behavior is the foundation of their future moral behavior. Those with questionable moral standards and behavior will lean towards self-gratification of lusts and desires, shunning commitment, and will think or say anything that will satisfy those lusts. Matthew 7:15 records a warning about false prophets, which can apply to politicians:

"Beware of false prophets, which come to you in sheep's clothing, but inwardly they are ravening wolves. Ye shall know them by their fruits."

So how do you find out about a candidate? A good place to start looking for this information is with the various groups that track the positions of the candidates. The following organizations usually distribute voter guides that show where the candidates stand on a range of moral/Biblical issues (such as prayer in school, abortion, homosexuality, marriage / family, and school choice):

- The Christian Coalition,
- Eagle Forum,
- American Family Association,

194

- Traditional Values Coalition (in California)
- Heritage Alliance

At the local level, this type of information is harder to find. You will need to go to candidate forums, listen closely to what they say, and ask those key questions that will show you their positions on the important issues. For state and federal elections, investigate the candidates' websites for their policy stances. Finally, find wise counsel from those who are more educated on the issues and are in agreement with your core values.

In conclusion, to determine the best candidate to support:

1. Ask the Lord for His wisdom and knowledge.
2. Do your homework and learn about the background and policy positions of the candidates.
3. Ask these questions: Are they morally qualified? Do they have the skills to govern? What groups or individuals are supporting that person? Are there hidden agendas?
4. If both candidates are morally unacceptable, I personally would not support/promote either of them, but I would vote for the lesser of the two "evils." Unfortunately, there are times when neither candidate is morally acceptable. When this occurs, we have to settle for the best one of the two. If you decide to not vote for either or for a third party candidate, then essentially you are voting for the least acceptable candidate. For Christians, who are mandated to be salt and light in the earth (and to rulership), voter abstinence is not an option...not even in protest. Choosing not to vote has proven to have many negative and unintended consequences.

It is easy to get disgusted with all the elected officials and just vote in anger against all incumbents. I know people who have done that and later regretted it when things got even worse.

If both candidates are morally acceptable within the Judeo-Christian concept of good government, evaluate their skills and qualifications on the next tier of issues such as national security, taxes, immigration policy, border security, welfare reform, foreign policy, and other issues of prominence during the campaign. Just as a doctor prescribes medicine properly to not injure the patient, those who assume governmental authority must have the ability to govern with mercy, truth, and justice without damage to those governed.

> Note: Always keep in mind the number one job of the federal government is to protect the citizens. This would include such things as border security and missile defense.

Be an informed voter! The future of the nation is depending on you and every future generation to guard America's Judeo-Christian values and freedoms.

Government is serious business. Prosperity and the economy are spiritual matters not political. Prosperity comes from God (Deuteronomy 8: 18). As Christians, we live under God's economy which is not dependent on which party is in control of Congress. The more Christians obey God's command to tithe, the more the economy of this nation prospers. However, when Christians give credit to the government for their prosperity, they are trading trust in God for trust in government. Unfortunately, many Christians choose to ignore the corrupt side of certain administrations or parties and vote their pocketbooks (money).

As a Christian, it is wrong to vote for what government can do for you personally. In the election of 2004, many voted for the candidate who could give them the most in government benefits, choosing to ignore the threat of worldwide terror that is attempting to destroy our very existence. We can not afford to be this shortsighted during a war against worldwide terror networks.

In reality, there is no government apart from God. We examined this in chapter one. When this country was founded, God established a destiny (mission) for this nation. He ordained it and He is still in control. There is no other nation like America on earth and there never will be, at least not until other nations are able to put their trust in God instead of man/government. As His people, we should not leave control of our country to the world. Instead, we must stand up for what God desires to do with it and through it. Remember, God is a God of good government – He ordained it. Moreover, He ordained us to be responsible for it. With responsibility comes accountability, and be assured He will hold us accountable.

"For everyone to whom much is given, from him much will be required; and to whom much has been committed, of him they will ask the more" (Luke 12:48b).

We, as a nation, have been given much and currently are in danger of losing much if we don't wake up.

Christians in Public Service

One of the major contributing factors in the collapse of the Roman Empire was the withdrawal of Christian's involvement in the secular government. Once Christianity became a recognized religion, Christians became involved in government and held positions of authority and the Empire prospered. When the Church of Rome withdrew from their involvement in their government, the Roman Empire slowly began to decline and then collapsed altogether.

The Church in the United States began withdrawing from the public square over a hundred years ago. Because of that, there has been a gradual collapse in the moral fiber of the nation and its leaders. The traditional family unit has disintegrated, especially among minority communities. Our educational system has declined to its lowest levels, and in many cities the schools are literal battlegrounds. We are a nation in decline.

The movement in the nation to remove God from every aspect of society, especially the public square is dangerous indeed. Many would have us believe that the government can meet all of our needs; all we have to do is trust in them, because they know what is best for us. They do not believe we can govern our own lives.

As Christians, we are taught to govern our own lives wisely according to the Word of God, not according to government dictates. According to I Timothy 2:1-2, we are commanded to pray for our leaders, our nation and those in authority over us so that we can live peacefully and guarantee that the gospel is able to go forth in godliness and holiness. We are also called to be active in the political process. We must educate ourselves on the issues and candidates, write letters regarding legislation, and work for sound public policy and good candidates.

As Christians, we have a responsibility to attain the greatest productivity with the gifts God has given us in order to affect the greatest good for the individual and the nation. The parable of the talents in Matthew 25:14-30 is our example of how God views what we do with what He gives us. Just as the lazy servant was judged, we will be judged by what we have done with the talents He has given us. I ask myself regularly if I am using the gifts He has given me exactly how He wants me to.

The Christian body of believers has been given, by the "Creator", a nation and government which provides for citizen government. As citizens, we can direct the course of the nation, either along the path of righteousness, life, and prosperity, or over the precipice of death and destruction. Our God has provided a nation whose citizen government can change world history for the better; protect the lives of the unborn, and implement sound fiscal, social, military and foreign policies. In addition, this nation's citizen government is to be a leader in establishing positive role models in government and society for the world and future generations. It is almost overwhelming when you think about what God has given us in our great nation. Stewardship is all about responsibility and accountability. Are we being good stewards of America?

The fruit of citizen involvement will be as jewels in the crown of salvation for those who take this responsibility seriously. For those who don't, it will be as wood, hay and stubble. We are given the opportunity to choose. The lazy servant lost everything, including his soul.

God is expecting us to use whatever abilities and gifts we have been granted to effect positive change and moral truths in government. Some of you will be called to run for office, others simply to write letters to your elected representatives or answer telephones for political candidates. Everyone is asked to do something no matter how little it may seem. When we all work together, giving what we can, then we can expect to accomplish the greater good for the nation and all humanity.

Many nations and people have tried to confine the worship of God to the four walls of a church building (separate from civil society). Currently, there are those who would like to hinder Christians from public service. In reality, the prosperity of a nation always has been determined upon its submission or rebellion to the laws of Nature and Nature's God. The former Soviet Union tried to separate the church from the state. Ultimately, this was a disaster for the good people of the Soviet Union, bringing the utopian experiment to collapse within forty-three years. The "Evil Empire" collapsed and the Church was victorious. Utopian ideas never succeed.

With the absence of moral absolutes, there is a void that is filled with confusion and a focus on self-gratification that does not take into consideration the ultimate consequences of decisions, policies, and positions. There has been no accountability and no forward thinking about long-term effects on the nation and what is best for all the people. When the Church withdraws from civil society into its own four walls, nations suffer. About 90 years ago, the American church started withdrawing from the civic arena. Since then there has been a slow decline or coarsening of society's standards. It is time to take society back and raise the standards. How can we "love our neighbors" while ignoring our civic responsibilities? We are the salt and light in society. If we do not do it, who will?

PATRIOTIC PORTRAIT

Thomas Jefferson (1743-1826) was born to
a warm and affectionate family in Virginia.
He greatly admired his father who provided a
classical education for Thomas, but not much
is known about his fathers' religious beliefs.
Jefferson grew up with a firm faith in God, a
strong sense of moral obligation, a love for
the outdoors, an appreciation and capacity for
hard work, and a love for classical learning.
His father died when he was fourteen years
old and at age 16, Jefferson enrolled in
William and Mary College at Williamsburg,

Virginia. Most of the professors at William and Mary were ministers of the
gospel; however, because of Jefferson's love for classical learning, he was
drawn to three professors who were not clergy. Through their writings, these
three men shared their ways of thinking and looking at the world with
Thomas. It was the writings of Sir Francis Bacon, Sir Isaac Newton and John
Locke that formed the basis of Jefferson's philosophical beliefs.

Jefferson's strong emphasis on the role of reason created a barrier that
prevented him from accepting the full truth of Christian doctrine. He did,
however, recognize that people are not always good (perhaps he was
influenced by the Biblical view of sin) and are not always governed by reason.
Most importantly, Jefferson's faith in human reason did not hinder his basic
belief in God.

Thomas Jefferson was an author, architect, educator, scientist, diplomat, and
the third President of the United States. In 1774, while serving in the Virginia
Assembly, he personally introduced a resolution calling for a Day of Fasting
and Prayer. Influenced by a committee of other statesmen in what to write,
Thomas Jefferson wrote the words of the Declaration of Independence. He
also served as Governor of Virginia. Jefferson believed the government
should not interfere with religion in favoring one religious sect over another.
On January 1, 1802, Jefferson wrote a letter to the Baptist Association of
Danbury, Connecticut, calming their fears that Congress would choose a
single Christian denomination to be the "state" denomination, as was the case
with the Anglican Church of England and Virginia. Jefferson's letter included:

"Believing with you that religion is a matter which lied solely between man
and God, that he owes account to none other for faith or his worship, that the

200

legislative powers of government reach actions only, and not opinions, I contemplate with solemn reverence that act of the whole American people which declared that their legislature should "make no law respecting an establishment of religion, or prohibiting the free exercise thereof," thus building a wall of separation between Church and State."[1]

Thomas Jefferson was not a signer of the Constitution nor did he attend the Constitutional Convention. Neither was he present when the First Amendment and religious freedom were debated in the first session of Congress in 1789. He was out of the country in France as a U.S. Minister. Since he was not there, all his information regarding the debates on these matters was secondhand. Today, he is held to be the authority on the Constitution, and his quote regarding the "wall of separation" is actually being attributed to the Constitution when it was only used in this letter of reassurance to the Danbury Baptists.

The so-called "wall of separation" was only meant to protect the Church from intrusions of the government. It was never Jefferson's intention to remove religion from all public life. At the time this letter was written, religious services were being held in the U.S. Capitol Building and several other government buildings in Washington, D.C. Almost every government building in Washington, D.C. has references to God and Scripture etched in stone.

At that time, the federal government actually encouraged religion. In addition, President Jefferson offered A National Prayer for Peace, gave special land to Christian Indians and Moravians, upheld the mandatory religious services for those serving in the military, and appropriated financial support for chaplains in Congress and the armed services. He was devoted to the morals of Jesus, and firmly believed they went hand in hand with a representative democracy. The liberal academics play up Jefferson as not being a religious man. However, even though he was not an evangelical Christian, by today's standards he would be classified as a religious man, a man of faith.

Jefferson referred to himself as Christian because of his respect and adherence to Jesus' moral philosophy although he denied the supernatural miracles of Jesus' life and resurrection.

This quote in a letter to William Jarvis (1820) on the judiciary is quite prophetic in its depth of insight in light of where we are today.

"You seem…to consider the judges as the ultimate arbiters of all constitutional questions; a very dangerous doctrine indeed, and one which would place us under the despotism of an oligarchy. Our judges are as honest as other men and not more so…and their power is the more dangerous, as they are in office for life and not responsible, as the other functionaries are, to the elective control."[2]

In a letter to Justice William Johnson in 1823, Jefferson wrote on the meaning of the Constitution:

"On every question of construction, carry ourselves back to the time when the constitution was adopted, recollect the spirit manifested in the debates, and instead of trying what meaning may be squeezed out of the text, or invented against it, conform to the probable one in which it was passed."[3]

Finally, Jefferson (though not a Christian) declared that religion is:

"Deemed by other countries incompatible with good government and yet proved by our experience to be its best support."[4]

Jefferson wrote this for his tombstone:

"Here lies buried Thomas Jefferson, author of the Declaration of Independence, author of the Statutes for Religious Freedom in Virginia, and father of the University of Virginia."

What obvious achievement is left off Jefferson's tombstone?

RECOMMENDED READING

Liberty and Tyranny, by Mark Levin

POLITICAL PARTY COMPARISON CHART

On the following page compare the basic philosophy of the Republican and Democrat Parties. Go to each party's websites to read their platforms for yourself. Analyze each issue in detail and then decide which party best reflects your Biblical perspective.

Republican Party Beliefs:	**Democrat Party** Beliefs:
Our Nation and the States were founded on the fundamental principle that individuals have certain rights and freedoms which cannot be infringed and may be restricted only to the degree necessary to preserve the rights of others.	That our Founding Fathers did not really mean what they said when they guaranteed certain constitutional rights such as the right to freedom of religious expression, the right to bear arms, and the right to retain use of private property.
The money you earn is yours and that government in a free society has the right to take only as much as is needed to perform those limited functions which are appropriate to it.	The government has a right to use your money as it sees fit to fund welfare programs, redistribute wealth and to return to you only that portion which it sees fit.
That the traditional family and the values it fosters are the foundation of American society and their preservation essential to our Nation's continued success.	American society must redefine its values and the role of the family to fit new lifestyle concepts which have resulted from the 60's counterculture movement.
That parents have the right to determine the values with which their children will be raised and to have the widest possible choice among public, private, and religious schools and that competition will improve public education.	The federal government has the right to determine the values that children will be taught in public schools. They oppose school choice proposals that would give parents a choice of schools and encourage real reform in public education.
The free enterprise system is the most effective engine of economic progress.	Government regulation and control of economic activity can better distribute wealth and services like health care.
High taxes, runaway government spending, and over-regulation of business and farming punish initiative and stifle economic growth.	That penalizing achievement with higher taxes and increased government bureaucracy and spending will not stifle economic growth.
That with freedom comes responsibility and that individuals must take personal responsibility for their own actions and our criminal justice system must be based on this idea.	Individual behavior, including criminal behavior, can be blamed on "society" and that spending on social welfare programs and improvements in prison living conditions can combat crime.
Your property is yours and you have the basic right to make use of it without unreasonable government restrictions.	The government has the right to regulate the use of private property in accordance with narrow special interest without giving just compensation to owners.
Human life is sacred and worthy of preservation.	There should be no restrictions on abortion.
The preservation of our rights and freedoms must be entrusted to a strong national defense and the ability of the United States to negotiate with other nations from a position of strength.	We can afford to drastically weaken our military despite the threats present in a unstable, post-Cold War international environment and that the U.S. must subjugate its interest to those of the U.N.
It is imperative to reaffirm the traditional freedoms and values of Americans to preserve our great Republic.	America must adopt a "politically correct" multi-cultural set of values which denies a common American heritage and will further divide American society.

QUESTIONS for THOUGHT and DISCUSSION

1. Carefully examine the side by side philosophical comparison of the two most influential political parties in the United States.

2. How does each party measure up to Biblical principles?

3. Why is it important to measure a party platform from a Biblical standpoint?

4. Why is it important to have representatives who honor and fear God?

5. Can you think of local ordinances/laws that can have a negative impact on your community? For instance, how does a non-smoking ordinance affect your restaurant businesses? (Think critically and not with your emotions.)

6. What are some reasons why it would be acceptable to vote for the least acceptable candidate? Try to look at the big picture and the consequences that would result from sitting out the election, such as happened in 2006 when many who were angry with Republicans did not vote. What happened as a result of that election?

7. Should the government tell us what we can think or not think? Say or not say?

8. What is the tool being used to divide this nation along racial and ethnic lines?

9. Can the movement towards political correctness and multi-culturalism (cultural Marxism) be used against us by our enemies? How?

10. What gifts and talents do you have that could be put to work for the good of this nation?

11. Do you know Christians who are politically active?

12. What do they do and why do they do it?

Foundational Truths – Chapter 12

"We are spending less time in the classroom on the Bible, which should be the principal text in our schools ... the Bible states these great moral lessons better than any other manmade book."

> - Fisher Ames, Writer of the House Language that became the First Amendment, as stated to Palladium Magazine in 1789

"No people will tamely surrender their Liberties, nor can any be easily subdued, when knowledge is diffused and virtue is preserved. On the Contrary, when People are universally ignorant, and debauched in their Manners, they will sink under their own weight without the Aid of foreign Invaders."

> - Samuel Adams

" The virtues of men are of more consequence to society than their abilities; and for this reason, the heart should be cultivated with more assiduity than the head."

> - Noah Webster, On the Education of Youth in America, 1788

Chapter 12

Understanding the Times

How Did We Get to Be a Nation in Decline?

The United States of America is on the verge of becoming a Socialist/Marxist nation. Capitalism, free markets, and individual freedoms are being dismantled and half the people of America are embracing the welfare state/socialism of the European Union (EU). At the same time, the EU economy is failing and they are now moving back towards a free-market, less taxes mentality. With each election more conservative leaders are elected. But it is hard to turn the tide of socialism and their efforts may or may not succeed. That should send us a strong warning against going down that road.

In order to understand how we have arrived at this crossroad between capitalism and socialism, a brief explanation of Western Civilization is needed. Western civilization was the result of the growth/spread of Christianity which resulted in bringing about reformation in how governments were run and how law was applied. It brought order into what had been countries or regions dominated by feudal lords vying to rule over the others which instigated many gruesome wars. From the Protestant Reformation came the official formation of the countries we now know as the European Union.

Out of the same reformation came great philosophers and legal thinkers who wrote important works read by most of our Founding Fathers. British law came from the writings of these men. Great advances in technology, education, industry, medicine, and literature all came out of the countries of the West. Capitalism and free enterprise, which came out of the Protestant Reformation, created wealth in every country that applied its principles.

So why is Western Civilization not taught in our universities anymore? Why is there such infatuation with third world nations, their cultures and their dictators? The answer lies in a term we are all familiar with: "political correctness" (PC). Marxists first used this term about 80 years ago to disguise the worldview of cultural Marxism. They knew if they called it by what it really is; they would not be able to move their agenda forward. Everything PC (including tolerance, diversity, multiculturalism and feminism) is all about destroying the American family and replacing the role of the father with the role of the state.

Political Correctness creates victim groups that separate Americans from each other by pitting one group against another. It is used to tear down traditional values and morals that stem from Christianity, it also normalizes sexual perversion and creates chaos to justify more government controls in our lives.

> **The Goal**: Create an all-powerful government that robs the people of freedom and liberty.
> **The Tool**: Public/Government education.

In other words, political correctness is all about creating a powerful invasive government that robs us of our freedoms and liberty. PC's ultimate goal is achieved through public education. The plan to undermine America's moral/spiritual roots started in 1933 when to escape Hitler, a group of Marxist German intellectuals came to America at the invitation of John Dewey who was on staff at Columbia.

Columbia University, with the help of Dewey's friends in academia, placed these men in teaching positions specifically in education and journalism. They knew the means to instill their worldview into millions of Americans and the culture was through education and the media.

John Dewey, best known as the father of modern education in America, was an honorary president of the National Education Association (NEA) and co-author of the Humanist Manifesto I. Dewey, with the help of Edward R. Murrow spread these German Marxists around the nation. At the age of 26, Murrow became the Assistant Secretary of the Emergency Committee in Aid of Displaced German Scholars. He had also been the Assistant Director of the Institute of International Education, established through a grant from the Carnegie Endowment for International Peace.

Stephen Duggan, an advisor to the Soviet government on workers' college issues, hired him. It is ironic that Edward R. Murrow destroyed U.S. Senator Joseph McCarthy for investigating the infiltration of Communists into our government, education, media, and Hollywood. His destruction of McCarthy appears to have been a means of self-preservation of the anti-American agenda of Dewey, Murrow, and their friends. This has been a pattern of the left throughout history.

You could say we have these German Marxists to thank for the radical 1960's counter-culture revolution. Many of these flag-burning, anti-American, pot-smoking, pagan spiritualists of the 1960's are now college and university presidents, professors, and textbook authors. And we wonder why our history has been distorted with untruths and has been re-written. The result is evident in the strong foothold of Cultural Marxism in American culture today. All these things have been done incrementally over the years while we have reacted just like the frog in the pot of water slowly being boiled to death without realizing what is happening.

They have been far more committed to changing the culture than most Americans have been in preserving American values. What better way to change things we hold dear than to create division between racial groups and special interest/victim groups. This has been the legacy of the radical '60's. Dr. Martin Luther King's dream was of a colorblind society; however, what happened is the opposite where everything is now defined by skin color and victim status.

The real enemy is Satan who has kept the church (you and me) divided first along sectarian or denominational lines and then along racial lines. If the church were truly united and thinking like Jesus (Biblically), we would not be in this crisis. Unity is our most powerful force. Satan knew this from the beginning and has done everything possible to keep Christians divided amongst themselves.

Therefore, today we are categorized as Asian-American, Hispanic-American, African-American, and so on depending on our ethnic heritage. This would be abhorrent to the founders of this nation. What happened to just being American? We have certainly been divided and what better way to conquer a nation without shedding blood.

Everywhere we turn, we can see the evidence of our being conquered by the years of indoctrination in our schools and universities. It is most visible by all the calls for government to do something with every crisis. There is never a cry for personal responsibility. With every fabricated crisis, the government grabs more power.

> A few examples of textbook errors, fabrications, and indoctrination in Texas textbooks:
>
> "Greenpeace is a mainstream organization." (Then the textbook proceeded to give out the 1-800 number to school children.)
>
> "Ronald Reagan's policies helped the rich but hurt the poor."
>
> "Many children today no longer pledge their allegiance to a particular nation or country; they now pledge their allegiance to the planet that keeps us alive."

In order to combat this anti-Christian, anti-American worldview; it must be called what it is – cultural Marxism. We need to take a stand and expose it for what it is and refuse to be cowed into being "PC" (politically correct).

Expose …
- Sensitivity training as a tool to destroy freedom of speech and religion,
- Tolerance as moral relativism and intolerance to those who do not conform to their dictates.
- Feminism as anti-family, anti-marriage, anti-father.
- Homosexuality as sin.

Then educate your friends and family to the consequences that cultural Marxism is having on our faith, family, and freedoms.

A population that has been dumbed down and not taught to think critically about issues is easier to manipulate and dupe. We need to reject anything that comes from the Department of Education because education decisions belong first to parent and then at the local level.

The latest push from the federal government is Common Core Standards and Curriculum that they did not even take the time to beta test to see if it actually works. The reason, it is not about education done right but about indoctrination and making sure future citizens fall in lock step with cultural Marxism.

As a result of their efforts we are seeing a bloodless revolution with half the American people willingly buying all the empty rhetoric while those who do think something is wrong sit back unwilling to fight to maintain the American dream of liberty and freedo m. But God is not finished with us yet and there is a growing remnant of citizens who waking up and getting informed in order to engage in this battle for the hearts and minds of America.

The Great Motivator: Self-interest

Another tool being used against American capitalism, independence and ingenuity is the vilification of self-interest. Making corporations and businesses out to be greedy bad people is one way to convince us that self-interest is bad. The reality is self-interest causes us to invent things, be creative and start businesses that ultimately create jobs. Our ingenuity and creativity fuels capitalism. This is a good thing. What is good for us financially benefits those around us as well as the total community. This God given ability to dream has brought about all the great inventions and innovations in the twentieth century. America was built on a dream of life, liberty (freedom to create, freedom to earn as much as we can, freedom to make decisions, etc.) and property.

Today's culture is trying to tell us that self-interest equals greed / selfishness and is bad, even evil. They dictate that we share (sacrifice) what we have worked hard to build for our families with those who do not work hard or do not work at all. This is not a foundational American principle. When the Pilgrims tried sharing everything in common, they starved! Marxist/Communism has never succeeded.

> Capitalism = liberty / freedom
> Socialism = bondage / slavery

Conservatives have been split between two camps in the last thirty years. There are social conservatives whose main focus has been abortion, family values and gay marriage as moral issues. Then there are the fiscal conservatives whose concerns have been economic issues only. Economic issues have not been viewed as a moral issue. But in his new book *The Battle: How the Fight between Free Enterprise and Big Government Will Shape America's Future*, Arthur Brooks, president of the highly influential American Enterprise Institute, says it is time to change that and I think he is right.

He says capitalism and the free enterprise system are under heavy assault today by forces on the left who believe these systems to be morally flawed. Consequently, those of us who believe the free market system is good and right need to fight back by learning to defend it on moral grounds. Capitalism should not just be presented as the best way to make money, but as the best system to ensure a country's citizens thrive and prosper and that they are free and able to pursue happiness unfettered. This is what the founder's meant when they used the phrase, "life, liberty and the pursuit of happiness." The free enterprise system is also what guarantees our freedoms. As the free enterprise of a nation is destroyed so are personal liberty and freedom.

Free Markets benefit every socioeconomic group. They allow for opportunities for everyone regardless of race, education, or socio-economic status. All income groups did better under the Reagan tax cuts, from the lowest 20 percent to the highest 20 percent, precisely because marginal tax rate cuts provided an incentive for production by enhancing the connection between efforts and rewards. People work harder when they are allowed to keep greater portions of the fruits of their labor. Production increases across the board, as does prosperity, thus the term "trickle down."

> "When government decides how much money each of us should have, we are no longer free."
> David Limbaugh, 3/17/09 Townhall.com

Socialism or "spreading the wealth" is actually plundering of productive citizens, which actually discourages hard work and the development of new ideas. The incentive to work hard to achieve your dreams – a key foundational principle of the American system – is squashed. This produces a bottom up approach. Giving money to unproductive people believing they will rise up and each successive group (working class, middle class, upper class) will also elevate and prosper does not stand up to critical thinking and / or logic. However, this is precisely the view of the political elite leftists in this nation. Poor people do not create jobs or wealth.

When we, the productive workers, have to spend the first five or six months out of the year working to pay the government confiscatory taxes, the whole nation suffers economic malaise. As the tax/confiscatory burden increases along with increased spending of government, the wealthy become less wealthy and entrepreneurship slows down. Thus, jobs are lost and new jobs are not created. The only new jobs come from the growth of government, but who pays for those jobs? As the taxpayers pay for more and more government jobs, the ever-growing deficit is passed on to our children's children.

People are naturally motivated by rewards. When hard work is penalized, as we see in today's political climate, motivation is diminished. Europe has experienced this exact situation and those governments are bankrupt.

Punishing high-income earners so that they make less and keep less sounds good to the class envy camp but it has unintended consequences for everyone else. For example, several times over the years, I have been blessed to be able to hire someone to clean my house. This is a luxury I cherish. A little over a year ago, as the economy slowed down this was an expense I could not afford so I had to let my housekeeper go. The downturn in my lifestyle due to the economy did not just affect me and my family but that of my housekeeper who lost a client and income.

In the same way when those we consider wealthy come under heavy government penalties, they have to cut back both in their businesses with layoffs and on personal spending/purchases that affect local businesses (auto dealers, restaurants, luxury ticket item makers, department stores etc.) which then results in further lost jobs. If the nation continues on this path, it will not be long before we have a nation of citizens totally dependent on government from the cradle to the grave.

When the coercive power of government equalizes incomes, it guarantees less prosperity across the board and spreads the misery, which is one of the many reasons Marxism and socialism have failed everywhere they have been tried.

> When economic freedom is lost, political freedom is lost and totalitarianism soon takes over.

Secular America and the Christian

When we are born again, the Bible says we become citizens of heaven and ambassadors for Christ influencing the culture where we live. Many Christians live with the idea of being citizens of heaven and do not bother to get involved in the communities in which they live. When we live this way, we risk having no impact on our culture, which allows the secularists to control the culture and government. Sometime after the civil war, the church in America began to withdraw from the public square. As pastors neglected preaching diligence and accountability in all areas, especially the moral issues of the day, the door to our freedoms opened and slowly were taken from us. Somehow, during this period, the church became marginalized; and today we see the result of that marginalization where right is called wrong, and what is clearly wrong (sinful) is called right and acceptable. In the last sixty years, our education system has slowly drifted away from morality and value based education to one that is valueless and void of God.

The teaching of our heritage has been replaced with a watered down version that eliminates the Biblical foundation of the founding of this nation. The Lord said in Hosea 4:6: *My people are destroyed for lack of knowledge.* This is true today. Because we do not have the knowledge of our heritage, history and Constitution, our nation is being destroyed. Little is taught in our schools and universities

214

regarding the importance of our Constitutional system, responsibilities of citizenship, free enterprise, property rights, or the value of life issues. Because of revisionist historians, the truth regarding the founding of this nation and our free enterprise system has been replaced by a negative view of the American system. Often patriotism is vilified in our universities.

Because of this bias against the American system (and everything Christian), there has been a gradual move towards a more secular and socialist (even Marxist) philosophy in government and those who make our laws. If this philosophy is allowed to take root, America will trend farther away from a God fearing nation and towards becoming a European styled secular socialist nation.

The bottom line is that it is all about freedom and liberty. If we do not understand the very foundations of this nation, we are ripe to lose it all and become the same as the European nations. For the most part, western European nations have exchanged their belief and trust in God for trust in government to take care of them from cradle to grave (socialism). As a result, they are facing financial collapse. When government mandates exorbitant vacation time, family leave with pay, healthcare for all, and impose high taxes and regulations on businesses there is little incentive to work or create wealth. As a result, their national productivity, creativity, and ingenuity is down, marriage and family is devalued, and birth rates are down as fewer people get married and have children. They are in danger of becoming extinct if these trends continue. However, the immigrant Muslim population in the EU is exploding due to their high birth rates. As this trend continues, Europeans will become the minority in their nations and their nations will become Muslim states.

At the same time, European nations have high unemployment especially among the immigrant communities. The growing burden on society is beginning to cause unrest and, in some cases, violence. Anti-Semitism is on the increase and more and more of their young are turning to religions other than Christianity with no hope. Is this the future we want for America? I sincerely hope not!

The crux of the problem is that the state cannot support us. It has no power to generate income except by taking from the productive populace and giving it to the people trained by tradition (and government schools) to expect the government to provide their basic needs. This is a form of voluntary slavery. When we allow the government to become larger and more invasive in our lives, we are willingly giving up our freedom. We then become a dependent people who cannot think for ourselves and must be told what to do and how to do it. We become like children and disavow all adult responsibilities in favor of a nanny-state.

It is time for us to take a close look at how we think, and examine whether we have fallen into the deception that government knows best how we should live our lives. Our founding fathers believed that God created us to prosper through the gifts, talents and creativity He has put in each of us. We need the freedom to be creative and produce income, own property; and generate wealth and jobs free from strict government regulations and programs that discourage incentive. We need to be a society that values liberty instead of dependency. It is time to take responsibility for ourselves and act like adults.

Even God's Word is direct and unswerving about personal responsibility.

For even when we were with you, we used to give you this order: if anyone is not willing to work, then he is not to eat, either.
2 Thessalonians 3:10

But if any provide not for his own, and specially for those of his own house, he hath denied the faith, and is worse than an infidel.
1 Timothy 5:8

> Depending on anyone or anything other than
> God is a form of idolatry.

Without knowledge of the truth concerning our system of government, we are unable to stand up and truly fight to keep the liberty and

216

freedom upon which this nation was founded. When we do not know the truth, we are easily led astray. If we closely examine the Constitution and the duties it assigns to the federal government, and then compare it to all the programs and duties assigned to it today; we might believe that over the years our elected representatives in Washington have indeed been led astray. Their votes do not line up with our Constitution and many do not line up with party platforms either. When elected to office, a person may mistakenly be seduced into thinking that government can solve all problems.

We must continuously seek to find good, upright candidates who know and respect our Constitution and will defend it. Only a strong person can resist the seduction of big government, recognize and say that the private sector is better equipped to solve most of the country's problems. A strong commitment to the principles of the Constitution always guides men willing and able to initiate good legislation.

Because our Constitution was written using Biblical principles, it is a timeless document. That means that just like the Bible it remains relevant throughout every age of history. Therefore, the need to constantly update its principles and make it relevant to current times is rarely necessary. The writers of the Constitution knew that some things would need to be added over time, which is why they provided an amendment process. Again, let me state, the Constitution is not a living, breathing document, changeable with time. No, it is a timeless document meant to stand the test of time.

Now that we have a good understanding of truth, our Christian heritage and what it means to have a Biblical worldview; we must firmly establish which absolutes we are unwilling to compromise when it comes to our daily decisions as well as our voting decisions.

Critical thinking is crucial in our ability to make good decisions. Unfortunately, critical thinking using reason and logic is not taught in our schools, but has been replaced by emotional thinking. When we vote emotionally or from family tradition without a thorough examination of the issues (thinking critically using common sense, reason and logic); we reap the consequences of bad policies and laws passed by those we elect to office.

It has been said that when we are steeped in "tradition," we cannot see truth when it is put before us. This is not to say that traditions are bad because there are many good traditions. However, we must discern whether some of our traditional thinking is keeping us in bondage. The Apostle Paul was in bondage to a cruel religious system until his Damascus road experience. Because of his experience, he did not turn to man to find out about Jesus but went straight to the desert of Sinai to encounter God for himself and allow the Lord Jesus be his teacher. He did not want man to bias his opinion and relationship with Jesus. Once his relationship was established, he went to the disciples and began his ministry. We need to do the same with our lives and look critically at what, through tradition, is keeping us in bondage unable to receive truth.

> *"The time has come that Christians must vote for honest men and take consistent ground in politics or the Lord will curse them...Christians have been exceedingly guilty of neglect in this matter. The time has come when they must act differently ... God will bless or curse this nation, according to the course Christians choose to take."*
>
> Rev. Charles G. Finney (1792-1875), revivalist in the Second and Third Great Awakenings, College President.

This book was designed to give you the basic knowledge of God's involvement in government, the founding of this nation, the constitution and how to form a Biblical worldview so you are prepared to step up to the plate and be a responsible citizen. God has given us the gift of a United States of America and He expects us to be stewards of this gift. Rest assured that we will be held accountable.

One of the first things we are to do according to the Apostle Paul is to pray for our leaders whether we like them or not (I Timothy 2:1). At age eighteen, American citizens are eligible to vote, join the armed services, serve on jury duty and even run for public office at the local level. These things are not to be taken lightly. Yet, how often do we try to get out of jury duty? It is a privilege to vote and serve on jury duty, and it is an honor to serve one's country. In recent years, people in other countries (who have never been allowed to vote for their leaders) turn out to vote in record numbers even at the risk of their lives. If they are willing to risk their lives to have a voice in their government, then how can we take such freedom for granted?

It is equally as important for us to stand up and vote for those who will represent our values in our city, our county, our state and our nation. Always remembering there are those who will say all the right things to get elected and then there are those who will do what they say they will do. It is up to us to do all we can to recognize which is which and get the latter elected. Then we need to stay engaged with them to help them stay true to their core values.

And don't forget that we need good representatives at all levels of government because the axiom that "all politics is local" is true in the sense that the policies that affect us first are the ones developed and in practice as local policies.

PATRIOTIC PORTRAIT

Abraham Lincoln (1809-1865, assassinated) was the 16th President of the United States of America. Under his courageous leadership, America survived the Civil War and remained the "United States."

Abraham Lincoln never lost touch with the common people and was regarded as a man of highest moral character. Hence, his nickname: "Honest Abe." He was raised in a log cabin and worked at clearing land and splitting rails while teaching himself law. He gained a respected reputation as a lawyer, and became Eighth Circuit Judge in Illinois. Abraham Lincoln was elected to the Illinois State Legislature, to the United States Congress, and, after becoming a national figure by debating against Stephen A. Douglas' pro-slavery bill; he was nominated as the Republican candidate for President.

Lincoln's anti-slavery position was formed as a youth. At age 28, he wrote to Joshua Speed, both a friend and slaveholder:

"I also acknowledge your rights and my obligations, under the Constitution, in regards to your slaves. I confess I hate to see the poor creatures hunted down and caught and carried back to their stripes and unrewarded toils; I bite my lip and keep quiet. In 1841, you and I had together a tedious low-water trip on a steamboat from Louisville to St. Louis. You may remember, as I well do, that from Louisville to the mouth of the Ohio, there were on board ten or a dozen slaves shackled together with irons.

"That sight was a continual torment to me: I see something like it every time I touch the Ohio, or any other slave border. It is hardly fair for you to assume that I have no interest in a thing which has, and continually exercises, the power of making me miserable."[1]

Abraham Lincoln, in closing remarks of a debate with Judge Douglas, asserted:

"That is the issue that will continue in this country when these poor tongues of Judge Douglas and myself shall be silent. It is the eternal struggle between these two principles – right and wrong – throughout the world. They are the

Understanding the Times*

two principles that have stood face to face from the beginning of time, and will ever continue to struggle."[2]

Lincoln had a well-developed sense of right and wrong and was well versed in scriptures. Most of his speeches were filled with Biblical phraseology. He believed the Bible to be the true Word of God, and religion was important to maintaining liberty. It is rumored that he was not a Christian because he did not attend a local church. In August of 1846, he made this public statement in the Illinois Gazette:

"That I am not a member of any Christian Church is true; but I have never denied the truth of Scriptures; and I have never spoken with intentional disrespect of religion in general, or of any denomination of Christians in particular. I do not think I could, myself, be brought to support a man for office whom I knew to be an open enemy of, and scoffer at religion."[3]

Only one week after he was inaugurated as President, the southern states formed the Confederacy. Within a month, the Civil War began when the Confederate Army fired on Fort Sumter on April 12, 1861. The Civil War ended four years later on April 9, 1865 with the surrender of General Robert E. Lee to General Ulysses S. Grant at Appomattox, Virginia. By the end of the war, over a half million men had died, which is more than the combined casualties of all other wars in which America has participated to date. On April 14, 1865, five days after he had freed millions of slaves, John Wilkes Booth assassinated Abraham Lincoln in Ford's Theater.

Lincoln understood that without "the assistance of that Divine Being who ever attended him, I cannot succeed....Trusting in Him who can go with me, and remain with you, and be everywhere for good, let us confidently hope that all will yet be well."[4]

On February 22, 1861, Abraham Lincoln replied to William Dodge: "With the support of the people and the assistance of the Almighty, I shall undertake to perform it.... Freedom is the natural condition of the human race, in which the Almighty intended men to live. Those who fight the purpose of the almighty will not succeed. They always have been, they always will be, beaten."[5]

Truly, he was a man who spent time on his knees in prayer as he carried the weight of the United States on his shoulders. He knew he was not capable of solving the issues within his own wisdom. However, it was the illness and death of his 12-year-old son in 1862 that pushed him closer to God and the Holy Scriptures. "Many noticed that he was seen more frequently with a Bible in his hand, and that he spent more time in prayer. From that time on, Lincoln regularly attended the New York Avenue Presbyterian Church on Sundays – often going to the Wednesday evening prayer meeting – until his death three

221

years later." Dr. Phineas Gurley, Lincoln's pastor at the New York Avenue Presbyterian Church, affirmed, "The death of Willie Lincoln in 1862 and the visit to the Gettysburg battlefield in 1863 finally led Lincoln to personal faith in Christ."

Some observations attributed to Abraham Lincoln, but not confirmed are:

- No man is poor who has had a godly mother.[6]
- The philosophy of the school room in one generation will be the philosophy of government in the next.[7]
- The only assurance of our nation's safety is to lay our foundation in morality and religion.[8]

Abraham Lincoln's own words are inscribed into the walls of the Lincoln Memorial in Washington D.C.:

"That this Nation, under God, shall have a new birth of freedom, and that government of the people, by the people, for the people, shall not perish from the earth."[9]

RECOMMENDED READING

www.WorldviewWeekend.com offers great materials that will give equip you to teach/train your children, grandchildren and great-grandchildren.

QUESTIONS for THOUGHT and DISCUSSION

We must ask ourselves some hard questions.

1. Who benefits from a population where the majority of the people are looking to Uncle Sam for handouts (social security, welfare programs, Medicaid, Medicare, agricultural subsidies, corporate subsidies, subsidized housing, prescription programs, subsidized education, and many other programs)?

2. Are these programs beneficial for the long-term good of the nation?

3. How long can government increase the tax burden on the wealthy before they are no longer wealthy or flee?

4. Who are the ones who create jobs?

5. When there are no more wealth-producing citizens, who will create jobs for the rest of us?

6. What has proven to work in the past to increase job creation and wealth creation?

7. Our leaders know what works to increase government income because it has worked in the past. When they do the opposite of what works what does that say about their true motives?

Foundational Truths – Chapter 13

"Nothing so strongly impels a man to regard the interest of his constituents, as the certainty of returning to the general mass of the people, from whence he was taken, where he must participate in their burdens."

> - George Mason, speech in the Virginia Ratifying
>   Convention, June 17, 1788

"The hour is fast approaching, on which the Honor and Success of this army, and the safety of our bleeding Country depend. Remember officers and Soldiers, that you are Freemen, fighting for the blessings of Liberty - that slavery will be your portion, and that of your posterity, if you do not acquit yourselves like men."

> - George Washington, General Orders, August 23,
>   1776

" Guard against the impostures of pretended patriotism."

> - George Washington, Farewell Address,
>   September 19, 1796

Chapter 13

Securing The Future

What does it Mean to be an American?

Too many citizens today mistake 'living in America' as 'being an American.' However "America" has always been more of an idea than a place. When you sign on, you do more than buy real estate. You accept a set of values and responsibilities. America was founded on a set of principles that were derived from the Bible, traditional Judeo-Christian thought and the great legal thinkers of the time. The principles set out in our founding documents are what made America great. The American people who embody these principles and values are what keep America great. No other nation has the freedom and liberty we have. No other nation is able to send the gospel around the world as we have. No other nation has helped the peoples of the world as we have. We are the most generous and giving nation in the world. America is a great nation and we should never be ashamed of that fact.

Years ago, immigrants came to America to become Americans and embrace the principles and values that make America great. Today, that is not so. Many are coming here to simply take advantage of our freedom, economy, and to better themselves and help their families. So, you might ask, what is wrong with that? There is nothing wrong with that if they are learning our language and adopting our values. Too often these days, they are not willing to learn our language or adopt our values. They are not becoming Americans. Our motto is, "Out of many, One". Today, there are those who are promoting the opposite, "Out of One, Many". How can we be a unified nation if half of the population celebrates their ethnicity first, over being American? It is time for the Church to set aside all racial, traditional and denominational divisions and work together to see true transformation in our nation.

Yes, America is a world power. This is not a bad thing. We are not an evil empire with a plan to take over other countries or cultures of the world. We do more good for the world than any other country. Yet, there is an element in our nation that wants to vilify America and blame every problem in the world on us. They would seek to make us like every other nation in the world, and would have us submit our sovereignty to the United Nations. They do not embody what it means to be American because they want to change the very values and principles that made this nation great. America was created to be that "City on the Hill" that shines its light for all to see. That light is actually the light of the Gospel of Jesus Christ.

How to Secure the Future

As parents, grandparents, aunts and uncles, we want the best for our children, grandchildren and other relatives. We want them to love God/Jesus, love their country and be responsible citizens who will preserve the nation given to them. Sadly, today we are passing on a nation in decline to the next generation. Therefore, it is vitally important for us to teach our children and grandchildren America's rich Christian heritage and the principles and values that made American great.

The founders of this nation never intended for the state to control education because at that time it was common knowledge that parents were responsible to train up their children to be self-governed Christian citizens with the understanding they are to do the same when they have children. Education is the sole responsibility of the parents and not the state. When children attend state run schools it is still the responsibility of the parents to make sure they learn to think Biblically and become adults who filter their decisions according to God's perspective.

Each generation is charged with the responsibility of making things better for the next. We have not only failed to pass on our Christian Heritage, but in many cases, we have failed to pass on our faith. These are the two best things we can pass on to our children. Unfortunately, many times we pass on the negative things instead such as generational curses, traditions, & prejudices. These things are supposed to stop with us when we become believers – but we have to break these curses and declare that they stop now! My children will not be in bondage to these things as I was. My children will be free!
Generally speaking, the church has not done a good job of challenging us to think like Jesus. God's purpose for redemption was to return us

back to the garden relationship that Adam had with God. They were one just as Jesus and God, the Father were and are One. This initial relationship between Adam and God is our example of the relationship we are supposed to have with Him. It was God's intention all along that we would walk as one with Him.

Somewhere along the way, the church lost this original intent. As a result, the church sends out a watered down message with no emphasis on our personal responsibility to study the Word of God, which is our highest worship. The Word washes us clean and sets us free because it is Truth and empowers us to be citizens of the Kingdom. With citizenship comes responsibility. We have become lazy and easily distracted by the things of this world. As a result, we are ineffective at changing our culture. How can we change the culture when we have not changed ourselves through devotion to the Word of God?

So how do we change? We start by looking within ourselves and examining the areas passed down to us from our family line. Then we identify those that do not line up with God's Word, repent and break free from that generational curse. Next, we purpose that we will not pass these negative behaviors on to our children. It is extremely sad when you see prejudiced people teaching their children by example to be prejudiced, hate filled and victims - especially if they profess Jesus Christ as Lord. Jesus has set us free from being victims of our past! We are free from bitterness, unforgiveness, self-hatred, addictions, prejudices, immorality, physical infirmities, and depression. Whom the Lord sets free is free indeed!

We will then be free to love God, love ourselves and love others. By allowing the Holy Spirit to change our thinking to line up with God's perspective, we will be empowered to think, speak and act in a consistently Biblical way that will change the culture.

So examine yourself, let the Holy Spirit reveal these things to you and then confess, repent, forgive and break the curse. Let it stop with you.

Regardless of denomination and race, Christians must become unified. Satan has done an excellent job for centuries creating divisions within the church body because he knows a unified body of Christ would be unbeatable. As long as the body of believers lives incongruently and divided, the enemy wins and we lose.

One recent example of incongruence was the 2008 election in California regarding same-sex marriage. Christians lined up against same-sex marriage on the ballot and then voted those into office who support same-sex marriage! Doesn't that make us politically schizophrenic? And we wonder why we are losing the culture war. When we purpose to think like Jesus, live, and act accordingly in unity, we will then see victories.

Now that we know the past, understand the present and purpose to think like Jesus; we can fight the good fight of faith for this nation. To begin the battle, we must pray for a spiritual awakening of the nation and true revival within the church. True revivals last for decades and require hard work. Often, we do not recognize we are in revival until the revival ends. Even though the media tries to convince us that the church is dead, we have been experiencing revival. Now it is time for true reformation, the kind that will effect change in the nation.

According to David Barton, there are four principles of reformation that are needed to see a reformed America. We must:

1) Develop a **Sense of Duty** (Luke 17:5-10). This old-fashioned idea is no longer emphasized in families. When we are duty driven, our faith increases because the duty is ours and the results are God's. After John Q. Adams served as President, he re-entered politics to serve as a Congressman where he adamantly fought slavery. He did not see much progress but he did his duty and, at the right time, God ended slavery through President Lincoln.

   When we are results-driven, it is too easy to get depressed and give up. Galatians 6: 9 says we will reap if we faint not. Sam Adams believed we were to do our duty with joy regardless of the outcome. We need to adopt a "long-haul" outlook. Never give up!

2) Adopt the **Principle of Incrementalism** where we take ground little by little, bit by bit. The socialist/Marxists in this country

have used this practice since the 1930's. The Pilgrims adopted this attitude and were happy to see themselves as stepping-stones for their succeeding generations. Too often, the pro-life movement will not settle for a little here and a little there in advancing the pro-life agenda. If they cannot be successful immediately, they quit and go home, thus not accomplishing anything. Incrementalism works!

3) Have an **Offensive Mentality** (Proverbs 21:22). This is one of the nine principles of war. In case you have not realized it yet, we are in a war. Defense is not one of the nine principles of war. It seems we spend most of our time in a defensive mode while our opponents take the offensive consistently.

4) Be **Transgenerational** (Judges 13:5) by training up future generations to carry on the fight to victory. John Q. Adams trained Abe Lincoln who then went on to end slavery.

> "It behooves you, therefore, to think and act for yourself and your people. The great principles of right and wrong are legible to every reader; to pursue them requires not the aid of many counselors. The whole art of government consists in the art of being honest. Only aim to do your duty, and mankind will give you credit where you fail."
>
> Thomas Jefferson, A Summary View of the Rights of British America, 1775

If we will adopt these principles and put them into practice, we will see changes. It is up to each and every generation to be vigilant in protecting liberty, freedom, and the American dream. Now it is time to act on all we have learned and get involved.

Practical Application – How to Get Involved

Pray for our elected officials as commanded in I Timothy 2:1-3 and then pray for God to reveal how we are to get involved and of course who to vote for.

Step One: Register to vote!

Step Two: Educate yourself on the issues and decide where you stand. The following organizations offer educational information on the moral/cultural issues of the day. Some even have workshops on community activism.

- ➤ Focus on the Family
- ➤ Eagle Forum
- ➤ Free Market Foundation
- ➤ Family Research Council
- ➤ The Center for Self-Governance
- ➤ Justice at the Gate
- ➤ Traditional Values Coalition
- ➤ Tea Party Organizations

The following publications will offer a broader understanding of economic, foreign policy, immigration, military issues, and national security among others.

- ➤ Imprimis – a free monthly newsletter from Hillsdale College (www.Hillsdale.edu)
- ➤ Human Events – a weekly online newspaper out of Washington D.C. (www.Humanevents.com)
- ➤ National Review – magazine
- ➤ TownHall.com

We must know where we stand Biblically on war and national security in order to know which candidates will keep us safe (the main role of the federal government.)

Is war consistent with the Christian faith? God is a God of war; He sent the Israelites to war repeatedly and in the New Testament, He sends believers into war against Satan and his demons.

Would we be willing to make a treaty with a demon? Can you trust them?

No! The only thing that demons understand or submit to is force; because that is the way they operate. Therefore, it is impossible to make a peace treaty with them. Talking just does not work. They are defeated only by force. So it is with enemy nations who have leaders that are demonized by the gods they worship.

In many cases, the only thing that will stop them is the strength of the United States of America. In order to gain peace, you first must defeat the enemy who wages or threatens war. In most cases, just because they know we have a strong military and are willing to fight, will keep rogue nations from attacking us. Even in peaceful times, a strong military is a strong deterrent to war. However, when we do fight, we should always fight to win.

Step Three: Decide which political party you can support. Get
                  involved.
Both parties have local clubs and a local party headquarters (listed in the phone book.) It is impossible to float between the two parties and be effective. We must evaluate the platforms and decide which ones line up with our core values.

Step Four: Vote in your party's Primary Election.   The primary process is how each party selects candidates to run for specific offices from the county level up to the national level. Primary elections are held every other year. In both the presidential election years and non-presidential years, the primary election allows you to vote for who you want to represent your party in the November general election. The primary is your one opportunity to vote for the candidates that best reflects your beliefs (not necessarily for the candidates that you think can win). It is very important for everyone to vote in the primary election.

> **TIP**: Parents use the primary election season to sit down with your children and watch interviews with the candidates and/or debates. These can be great teaching tools on a scriptural worldview.

Most states hold either precinct meetings or caucuses after the polls close on primary election day. This is the first level of involvement in the party process. This is the entry point of choosing delegates to state and national conventions as well as writing the party platform. This precinct/caucus is where resolutions to change the party platform are first introduced. The resolutions then work their way up through each convention - senatorial or county, state and then national. The national platform does not always reflect each state platform.

These meetings are vital to our political process and deserve your participation. They can be boring especially at the county/senatorial level (I always take reading material) but they are vitally important in the political
process. This is also your chance to meet your elected representatives, make your opinions known, and show your willingness to get involved.

Step Five: Educate yourself on the candidates. The organizations listed in step two will usually have voter guides to help you. If your state elects judges, you may have to take time to call them individually to ask questions on their judicial philosophy. You can also call candidates for local, county, state and federal offices (especially if they are not an incumbent) to ask specific questions about their stances on issues. Check out their websites and email them your questions. There are always candidate forums held in the 6-8 weeks prior to an election. Take advantage of these. Be informed!

Caution: We as Christians need to be careful of being charmed by charismatic leaders. Pray for discernment because we shouldn't go by what we see on the surface. We must do our own thinking. Compare where the candidates stand in comparison to your core values, the absolutes in your belief system on which you refuse (or should refuse) to compromise. Look at their past voting record. Is there a consistent pattern of avoidance on specific issues? Check out their mentors, pastors, people of influence in their life, and organizations they align with; this will give you an idea of their worldview. Apart from the core moral issues on which we should not compromise, how does the candidate stand on basic economic/tax issues, right to bear arms, immigration, military/defense, foreign policy, etc.? Educate yourself on basic economics and know what helps and what hurts the economy and job creation.

> The following quotes are from one of the most charismatic leaders in the 20th century:
> - "How fortunate for leaders that men do not think."
> - "Great liars are also great magicians."
> - "Make the lie big, make it simple, keep saying it, and eventually they will believe it."
>
> Adolph Hitler, German Chancellor and mass murderer

Step Six: Always let your voice be heard.

➢ Write letters or call your elected officials. Hold them accountable for their positions.

➢ Visit your lawmakers when you are in your state capitol or Washington D.C.

➢ Write letters to the editor of your local newspapers.

➢ Call in to radio talk shows.

➢ Voice concerns to media when you see or hear things that are offensive, blatantly biased or not factual.

➢ Voice concerns to local businesses and corporations when they support anti-Christmas views, homosexual agenda, sexualize youth, pro-abortion stances etc.

Be sure to always speak and write truthfully, but with grace, good will, and self-control. An angry voice is often ignored, but a soft answer turns away wrath. A little honey goes a long way.

Step Seven: Volunteer

➢ Volunteer for candidates that you like.

➢ Volunteer to work at party headquarters.

➢ Apply for city and/or county boards and commissions

➢ Volunteer at city workdays

> ➤ Volunteer to be on the board of your neighborhood association.

> **TIP**: Parents, you can train your children in civic duty by setting an example:
> - Take them with you when you vote.
> - Take them when they are old enough to stuff envelopes to help with campaigns.
> - Encourage them to write letters to editors when issues affect them and they have strong opinions to express.
> - Pray together as a family for our leaders.

Go to www.WallBuilders.com and search for *"Ten Steps to Change America"* by David Barton. This is a great resource filled with valuable ideas on prayer, teaching your children to pray, how to write letters to elected officials and much more.

The Challenge – Are You Ready?

In conclusion, I would like to challenge you with this passage from the preface of Noah Webster's *Common Version of the Holy Bible, containing the Old and New Testament, with Amendments of the Language, 1833*. He makes it very clear what our responsibilities are concerning maintaining the republican government the founding Fathers intended. It reads:

> "The Bible is the Chief moral cause of all that is good, and the best corrector of all that is evil, in human society; the best book for regulating the temporal concerns of men, and the only book that can serve as an infallible guide to future felicity. It is extremely important to our nation, in a political as well as religious view, that all possible authority and influence should be given to the scriptures, for these furnish the best principles of civil liberty, and the most effectual support of republican government."

I challenge you to a life of personal responsibility before God, to pray diligently for this nation and to get involved and stay involved in the election process.

- Let your voice be heard.
- Educate yourself on history and the issues.
- Pray for wisdom at each election cycle.
- Speak out on issues that reflect the Biblical worldview.
- God may even lead you to run for office or work on local government boards or committees.
- Teach your children and grandchildren their Christian heritage, Biblical worldview, and the importance of civic duty.

God desires us to have godly leadership so we will be a righteous nation. Proverbs 14:34 says, *"..righteousness exalts a nation; sin is a disgrace to any people."* Above all, pray for our leaders.

If you are willing to meet this challenge, sign here:

I agree to meet the challenge. _____

Final Word

It has been said that "God has no grandchildren" which should give us pause to really examine what that means. How many people do we know who think that coming from a Christian family or going to a certain church guarantees their salvation? When we are truly born again into Christ we become God's children. There is no mention of our children automatically becoming born again just because they are born to those who are born again.

The reality is that each person is responsible for his/her salvation decision. As parents our number one responsibility is to lovingly lead our children to Christ and then raise them up in His wisdom and revelation. So they will go forth into the world with a firm faith in

Christ and a solid foundation in His Word. This is our call as parents and it requires diligence on our part because we have to then be consistent in our time with the Lord so that we set the tone and example in the home.

If you are born in America you automatically become a citizen of the United States but when you are born into a Christian home you do not automatically become a Christian. God gave us a free will and wants each of us to choose Him out of our own free will. This happens as parents pour God's love into their children and provide opportunities for them to discover God's loving presence in their lives.

Loving America and becoming a true patriot happens in much the same way. As Ronald Reagan famously said "it isn't passed to us through the bloodstream". It is up to parents to set the example on what it means to be a good citizen and provide opportunities for their children to discover the exceptional greatness of America. Teaching the true history of the beginning of this nation is one way to instill love for the country especially when they understand God's role and purpose in it all.

As we become diligent in teaching these things to our children and instilling in them the sense of duty to pass this on to their children then we will begin to see the generations working together to preserve our God given rights (life, liberty and happiness). The motto of the military is to preserve and protect and as Christians and citizens this should also be our daily duty to our families and our nation. This is how we secure the future of freedom for America and all future generations.

PATRIOTIC PORTRAIT

Noah Webster (1758-1843) was a statesman, educator, lexicographer and the author of *Webster's Dictionary*. He was affectionately known as "the Schoolmaster of the Nation", and published the first edition of his *American Dictionary of the English Language* in November 1828. It contained the greatest number of Biblical definitions given in any secular publication.

Noah Webster served as a soldier during the Revolutionary War, was elected to the Connecticut General Assembly for nine terms, the Legislature of Massachusetts for three terms, and served as a judge. He was also largely responsible for Article I, Section 8, of the United States Constitution, which outlines the duties of Congress. During his time in the Massachusetts Legislature, he fought to have funds set aside for education. He declared that government was responsible to: "Discipline our youth in early life in sound maxims of moral, political, and religious duties."[1]

In 1832, Noah Webster published his *History of the United States*, in which he wrote:

> "The brief exposition of the constitution of the United States, will unfold to young persons the principles of republican government; and it is the sincere desire of the writer that our citizens should early understand that the genuine source of correct republican principles is the Bible, particularly the New Testament or the Christian religion.

> "The religion which has introduced civil liberty is the religion of Christ and His apostles, which enjoins humility, piety, and benevolence; which acknowledges in every person a brother, or a sister, and a citizen with equal rights. This is genuine Christianity, and to this, we owe our free Constitutions of Government.

> "The moral principles and precepts contained in the Scriptures ought to form the basis of all of our civil constitutions and laws...All the miseries and evils which men suffer from vice, crime, ambition, injustice, oppression, slavery and war, proceed

from their despising or neglecting the precepts contained in the Bible.

"When you become entitled to exercise the right of voting for public officers, let it be impressed on your mind that God commands you to choose for rulers just men who will rule in the fear of God. The preservation of a republican government depends on the faithful discharge of this duty. If the citizens neglect their duty and place unprincipled men in office, the government will soon be corrupted; laws will be made not for the public good so much as for selfish or local purposes...

"Corrupt or incompetent men will be appointed to execute the laws; the public revenues will be squandered on unworthy men; and the rights of the citizens will be violated or disregarded.

"If a republican government fails to secure public prosperity and happiness, it must be because the citizens neglect the divine commands, and elect bad men to make and administer the laws."[2]

Noah Webster was a man of great insight and a true statesman. In 1843, just before his death, he professed:

"I know whom I have believed, and that He is able to keep that which I have committed to Him against that day."[3]

RECOMMENDED READING

The Ten Big Lies About America" by Michael Medved -and-
The Ten Big Lies About American Business" by Michael Medved

QUESTIONS for THOUGHT and DISCUSSION

1. What does it mean to be an American to you?

2. What is a patriot and is patriotism esteemed today?

3. How will you teach your children and grandchildren true patriotism?

4. Are you personally challenged to pass on to the next generation your faith and your heritage as an American Christian?

5. In what ways will you become more pro-active in the American political and public policy process?

6. Has this book challenged your traditional thinking regarding your faith and public/civic responsibilities? How?

7. Do you now believe that you can make a difference if you get involved?

BIBLIOGRAPHY

Jesus, Politics and the Church by Tony Nassif, Published by Winepress

The Ten Offenders by Pat Robertson, Published by Integrity

The Light and the Glory by Peter Marshall & David Manuel, Published by Revell

Of Plymouth Plantation by William Bradford, Boston: Wright and Potter, 1901

Religion and the Founding of the American Republic by James H. Hutson, published by the Library of Congress

America's God and Country, Encyclopedia of Quotations by William J. Federer, published by AmeriSearch

Christianity and the Constitution, The Faith of Our Founding Fathers by John Eidsmoe, published by Baker

Think Like Jesus, Make the Right Decision Every Time by George Barna, published by Integrity

American History in Black & White, by David Barton, published by WallBuilder Press

Black Patriots of the American Revolution by David Barton, The WallBuilder Report, African American History Issue 2004

Honoring Godly Heroes, African American Pastors by David Barton, The WallBuilder Report, African American History Issue 2005

www.insuredemocracy.com, source for election voting facts.

The Founders Key, by Dr. Larry Arnn, published by Thomas Nelson

SOURCE NOTES

Chapter 1

1. Information under the Ten Commandments section was taken from *The Ten Offenders* by Pat Robertson (Integrity Publishers, 2004)

2. Noah Webster. *America's God And Country Encyclopedia of Quotations*, William J. Federer (St. Louis, MO, Amerisearch, Inc., 2000), p.677, from the 1828 preface to his *American Dictionary of the English Language*.

3. John Adams. *God And Country Encyclopedia of Quotations*, William J. Federer (St. Louis, MO, Amerisearch, Inc., 2000), p. 10. July 26, 1796, writing in his diary a disapproval of Thomas Paine's assertions. Norman Cousins, In God We Trust – The Religious Beliefs and Ideas of the American Founding Fathers (NY: Harper & Brothers, 1958), p. 99.

4. John Witherspoon. *God And Country Encyclopedia of Quotations*, William J. Federer (St. Louis, MO, Amerisearch, Inc., 2000), p. 703. May 17, 1776, in his sermon entitled, "The Dominion of Providence over the Passions of Men." Varnum Lansing Collins, *President Witherspoon* (NY: Arno Press and The New York Times, 1969), I:197-98.

5. John Witherspoon. *God And Country Encyclopedia of Quotations*, William J. Federer (St. Louis, MO, Amerisearch, Inc., 2000), p. 704. John Adams. Roger Schultz, "Covenanting in America: The Political Theology of John Witherspoon," Master's Thesis, Trinity Evangelical Divinity School, Deerfield, Illinois, 1985, p. 149.

Chapter 2

1. Ronald Reagan, January 11, 1989 Farewell Address, Washington D.C., Wikiquote.org.

2. Ronald Reagan. *God And Country Encyclopedia of Quotations*, William J. Federer (St. Louis, MO, Amerisearch, Inc., 2000), p. 528. 1980, "Our Christian Heritage", letter from Plymouth Rock (Marborough, NH: The Plymouth Rock Foundation), p. 7.

3. Ronald Reagan. *God And Country Encyclopedia of Quotations*, William J. Federer (St. Louis, MO, Amerisearch, Inc., 2000), p. 529. January 25, 1984, "Proclaim Liberty" (Dallas, TX: Word of Faith) p. 3.

4. Ronald Reagan. *God And Country Encyclopedia of Quotations*, William J. Federer (St. Louis, MO, Amerisearch, Inc., 2000), p. 530. August 23, 1984, at an ecumenical prayer breakfast at the Reunion Arena in Dallas, TX, on the occasion of the enactment of the Equal Access Bill of 1984.

Chapter 3

1. George Washington Carver. *God And Country Encyclopedia of Quotations*, William J. Federer (St. Louis, MO, Amerisearch, Inc., 2000), p. 96. November 19, 1924, in a speech given before 500 people of the Women's Board of Domestic Missions in New York City's Marble Collegiate Church. Ethel Edwards, Carver of Tuskagee (Cincinnati, Ohio: Ethel Edwards & James T. Hardwick, a limited edition work compiled in part from over 300 personal letters written by Dr. Carver to James T. Hardwick between 1922 and 1937, available from the Carver Memorial in Locust Grove, Diamond, MO, 1971) pp. 141-142.

2. George Washington Carver. *God And Country Encyclopedia of Quotations*, William J. Federer (St. Louis, MO, Amerisearch, Inc., 2000), p. 96. Ibid, pp.183,199.

3. George Washington Carver. *God And Country Encyclopedia of Quotations*, William J. Federer (St. Louis, MO, Amerisearch, Inc., 2000), p. 97. Ibid, pp. 157-160.

4. George Washington Carver. *God And Country Encyclopedia of Quotations*, William J. Federer (St. Louis, MO, Amerisearch, Inc., 2000), p. 97. Ibid, pp. 157-160.

5. George Washington Carver, *God And Country Encyclopedia of Quotations*, William J. Federer (St. Louis, MO, Amerisearch, Inc., 2000), p. 98. 1939, in the citation made at the presentation of the Roosevelt Medal. Henry M. Morris, *Men of Science – Men of God* (El Cajon, CA: Master Books, Creation Life Publishers Inc., 1990) pp. 81-83.

6. George Washington Carver. *God And Country Encyclopedia of Quotations*, William J. Federer (St. Louis, MO, Amerisearch, Inc., 2000), p.98. *Bless Your House*

Chapter 4

1. Information in Lessons V – IX from *The Light and the Glory*, *Of Plymouth Plantation* and *Religion and the Founding of the American Republic* (The Library of Congress, by James H. Hutson, 1998).

2. William Bradford. Peter Marshall and David Manuel, The Light and the Glory (Old Tappan, New Jersey: Fleming H. Revell Company, 1977) p. 144. Fleming, *One Small Candle*, p. 218.

3. William Bradford. Nathaniel Morton, New England's Memorial, Sixth Edition, with Governor Bradford's History of Plymouth Colony (Boston: Congregational Board of Publication, 1855), p. 239.

4. William Bradford: *America's God And Country Encyclopedia of Quotations*, William J. Federer (St. Louis, MO, Amerisearch, Inc., 2000), p. 64. July 1620, in a day of solemn humiliation prior to the Pilgrim's departure from Leyden, Holland. William Bradford (Governor of Plymouth Colony), *The History of Plymouth Plantation* 1608-1650 (Boston, Massachusetts: Massachusetts Historical Society, 1856).

Chapter 5

1. John Winthrop. Peter Marshall, David Manuel, *The Light and the Glory* (Old Tappan, New Jersey: Fleming H. Revell Company, 1977) p. 149. From the *Winthrop Papers*, Massachusetts Historical Society, Vol. 1, pp. 196.

2. Reverend Francis Higginson. Peter Marshall, David Manuel, The Light and the Glory (Old Tappan, New Jersey: Fleming H. Revell Company, 1977) p.155. William Warren Street, *The Story of Religion in America*, p. 48.

3. John Winthrop. Peter Marshall, David Manuel, *The Light and the Glory* (Old Tappan, New Jersey: Fleming H. Revell Company, 1977) pp. 161-162. Winthrop Papers II, pp. 292-295, Massachusetts Historical Society.

4. Thomas Hooker. *A Biographical Sketch of the Life of Thomas Hooker*, by William C. Nichols. Taken from "The Soul's Preparation for Christ", 1994 by International Outreach, Inc., www.intoutreach.org/biog.html.

5. Thomas Hooker. *A Biographical Sketch of the Life of Thomas Hooker*, by William C. Nichols. July 16, 1994, International Outreach, Inc. www.intoutreach.org/bio.html.

6. Thomas Hooker. Britania Biographies, Barbara Cross Mission to the Worlds, Chelmsford, England.

Chapter 6

1. Patrick Henry. Peter Marshall, David Manuel, *The Light and the Glory* (Old Tappan, New Jersey: Fleming H. Revell Company, 1977) p. 102. Bancroft, VII, p.274.

2. Taken from: Christianity and the Constitution by John Eidsmoe, Baker Book House, Chapter 5, pp72-73.

3.	Samuel Adams. Statement made in a political essay, printed in The Public Advisor, 1749. William V. Wells, The Life & Public Service of Samuel Adams (Boston: Little, Brown, & Co., 1865), Vol 1 p. 22.

4.	Samuel Adams. Statement made 1750. William V. Wells, The Life & Public Service of Samuel Adams (Boston: Little, Brown, & Co., 1865). *America's God And Country Encyclopedia of Quotations*, William J. Federer (St. Louis, MO, Amerisearch, Inc., 2000), p. 23.

5.	Samuel Adams. *America's God And Country Encyclopedia of Quotations*, William J. Federer (St. Louis, MO, Amerisearch, Inc., 2000), p. 24. Nov. 22, 1780 statement to T. ells, daughter's fiancé. Norman Cousins, *In God We Trust – The Religious Beliefs & Ideas of the American Founding Fathers* (NY: Harper & Brothers, 1958) p. 354.

6.	Samuel Adams. *America's God And Country Encyclopedia of Quotations*, William J. Federer (St. Louis, MO, Amerisearch, Inc., 2000), p. 25. In his last will & testament. Stephen Abbott Northrop, D.D., *A Great Cloud of Witnesses* (Portland, Oregon, American Heritage Ministries, 1987; Mantle Ministries, 228 StillRidge, Balverde, TX).

Chapter 7

1.	John Adams. *The Light and the Glory* (Old Tappan, New Jersey: Fleming H. Revell Company, 1977) Chapter 17, p. 310. Adams Family Correspondence, II pp. 28, 30-31.

2.	Samuel Adams. *The Light and the Glory* (Old Tappan, New Jersey: Fleming H. Revell Company, 1977) Chapter 16 p.309. Kistler, p. 71.

3.	General Nathaniel Green. *The Light and the Glory* (Old Tappan, New Jersey: Fleming H. Revell Company, 1977) p. 329. Lancaster & Plumb, *The American Heritage*, p. 320.

4.	Major Ben Tallmadge. *The Light and the Glory* (Old Tappan, New Jersey: Fleming H. Revell Company, 1977) p. 315. Sheer & Rankin, *Rebels and Redcoats*, p.171.

5.	George Washington. Christianity and the Constitution by John Eidsmore, Baker Book House, p. 121. Boller, *George Washington & Religion*, p. 69.

6.	George Washington. *America's God And Country Encyclopedia of Quotations*, William J. Federer (St. Louis, MO, Amerisearch, Inc., 2000), p.643. Aug. 20, 1778, in letter to Thomas Nelson in Virginia. Jared Sparks, ed., The Writings of George Washington, 12 Vols. (Boston: American Stationer's Company, 1837; NY: F. Andrews, 1834-1847), VI, p. 36.

7.	George Washington. *America's God And Country Encyclopedia of Quotations*, William J. Federer (St. Louis, MO, Amerisearch, Inc., 2000), p.635. 1745. *110 Rules of Civility and Decent Behavior in Company and Conversation (copied in his own handwriting at the age of 15) (Bedford, MA: Apple books, 1988, distributed by the Globe Pequot Press) p. 30.*

8.	George Washington. *America's God And Country Encyclopedia of Quotations*, William J. Federer (St. Louis, MO, Amerisearch, Inc., 2000), p.658. George Washington, 1752, in his personal prayer book, entitled "*Daily Sacrifice*", consisting of 24 pages in his own handwriting.

9.	Mary Washington. *America's God And Country Encyclopedia of Quotations*, William J. Federer (St. Louis, MO, Amerisearch, Inc., 2000), p.635-636. Nov. 1753, in his parting words from his mother, Mrs. Mary Washington. John N. Norton, "*Life of General Washington*" (1870), 6.34. Marian Harland, "*The Story of Mary Washington*" (1892), p. 87.

10.	George Washington. *America's God And Country Encyclopedia of Quotations*, William J. Federer (St. Louis, MO, Amerisearch, Inc., 2000), p. 636. July 18, 1755,

George Washington, in a letter to his brother, Jared Sparks, ed., *"The Writings of George Washington"* , 12 Vols. (Boston: American Stationers Company, 1837, NY: F. Andrew's 1834-1847), Vol. II, p. 89.

11. George Washington. *America's God And Country Encyclopedia of Quotations*, William J. Federer (St. Louis, MO, Amerisearch, Inc., 2000), p. 636-637. 1770. George Washington. Parke Custus, *"Recollections & Private Memoirs of Washington"*, Benson J. Lossing, editor, (1860) p, 303.

12. George Washington. *America's God And Country Encyclopedia of Quotations*, William J. Federer (St. Louis, MO, Amerisearch, Inc., 2000), p. 660. From Mt. Vernon, Sept. 9, 1786, in a letter to John F. Mercer. William S. Baker, *"Washington After the Revolution 1784-1799"* (1897), p.62.

13. George Washington. .*America's God And Country Encyclopedia of Quotations*, William J. Federer (St. Louis, MO, Amerisearch, Inc., 2000), p. 658. I

Chapter 8

1. Benjamin Franklin. *The Light and the Glory* (Old Tappan, New Jersey: Fleming H. Revell Company, 1977) Chapter 18, p. 342-343. *In God We Trust*, edited by Norman Cousins, p. 42.

2. *Christianity and The Constitution*, by John Eidsmoe, (Baker House Book Company, 1987) Chapter 21, pp. 355-377.

3. Benjamin Franklin. *America's God And Country Encyclopedia of Quotations*, William J. Federer (St. Louis, MO, Amerisearch, Inc., 2000), p.239. *Poor Richard's Almanac*. Carroll E. Simcox, comp.,*4400 Quotations for Christian Communicators* (Grand Rapids, MI: Baker Book House, 1991), p.185. John Bartlett, *Bartlett's Familiar Quotations* (Boston: Little, Brown and Company, 1855,1980) p. 347.

4. Benjamin Franklin. *America's God And Country Encyclopedia of Quotations*, William J. Federer (St. Louis, MO, Amerisearch, Inc., 2000), p.246. Tryon Edwards, D.D., The New Dictionary of Thoughts – A Cyclopedia of Quotations (Garden City, NY: Hanover House, 1852; revised and enlarged by C.H. Catrevas, Ralph Emerson Browns and Jonathan Edwards [descendent along with Tryon of Jonathan Edwards (1703-1758), president of Princeton]; The Standard Book Company, 1955, 1963) pp. 49, 338.

5. Benjamin Franklin. *America's God And Country Encyclopedia of Quotations*, William J. Federer (St. Louis, MO, Amerisearch, Inc., 2000), p. 247. April 17, 1787, in a letter. Albert Henry Smyth, ed., *The Writings of Benjamin Franklin*, 10 vols. (New York – Macmillan Co., 1905-7), 9:569, reprinted (NY: Haskell House Publishers, 1970),Vol. IX, p. 569.

6. Benjamin Franklin. *America's God And Country Encyclopedia of Quotations*, William J. Federer (St. Louis, MO, Amerisearch, Inc., 2000), p. 253. *Autobiography of Benjamin Franklin* (Note: Franklin's Epitaph, written by himself in 1728, is engraved on his gravestone), p. 401.

Chapter 9

1. James Madison. Speech, House of Representatives, during debate "On the Memorial of the Relief Committee of Baltimore for the Relief of St. Domingo Refugees (Jan. 10, 1794). *"A Century of Lawmaking for a New Nation: U.S. Congressional Documents and Debates"*, 1774-1875.

2. Frederick Douglass. American History in Black & White by David Barton (Wallbuilders Press, 2004) p. 11. Frederick Douglass, *"The Frederick Douglass*

Papers", John Blassingame, ed. (New Haven: Yale University Press, 1982), pp. 385-386, from "What to the Slave is the Fourth of July?", July 5, 1852.

Chapter 10

1. Thomas Jefferson. *America's God And Country Encyclopedia of Quotations*, William J. Federer (St. Louis, MO, Amerisearch, Inc., 2000), p.331. Thomas Jefferson, June 12, 1823, in a letter to Justice William Johnson. Thomas Jefferson, *Jefferson Writings*, Merrill D. Peterson, ed. (NY: Literary Classics of the U.S., Inc., 1984), p. 1475.

2. John Jay. *America's God And Country Encyclopedia of Quotations*, William J. Federer (St. Louis, MO, Amerisearch, Inc., 2000), p. 318. Benjamin Franklin Morris, "*Christian Life and Character of the Civil Institutions of the United States*", (Philadelphia: George W. Childs, 1864), p. 154.

3. John Jay. *America's God And Country Encyclopedia of Quotations*, William J. Federer (St. Louis, MO, Amerisearch, Inc., 2000), p. 319. John Jay. May 17,1829, in his final words to his children. William jay, *Life of John Jay*, with Selections from his Correspondence, 2 Vols. (NY: Harper, 1833), Vol I, p. 548.

4. John Marshall. *America's God And Country Encyclopedia of Quotations*, William J. Federer (St. Louis, MO, Amerisearch, Inc., 2000), p. 418. 1819, in the case of McCulloch v. Maryland, 4 Wheaton 316, 431. John Bartlett, *Bartlett's Familiar Quotations* (Boston: Little, Brown and Company, 1855, 1980), p. 402.

Chapter 11

1. Thomas Jefferson. *America's God And Country Encyclopedia of Quotations*, William J. Federer (St. Louis, MO, Amerisearch, Inc., 2000), p.325. January 1, 1802, in a personal letter to Nehemiah Dodge, Ephraim Robbins, and Stephen Nelson of the Danbury Baptist Association, Danbury, Connecticut, Reynolds v. U.S., 98 U.S. 164 (1878).

2. Thomas Jefferson. *America's God And Country Encyclopedia of Quotations*, William J. Federer (St. Louis, MO, Amerisearch, Inc., 2000), p.330. September 28, 1820, in a letter to William Jarvis. Thomas Jefferson, "Jefferson's Letters", Wilson Whitman, ed., (Eau Claire, WI: E.M. Hale & Company, 1900), p. 338.

3. Thomas Jefferson. *America's God And Country Encyclopedia of Quotations*, William J. Federer (St. Louis, MO, Amerisearch, Inc., 2000), p. 331. June 12, 1823, in a letter to Justice William Johnson. Thomas Jefferson, Jefferson Writings, Merrill D. Peterson, ed. (NY: Literary Classics of the United States, Inc., 1984), p. 1475.

4. Thomas Jefferson. *America's God And Country Encyclopedia of Quotations*, William J. Federer (St. Louis, MO, Amerisearch, Inc., 2000), p.334. Stephen K. McDowell and mark A. Beliles, "America's Providential History" (Charlottesville, VA: Providence Press, 1988), p.148.

5. Thomas Jefferson. *America's God And Country Encyclopedia of Quotations*, William J. Federer (St. Louis, MO, Amerisearch, Inc., 2000), p. 333. July 4, 1826, epitaph inscribed on his tombstone, which he authored himself.

Chapter 12

1. Abraham Lincoln. *America's God And Country Encyclopedia of Quotations*, William J. Federer (St. Louis, MO, Amerisearch, Inc., 2000), p. 374. 1837, at age 28, in a letter to a pro-slavery friend, Joshua Speed. Roy P. Basler, ed., *The Collected Works of Abraham Lincoln* (New Brunswick, NJ: Rutgers University Press, 1953), Vol. 2, p. 320.

2. Abraham Lincoln. *America's God And Country Encyclopedia of Quotations*, William J. Federer (St. Louis, MO, Amerisearch, Inc., 2000), p.376. 1858 in the closing remarks of a debate with Judge Douglas. Carroll E. Simcox, *3000 Quotations on Christian Themes* (Grand Rapids, MI: Baker Book House, 1989), p/202, No. 2455.

3. Abraham Lincoln. *America's God And Country Encyclopedia of Quotations*, William J. Federer (St. Louis, MO, Amerisearch, Inc., 2000), p. 375. August 15, 1846 , in a public statement published in the Illinois Gazette, during his race for the Congressional seat of the Seventh District of Illinois. P. Thomas Benjamin, Abraham Lincoln (New York: Knopf, 1953), pp. 108-109.

4. Abraham Lincoln. *America's God And Country Encyclopedia of Quotations*, William J. Federer (St. Louis, MO, Amerisearch, Inc., 2000), p. 377. February 11, 1861, Springfield, Illinois, in a *Farewell Address* to his home as he left for Washington, D.C. John Bartlett, *Bartlett's Familiar Quotations* (Boston: Little, Brown and Company, 1855, 1980), p. 521.

5. Abraham Lincoln. *America's God And Country Encyclopedia of Quotations*, William J. Federer (St. Louis, MO, Amerisearch, Inc., 2000), p. 377. February 23, 1861, in a reply to William Dodge. L.E. Chittenden (Register of the Treasury under President Lincoln), *Recollections of President Lincoln and His Administration*, p. 76.

6. Abraham Lincoln. *America's God And Country Encyclopedia of Quotations*, William J. Federer (St. Louis, MO, Amerisearch, Inc., 2000), p.392. *Bless Your Heart* (Series 11) (Eden Prairie, MN: Heartland Prairie, Inc., 1990), p. 8.17.

7. Abraham Lincoln. *America's God And Country Encyclopedia of Quotations*, William J. Federer (St. Louis, MO, Amerisearch, Inc., 2000), p. 392. Attributed. Herald Star, Steubenville, Ohio, 1984. Stephen K. McDowell and mark A. Beliles, *America's Providential History* (Charlottesville, VA: Providence Press, 1988), p.79.

8. Abraham Lincoln. *America's God And Country Encyclopedia of Quotations*, William J. Federer (St. Louis, MO, Amerisearch, Inc., 2000), p. 392. Attributed. Ibid, pp. 148, 179.

9. Abraham Lincoln. Inscription of President Abraham Lincoln's words on the walls of the Lincoln Memorial in Washington D.C.

Chapter 13

1. Noah Webster. *America's God and Country Encyclopedia of Quotations*, William J. Federer (St. Louis, MO, Amerisearch, Inc., 2000), p.675. 1828, in the preface to his *American Dictionary of the English Language* (reprinted San Francisco: Foundation for American Christian Education, 1967), Preface p. 22.

2. Noah Webster. *America's God and Country Encyclopedia of Quotations*, William J. Federer (St. Louis, MO, Amerisearch, Inc., 2000), p. 678. 1832, "*History of the United States*", (New Haven: Durrie & Peck, 1832), pp. 307-308, paragraph 49.

3. Noah Webster. *America's God and Country Encyclopedia of Quotations*, William J. Federer (St. Louis, MO, Amerisearch, Inc., 2000), p. 681. 1843. "*Memoir of Noah Webster*", Webster's Unabridged Dictionary.

GLOSSARY – *Definitions Matter*

Capitalism: Capitalism is an economic system in which investment in and ownership of the means of production, distribution, and exchange of wealth is made and maintained chiefly by private individuals and corporations. It is characterized by the following: private property ownership; individuals and companies are allowed to compete for their own economic gain; and free market forces determine the prices of goods and services. Such a system is based on the premise of separating the state and business activities. Capitalists believe that markets are efficient and should thus function without interference, and the role of the state is to minimally regulate and protect.

Charity: Charity is the voluntary act of giving help, such as money or food, to those in need; alms; a kindly attitude towards people. Charity is also synonymous with an organization set up to provide/deliver help to those in need such as the Salvation Army, Operation Blessing, Feed the Children etc. The key to charity is that it is a voluntary act.

Coercion/Plunder: The act of compelling by force the handing over of your goods/money to someone else. It could be by physical force as in war or by force of law. When government enacts laws that take your hard-earned money to give to those who do not work hard that is an act of plunder by force of law. It may be framed as government charity but government on its own does not make money (except that which they print on paper) so they must plunder the citizens who own businesses and those who work hard in order to provide for other citizens who do not work.

Conservative: Conservatism is a way of understanding life, society and governance. Just like the <u>definition of liberal</u>, the definition of conservative can be divided into 6 key principles:

1. **Belief in natural law:** Human beings do not make the laws of morality, nor are rights conferred upon us by governments but rather by a higher power. The majority believe they originate with God. Conservatives tend to believe that most political problems are spiritual/religious and moral problems. At the very root of the definition of conservative is a belief in the importance of virtue.

2. **Belief in established institutions:** American conservatives, for example, believe passionately that the Constitution and the Bill of Rights are works of profound genius, and that they provide the best system of law and government possible. More broadly, conservatives believe in the Anglo-Saxon tradition of rule of law and good government. A very important part of the definition of conservative is the deep respect conservatives hold for the cultural institutions of church and family maintaining that

these institutions are vitally important for the spiritual well-being of humankind.

3. **Preference for liberty over equality:** This concept is the most difficult part of the definition of conservative for most people to understand, particularly since liberty and equality are almost used as synonyms in our times. Put simply, all societies face a fundamental choice between emphasizing freedom or emphasizing equality. The reality is that we can be either equal or free, but we cannot be both. Though both the right and left wings claim to promote both freedom *and* equality, the right is most concerned with freedom and the left most concerned with equality. The upper most concern for conservatives is always: are we maximizing freedom?

4. **Suspicion of power—and of human nature:** The fourth principle that defines conservatives is their **suspicion of power** and their hatred of big government. In his First Inaugural Address, President Ronald Reagan declared, that government was the problem not the solution to the problems facing America and that if we are not capable of self-governing ourselves then who of us can govern someone else. Yet, conservatives recognize that government is a necessary evil, as without it the good are often at the mercy of the evil. Men are not angels, and the Founders knew that we are imperfect beings and easily corrupted. For this reason, conservatives believe power must be spread out and decentralized, with adequate checks and balances to ensure that government does not devolve into tyranny.

5. **Belief in exceptionalism:** This is based in conservative lack of belief in perfect equality. Conservatives realize that some people inevitably have superior abilities, intelligence, and talents, and they believe that those people have a fundamental right to use and profit from their natural gifts and that they in turn would benefit the growth in the economy by their spending, invention and creation of jobs. While it has become commonplace to regard the exceptional among us as "winners in the lottery of life" who are lifted up by the tired shoulders of average citizens, conservatives believe quite the opposite. Conservatives believe that exceptional people exist to lift us up, to improve our lives, and to give us hope. As such, they believed that genius could only breathe in an atmosphere of freedom.

6. **Belief in the individual:** Conservatives such as Barry Goldwater believed that each man regardless of his individual good and the good of his society is ultimately responsible for his own development. Only he can make those choices. To the conservative civil society or ordered liberty is paramount and private property and liberty are inseparable. The

248

civil society has as its highest purpose its preservation and continued improvement through the choices of each individual.

Critical Thinking: In short, critical thinking is self-directed, self-disciplined, self-monitored, and self-corrective thinking. It presupposes assent to rigorous standards of excellence and a mindful command of their use. It entails effective communication and problem solving abilities and a commitment to overcome our natural self-centeredness and society as the center of all things. It is using the logic and reasoning abilities that God gave us to come to logical and well thought out conclusions. Because critical thinking is not natural for us, we must work at developing this skill. Without it, our decisions will be based solely on our emotions, which do not always act in our best interest for the long-term.

Free market: <u>Business</u> governed by the laws of <u>supply</u> and <u>demand</u>, not restrained by <u>government</u> interference, <u>regulation</u> or <u>subsidy</u>. Also, a foreign exchange market not controlled by the government. When supply is low with high demand – prices go up and when supply is up and demand is low – prices go down. It is fair and balanced for all and thus benefits all. Unlike government controlled economies it allows people to fail in their ventures but it also encourages them to try again. There are no bailouts.

Liberal/Statist: The definition of modern liberalism can be divided into 6 key principles:

1. **Belief in positive law:** Rights are derived by written law, not a higher power. They do not believe that natural rights of life, liberty and property are important, as the conservatives believe they are. They believe government grants and guarantees rights. They believe that abstract rights are the most easily infringed upon. However, they have been known to read abstract rights into the Constitution that are not specifically mentioned. Separation of church and state is fundamental to the definition of modern liberalism.

2. **Faith in progress:** They believe they should use the government to change the world. What conservatives seek to preserve and improve, the modern liberal wants to replace through economic and social experimentation.

3. **Preference for equality over liberty:** While it is true that some forms of equality such as equality of rights and opportunity serve to enhance liberty, most modern liberals are willing to trade certain freedoms, such as greater personal choice, in favor of greater equality and social stability. The idea that all men are created equal is taken to its literal extreme as they attempt through government to equalize everything.

4. **Belief in the benevolence of government and individuals:** Modern liberals believe that human nature is essentially good; and that if an individual is corrupted, it is usually the fault of some social or economic injustice. Therefore, the government can and should play a positive role in the lives of its citizens, particularly the disadvantaged. The Founders disagreed and did not believe this was a function of government. They knew that human nature is not essentially good and only a Savior would return us to a perfect relationship with our Creator, God.

5. **Belief in the perfectibility of human beings:** Modern liberals believe that with the proper education, everyone can become virtuous and live a happy, meaningful life. Modern liberals define education quite broadly to refer to an individual's entire upbringing, as opposed to merely schooling. They want to mold society according to their philosophy by having government involved in all aspects of every life.

6. **Belief in the community:** a feeling that "we're all in this together." Modern liberals believe that individuals are stronger working together than they are working alone. At the root of modern liberalism is not merely the desire for equality, but for the social progress that the progressive believes only an egalitarian society can achieve. They have a need to control every aspect of society creating a culture of conformity and dependency. This nation was founded on individual liberty – initiative, self-reliance, and independence. The principles made America great.

The modern liberal believes in the supremacy of the state, therefore they can be more accurately called statist than liberal. The modern liberal/statist is far more authoritarian which causes discord with the principles of the Declaration and the order of the civil society in part. The Founders understood the greatest threat to liberty is an all-powerful central government, where the few dictate to the many. They also recognized the rule of mob would lead to anarchy and, in the end, despotism.

Libertarian: Libertarianism is, as the name implies, the belief in liberty. Libertarians strive for the best of all worlds - a free, peaceful, abundant world where each individual has the maximum opportunity to pursue his or her dreams to realize their full potential.

The core idea is simply stated but profound and far-reaching in its implications. Libertarians believe you should be free to do as you choose with your own life and property, as long as you do not harm the person and property of others. Libertarianism is thus the combination of liberty (the freedom to live your life in any peaceful way you choose), responsibility (the prohibition against the use of force against others, except in defense), and tolerance (honoring and respecting the peaceful choices of others). Thus, Libertarians advocate for decriminalization of illegal drugs feeling drug use does not harm others. Conservatives believe drug usage does harm society as a whole. Libertarians favor bringing the military home to secure our borders and protect us at our borders only. They take more of an isolationist view on foreign and trade policies.

Liberty: Freedom from arbitrary or despotic government or control; freedom from control, interference, obligation, restriction, etc. regarding governmental regulations and controls. Also, liberty is freedom from captivity, confinement, or physical restraint. The more liberty the people have, the smaller the government.

Marxism: The system of economic and political thought developed by Karl Marx, along with Friedrich Engels, especially the doctrine that the state throughout history has been a device for the exploitation of the masses by a dominant class, that class struggle has been the main agency of historical change, and that the capitalist system, containing from the first the seeds of its own decay, will inevitably, after the period of the dictatorship of the proletariat, be superseded by a socialist order and a classless society. The political and economic philosophy of Karl Marx and Friedrich Engels in which the concept of class struggle plays a central role in understanding society's allegedly inevitable development from bourgeois oppression under capitalism to a socialist and ultimately classless society. Marxism says there is no God.

Non-partisan: Refers to there being no political party affiliation needed or required to run for a particular office such as city council or school board.

Partisan: Simply put, partisan refers to political party affiliation.

Platform: The document proposed by each political party that outlines that party's core values and political philosophy. It lays out what types of policies are on their agenda.

Politician: A person who has a career in politics and either seeks or holds elective office. Politicians use public office to advance personal and partisan interests. Politicians are more concerned with personal gain rather than the good of the country.

Socialism: Any of various theories or systems of social organization in which the means of producing and distributing goods is owned collectively or by a centralized government that often plans and controls the economy. Socialists mainly share the belief that capitalism unfairly concentrates power and wealth among a small segment of society that controls <u>capital</u>, creates an <u>unequal</u> society, and does not provide equal opportunities for everyone in society. Therefore socialists advocate the creation of a society in which wealth and power are distributed more evenly based on the <u>amount of work expended in production</u>, although there is considerable disagreement among socialists over how and to what extent this could be achieved. Socialism says that government is god and provides for its citizens from birth to grave where as Marxism says there is no god.

Statesman: An experienced politician who usually holds public office at the national level. A seasoned public servant devoted to country, a patriot, who is highly respected and influential in the affairs of state. A statesman promotes the welfare of the nation not his own personal agenda.

Treason: Violation of allegiance toward one's country or sovereign, especially the betrayal of one's country by waging war against it or by consciously and purposely acting to aid its enemies. It carries the death penalty if convicted. Sedition is disloyalty or treachery (any act, writing, speech, etc. directed unlawfully against state authority, the government, or the constitution, or calculated to bring it into contempt or to incite others to hostility or disaffection) to one's own country or its government.

Tyranny: A government in which absolute power is vested in the government as a whole or in a single ruler. It results in a totalitarian and authoritarian approach to governing that limits individual freedom and economic growth. Tyranny can be defined in degrees as either soft or hard. **Soft tyranny** is what the European socialist countries have and hard **tyrannies** are seen in North Korea, Cuba, China, and the old USSR. Tyranny of any kind is dangerous because it doesn't take much for a soft oppressive tyranny to become a hard cruel tyranny.

Go to **www.G2g.org** to **sign up for Carol's Blog!**

For more information, to connect, or **invite Carol to speak at your event, visit:**

www.G2g.org

~ ~

Write a Review

1. Go to Amazon.com
2. Search for What Were They Thinking? By Carol Sewell
3. Scroll all the way to the bottom and click on the button, "Write a Review."
4. Rate the book (out of 5 stars) and write a review.
5. Submit

Note: You do not have to purchase the book on Amazon to leave a review. Anyone with an Amazon account is eligible to write a review for any book they have read.

Thank You!